GLOBALIZATION, SUSTAINABLE RURAL DEVELOPMENT AND COMMON PROPERTY RESOURCES

INTERNATIONAL ENVIRONMENTAL ECONOMICS

GLOBALIZATION, SUSTAINABLE RURAL DEVELOPMENT AND COMMON PROPERTY RESOURCES

Edited by

Dr. Ram Krishna Mandal
Associate Professor of Economics
Dera Natung Govt. College
Itanagar – 791 113
Arunachal Pradesh
(India)
e-mail: rkm_1966@yahoo.co.in

DISCOVERY PUBLISHING HOUSE PVT. LTD.
NEW DELHI-110 002

Published by:
Tilak Wasan

DISCOVERY PUBLISHING HOUSE PVT. LTD.
4383/4B, Ansari Road, Darya Ganj
New Delhi-110 002 (India)
Phone : +91-11-23279245, 43596064-65
Fax : +91-11-23253475
E-mail : parul.wasan@gmail.com
discoverypublishinghouse@gmail.com
web : www.discoverypublishinggroup.com

***First Edition:* 2012**

ISBN: 978-93-5056-102-7

Globalization, Sustainable Rural Development and Common Property Resources

Printed at:
Shree Balaji Art Press
Delhi

Dedicated

To

My Teacher

Prof. Chandan Kumar Mukhopadhyay

With Reverence and Affection

PREFACE

The present study is an attempt at a comprehensive and critical analysis for the role of Globalization, Sustainable Rural Development and Common Property Resources in the world. The current track record of UN institutions is not particularly inspiring. For example, the urgency of tackling climate change is not reflected so far in the outcome of negotiations to renew the Kyoto Protocol. The 1990s slide towards greater poverty and environmental breakdown, together with the dilution of powers of developing countries to manage their own affairs, led to a strong public reaction against global bodies deemed to be responsible. Common property resources (CPRs), though neglected by policy-makers and planners, play a significant role in the life of the rural poor.

The present volume is a collection of papers contributed by eminent scholars, academicians, policy-makers, bureaucrats and thinkers from different parts of the world. The publication of this book would not have been possible without their contributions. Their work is based on diverse source materials which consist of official reports, published journals, books and findings of field-work. Most of their writings are based either on the social structural aspects or on the social dynamism and rapid regional socio-economic transformation. I have felt the need to put some of their writings together so as to enable the readers to get an overall idea about the aspect. Some of their writings have been updated, revised and edited for the purpose. I hope that the readers will find it relevant for understanding the present problem raised by globalization. I hope, this book will benefit immensely the students, researchers, teachers, young scholars, planners and administrators in the area of sustainable rural development and common property resources. I am conscious of the bulk of the work which becomes largely inevitable on account of the intrinsic sweep of the subject. I acknowledge my gratitude to all contributors, whose works are consulted in the preparation of this volume.

I would be falling in my duty if I do not extend my gratitude to my Principal, Shri Tomar Ete, Dera Natung Government College, Itanagar, Arunachal Pradesh, India for generating in me an interest to edit this book.

I also acknowledge the inspiration received from my beloved teacher and guide, Prof. Chandan Kumar Mukhopadyaya, Department of

Economics, University of North Bengal, West Bengal. I extend my gratitude to him.

I have received support and cooperation from my colleagues Dr. A. I. Singh and Mrs. Madhuparna Bhattacharjee, I acknowledge a deep sense of gratitude to them.

I am also taking the opportunity to thank profusely to Shri Tilak Wasan, Discovery Publishing House (Pvt.) Ltd., New Delhi for publication this book.

Lastly, I am grateful to the members of my family: Mrs. Archana Mandal (wife) and Miss Anusree Krishna Mandal (Daughter) and Master Avinandan Krishna Mandal (son) for their untiring support and patience during the work of this volume.

Dr. Ram Krishna Mandal

CONTENTS

LIST OF CONTRIBUTORS

Prof. Pradeep Kumar Vaid, Department of Public Administration (ICDEOL), Himachal Pradesh University, Summerhill, Shimla, Himachal Pradesh, Pin code-171005, India

Prof. Kanakachala Billav, Department of Economics, Smt. Channamma Basappa Patil College, Chincholi – 585307, Dist: Gulbarga, Karnataka, India

Prof. Sangappa Hosmani, HOD, Dept. of Political Science, Smt.Chanamma Basappa Patil College, Chincholi- 585307, Dist: Gulbarga, Karnataka, India

Prof. Dipak Kr. Mandal, Ex-Head, Department of Geography and Applied Geography, University of North Bengal, Raja Rammohunpur, Darjeeling, West Bengal, India

Prof. Ravinder Sharma, Professor (Agri. Econ.) Department of Social Science, College of Forestry, Dr. Y. S. Parmar University of Horticulture and Forestry, Nauni (Solan) -173230, Himachal Pradesh, India

Prof. C. K. Roy, Apeejay Institute of Technology, School of Management, Greater Noida, U.P., India

Prof. Malabika Deo, Head, Department of Commerce, Pondicherry University, Puducherry - 14, India

Dr. V B Gupta, Reader, School of Future Studies and Planning, Devi Ahilya University, Khandwa Road, Indore, M.P., India, India

Dr. Ram Kumar Jha, Associate Professor, SAL Institute of Management, Opp. Science City, Bhadaj, Ahmedabad - 380060, Gujarat, India

Mr. A. K. Singh, Research Scholar, School of Future Studies and Planning, Devi Ahilya University, Khandwa Road, Indore, M.P., India

Dr. Hilaluddin, Chief Consultant (Forestry), Ministry of Agriculture, NRAA, D.P. Shastri Marg, New Delhi - 110 067, India

Dr. Naim Akthar, Scientific Officer, Central Zoo Authority, Bikaner House, Shahjahan Road, New Delhi - 110 003, India

Mr. Rashid Y. Naqash, Wildlife Warden, Central Wildlife Division, Department of Wildlife Protection, Government of Jammu & Kashmir, Srinagar - 11, India

Dr. Faiza Abbasi, Guest Faculty, Department of Wildlife Sciences, Aligarh Muslim University, Aligarh - 202 002, U.P., India

Mr. A.K.Biswas, Assistant Professor, Department of Political Science, A. B. N. Seal College, Cooch Behar, West Bengal, Pin-736101, India

Dr. Jagannath B Kukkudi, Assistant Professor, Government First Grade College, Kalagi-585312 Tq: Chittapur, Dist: Gulbarga, Karnataka, India

Mr. Veerendarakumar B, Guest Faculty, Government First Grade College Kalagi-585 312 Tq: Chittapur, Dist: Gulbarga, Karnataka, India

Md. Gazi Salah Uddin, Senior Lecturer, Department of Business Administration, East West University, 43, Mohakhali, Dhaka-1212, Bangladesh

Dr. Phouphet Kyophilavong, Associate Professor in Economics, Deputy Director of Economics Department, Faculty of Economics and Business Management, National University of Laos, Lao PDR, Laos

Dr. Watcharas Leelawath, Deputy Executive Director, International Institute for Trade and Development (ITD), Bangkok, Thailand

Mr. S. S. M. Sadrul Huda, Assistant Professor, Department of Business Administration, East West University, 43, Mohakhali, Dhaka-1212, Bangladesh

Manika Chakraborty, Lecturer, Department of Management Studies, University of Dhaka, Bangladesh

Kohinoor Biswas, Assistant Professor, Department of Business Administration, East West University, 43, Mohakhali, Dhaka-1212, Bangladesh

Dr. Komol Singha, Assistant Professor, Agricultural Development and Rural Transformation Centre, Institute for Social and Economic Change, Dr. V K R V Rao Road, Nagarabhavi P. O., Bangalore - 560 072, India

Mr. Bappa Ghosh, Research Scholar, Department of Geography and Applied Geography, University of North Bengal, Raja Rammohunpur, Darjeeling, West Bengal, India

Mr. Krishna Murari, Assistant Professor, MITS University, Laxmangarh, Sikar, Rajasthan, India

Ms. Pooja Kumari, Faculty, MITS University, Laxmangarh, Sikar, Rajasthan, India

Dr. Ram Kumar Jha, Associate Professor, SAL Institute of Management, Opp. Science City, Bhadaj, Ahmedabad-380060, Gujarat, India

Dr. G. Parimalarani, Assistant Professor, Dayanda Sagar Business Academy, Bangalore, Karnataka, India

Mr. Sudarshan Prasad Regmi, Ph. D. Research Scholar, Department of Social Science, College of forestry, Dr. Y. S. Parmar University of Horticulture and Forestry, Nauni (Solan)-173230, Himachal Pradesh, India

Dr. Mithilesh Kumar Jha, Head, Department of Economics, Yingli Government College, Longleng, Dist:- Longleng Nagaland, Pin - 798625, India

Ms. Kumari Anupma Jha, Department of History, Yingli Government College, Longleng, Dist:- Longleng Nagaland, Pin-798625, India

Mr. Dulal Ch. Karmakar, Assistant Professor in Economics, P. B. College, Gauripur, Dist. Dubri, Assam, India

Dr. Rahul Verma, Assistant Professor, Department of Geology, PUC, Mizoram University, Mizoram, India

Miss Rupali Rathod, Assistant Professor in Commerce, Government Womens' First Grade College, Jewargi Conoly, Gulbarga, Karnataka, India

Mrs. Safiya Begum, Assistant Professor in Commerce, Government First Grade College, Sulepeth, Dist Gulbarga, Karnataka, India

Mr. Sandeep Kumar Patnaik, Department of Commerce, B.B. College, Orissa, India

Dr. Upendra Nath Sahu, SLO, Deputy Secretary, Government of Orissa, Bhubaneswar, Orissa, India

Dr. Priti Ranjan Hathy, Department of Computer Application, Women's Polytechnic, Bhubaneswar, Orissa, India

Mr. T. Rajasekar, Ph. D Research Scholar, Department of Commerce, Pondicherry University, Puducherry-14, India

Dr. Ram Krishna Mandal, Associate Professor of Economics, Dera Natung Government College, Itanagar-791 113, Arunachal Pradesh, India

Rationale of Environment Education for Sustainable Development and Productivity of the Environment

—Prof. Pradeep Kumar Vaid

Introduction

Every 'living organism' is surrounded by environmentalanism and environment both are subjected to change with time. If these changes are within the adjustment capacity of environment or organism they do not leave any derogatory effect on them. Such changes are taking place from thousands of years. But in the recent world history of about 200 years rapid changes have occurred in the environment throughout the globe. These changes have resulted into global because of greenhouse gas emissions, acidification of soil and water, decline in the quality of air, soil and water, exploitation of natural resources through mining activities, drastic changes in land use and land cover through over exploitation of natural resources leading to desertification of landscape associated rapid depletion of biodiversity etc.

This deterioration in natural environment has already lead to extinction a variety of life forms on the earth. Therefore, top priority should be given to overcome environmental problems. Education in various forms and at various levels has the potential to solve environmental problems.

Education and Environment

People while dealing with nature and natural resources have accumulated a lot of empirical knowledge on the basis of their experiences; therefore people in traditional societies developed an eco-centric view which is widely reflected in their attitudes towards plants, animals, rivers and the earth. All this knowledge of man is communicated in different ways to the next generations.

Therefore, education in its various forms have been used to create, conserve and transfer knowledge from time to time, at the same time education has been used to develop human potential for self-development and also making useful for the society. It has been rightly said in National Policy of Education, 1986 that "Education is an investment in present and future". So for betterment of present environment and to handover that better environment to future generations environmental concerns must be incorporated at all levels of education i.e. (*i*) Pre-primary, (*ii*) Primary, (*iii*) Secondary and (iv) tertiary level of education. Steps in this direction have been initiated in the form of Environment Education worldwide since 1970s.

Principles of Environmental Education

Some guiding principles of Environmental Education are as follows:

(*i*) Environmental Education considers environment in its totality.

(*ii*) Environmental Education should be a life-long process.

(*iii*) Environmental Education should be considered a new approach to education. It should examine major environmental issues from local, national, regional and international point of view.

(*iv*) Environmental Education should focus on current and potential environmental situations while taking into account the historical perspective. It should also be considered that response to situational need vary between and within countries.

(*v*) Environmental Education focuses on complexity of environmental problems and develop critical thinking and problem solving skills.

(*vi*) Environmental Education should utilize variety of learning environments and educational approaches to teaching/learning with lots practical activities.

Objectives of Environmental Education

The overall objectives of Environmental Education are to develop in the learner:

(*i*) An awareness of environment and its problems;

(*ii*) basic knowledge and understanding of the environment and its inter-relationship with man including indigenous tradition and cultural practices related to the environment;

(*iii*) habits values, attitudes and emotions to maintain and promote quality environment for human survival;

(*iv*) skill to solve environmental problems;

(*v*) ability to assess the outcomes of environmental action and initiatives; and

(*vi*) A sense of responsibility and urgency to ensure appropriate action to solve environmental problems.

Environmental Education, therefore, aims at cognitive, affective and cognitive behaviour modification. This is an action-oriented, project-centred and participatory process leading to development of self-confidence, positive attitudes and personal commitment to environmental protection and its improvement. The concept of 'man-nature interdependence' highlights the dynamic nature of the relationship between human beings and environment. This should be the cornerstone of bringing about an understanding of environment leading to action for sustainable development. Environmental Education should be a compulsory subject in the school and at higher education curriculum. Accordingly, the syllabus at different levels of education needs to be suitably reviewed in order to identify linkages and to avoid overlapping of contents.

Environment Education and Sustainable Development

Environment belongs to each one of us and all of us have a responsibility to contribute towards its conservation and protection. Human beings, for whose development, there is much hue and cry, live in both natural and social world. When we talk of development, we should keep in mind two basic characteristics of development:

(*i*) It should be sustained. The benefits that we are getting now from it should be assured to future generations.

(*ii*) It should be ethical. Whatever the benefits, a person or species should into not harm other individuals or species thus, development has to be visualized in a holistic manner, where it brings benefits to all, not only for present generation, but also for the future generation.

The objective of development should not only be to raise the economic standard of life but to raise the social, economic, ethical and spiritual level of the people. Sustainable Development has become the fuzz words. The two aspects of sustainable development are Inter-generational equity and inter-generational equity. Inter-generational equity emphasizes that we should hand over a safe, healthy and resourceful environment to our future generations. This can be possible only if we stop over exploitation of resources, reduce waste discharge and emissions and maintain ecological balance. On the other hand inter-generational equity emphasizes that the development processes should seek to minimize the wealth gaps within and between nations.

In the rapidly changing environment, it is imperative that public should be made aware about various environmental issues and the protection of environment. Preparation of resource material in the form of pamphlets, broachers and boards and organization of seminars and work shops, establishment of eco-clubs, tree plantation activity, introduction of environment education, subject right from the school stage will inculcate a feeling of belongingness to earth. With such efforts 'Earth thinking' will gradually get incorporated in our thinking and action, which will greatly help in transforming our life styles to sustainable one.

Value based environmental education is one of the important recipe for transforming our life styles and attitudes. The basic values like; (i) Human values 'man in nature' rather than 'nature for work', (ii) Social values like love, compassion, tolerance, justice, (iii) Ethical values, (iv) Global values i.e. human civilization is a part of the planet as a whole and (v) Spiritual values highlighting the principles of self-restraint, self discipline, reduction of wants, freedom from greed and austerity, are incorporated into environmental education, we can go a long way in attaining the goals of sustainable development and environment conservation.

Conclusion

Environment protection and conservation is the moral duty of all of us living on this plant. All of us have to change our mental attitude, our way of thinking so as to attune our actions and our living style to the promotion of clean and safe environment and to contribute towards conservation of environment. Educational intervention through Environmental Education should Programmes in formal, non formal and informal settings can be one important remedy. But the initiative regarding implementation of Environmental Education programme has to be taken by educational institutions. University must take a lead in this area by framing suitable programmes for Environmental Education, personal training, material preparation for Environmental Education and execution of the whole programmes in a proper way. Environmental Education movement has gained momentum all over the world. To make this movement an observable reality in India, educational institutions from lower to higher levels should come forward and give Environmental Education its proper place in teaching, research as well as extension activities in all courses of study. It is only self-motivation and sense of duty in teachers to bring changes in knowledge, attitude, skill and behaviour of general masses towards sustainable development through Environment Education.

REFERENCES

Balagot, Dr. Beta P., "Environment Management in the Context of Sustainable Development", Source Book in *Environmental Education for Secondary School Teachers,* (1990).

Ramakrishnan, P.S., *Ecology and Sustainable Development,* N.B.T., New Delhi.

Sharma, R.C., and B. Mahajan (1994), *Source Book on Environmental Education for Elementary Teacher Education,* NIEPA, New Delhi.

Selvam, S.K. Panneer, "Environmental Education for sustainable Development", *University News,* Nov. 15-21, 2004, New Delhi.

Singh, Sunil Kumar, "Environmental Education: A remedy for environmental crises". *University News,* March 20-26, 2006. New Delhi.

Irrigataion and Economic Development

A Comparative Regional Analysis of Karnataka State

—Prof. Kanakachala Billav

ABSTRACT

The economic development of Karnataka is mainly dependent on the development of agriculture and irrigation is the main infrastructure for development of this vital sector. The modernization of agricultural practices vis-à-vis increase in productivity of crops cannot be conceived in absence of assured irrigation facilities. The importance of irrigation development in a State like Karnataka therefore, needs no special emphasis. Like other leading States in India, the programmes for development of irrigation in Karnataka has been launched under two heads, viz., Major and Medium Irrigation and Minor Irrigation. While the Irrigation Schemes are classified as Major, Medium and Minor, they are categorised as Surface Flow, Surface Lift (For Major / Medium and Minor) and Ground Water Lift (for Minor only).

Karnataka is one of the leading States in the country in terms of growth and development measured in all development indices, it has not been able to ward off the problems of regional imbalance therein. Although, historical antecedents like carving the state areas from adjoining states, differential degrees of fertility, climatic conditions, rainfall and natural resources are considered as factors, responsible for regional differences in pace and the level of development efforts need to be made to set right these imbalances by deliberate and purposive plans and allocation of developmental resources accordingly. The present paper attempts to identify the irrigation and agricultural development disparities in the state, regions which beset within the purview of other regions of the state and provide justification for renewed and reinforced as well as developmental focus on this region.

Introduction

Irrigation through canals, wells and other sources is considered as a catalyst of economic development of a country. Numerous studies have confirmed on the role of irrigation in increasing crop productivity, intensity of cropping in India since the evolution of planning. However, it also helps in reducing instability in crop production, changes the cropping pattern in favour of high valued crops, reduces inequality in income among various section farmers in the society. Agriculture in Karnataka has a wide diversity, from crop agriculture to plantations (such as areca nut, coffee, rubber, and coconut), sericulture, horticulture, livestock and poultry rearing. Therefore, a mix of region-specific strategy alone can bring about some solution to the problems of regional disparity on the agricultural front in the state. Regional imbalance has been conceptualized and conceived as having two major dimensions and is viewed in terms of material or physical and social conditions of the existence of people in a region.

The economic development of Karnataka is mainly dependent on the development of agriculture and irrigation is the main infrastructure for development of this vital sector. The modernization of agricultural practices *vis-à-vis* increase in productivity of crops cannot be conceived in absence of assured irrigation facilities. The importance of irrigation development in a State like Karnataka therefore, needs no special emphasis. Like other leading States in India, the programmes for development of irrigation in Karnataka has been launched under two heads, viz., Major and Medium Irrigation and Minor Irrigation. While the Irrigation Schemes are classified as Major, Medium and Minor, they are categorised as Surface Flow, Surface Lift (For Major/Medium and Minor) and Groundwater Lift (for Minor only). Karnataka is one of the leading states in the country in terms of growth and development measured in all development indices, it has not been able to ward off the problems of regional imbalance therein. Although, historical antecedents like carving the State areas from adjoining states, differential degrees of fertility, climatic conditions, rainfall and natural resources are considered as factors, responsible for regional differences in pace and the level of development efforts need to be made to set right these imbalances by deliberate and purposive plans and allocation of developmental resources accordingly. The present paper attempts to identify the irrigation and agricultural development disparities in the State, regions which beset within the purview of other regions of the state and provide justification for renewed and reinforced as well as developmental focus on this region.

Land Utilization Pattern in Karnataka

Land utilization pattern in Karnataka is not homogeneous. The total geographical area of the State is 1, 90,49,836 hectares, the land utilization pattern in the State is explained in the following Table 2.1. The table reveals that the net area sown in the state is 1,24,38,309 hectares and it accounts 52.85% of the total geographical area (61.14 lakh hectares in North Karnataka Region (NKR) and 41.44 lakh hectares in South Karnataka Region (SKR). On the other hand, 46.15% of the geographical area is distributed to other activities like, forest (16.08%), land not available for cultivation (11.01%), other uncultivated land (9%) and fallow land (10%). But, geographical area is not equal distributed between SKR and NKRs. NKR has highest geographical area than the SKR, where as 44.36% of geographical area in Hyderabad Karnataka Region (HKR) to the total NKR geographical area. Forest, land not available for cultivation and other un-cultivable land is more in SKR than NKR but fallow land and net are sown area is more in NKR than the SKR. HKR has less in all activities of land utilization in NKR. It shows nature also created regional disparities in the state.

Table 2.1: Land Utilization Pattern in Karnataka, 2006-07

(Hectares)

Activities	Karnataka	South Karnataka	North Karnataka	Hyderabad Karnataka
Total Geographical area	1,90,49,836	92,36,720	98,13,116	43,53,507
Forest	30,71,833	16,27,977	14,43,856	2,41,431
Land not available for cultivation	21,50,894	13,92,316	7,58,578	3,90,484
Other uncultivated land	16,42,609	13,34,889	3,07,720	1,90,989
Fallow land	20,80,038	9,93,663	10,86,375	6,58,129
Net area sown	1,24,38,309	45,82,552	78,55,757	35,64,029

Source: *Karnataka at a Glance*, 2007-08, pp. 32-38.

Major and Medium Irrigation Schemes in Karnataka

The State has five major river basins, namely Krishna, Cauvery, Godavari, several west flowing rivers and north and south pennar. Of the total estimated yield under catchments rainwater of 98,406 million cubic metre about 48,000 mn. cum, of water is economically utilized within the State. The development of major and medium irrigation system is based on the field situation at the river basin.

River Krishna has highest irrigated area under planned and ongoing projects, which compared to other river basins. The area of 39.89% are balanced of major ongoing projects and 71.13% of area is balanced in medium ongoing projects, when compared to Cauvery basin it is very less i.e., 38.64% area is balanced in major and 49.93% area in medium ongoing projects. The ongoing and medium projects are very high in Krishna river basin compared to Cauvery river basin due to lack of administration, corruption and political influences. In Godhavari river basin, the entire potential is to be exploited. On an average, both the Krishna and Cauvery river basins 38 to 39% of the potential under ongoing major irrigation projects. The ongoing medium irrigation projects in both Krishna and Cauvery river basins the area of 71% and 50% are yet to achieved. According to Nanjundappa Report on "Regional Imbalance", the remaining area of 11.62 lack hectares can be covered under major and medium irrigation schemes, at an additional cost of Rs. 13,088 crores. These projects can be fully implemented in several districts of Krishna and Cauvery river basins.

Minor Irrigation Schemes in Karnataka

Minor irrigation schemes consists of tanks, lift irrigation, anicuts, pickups, bhandaras, salt water exclusion dams, vented dams etc. under minor irrigation schemes, the other water related problems can be solved. The minor irrigation schemes can be implemented in 9,25,645 hectares. The area of 75 to 79% of the minor irrigation schemes are implemented in South Karnataka region, but the area of 24.21% is implemented in North Karnataka region.

Status of development in all irrigation schemes is expressed in the Table 2.2 by taking into consideration of three indicators of North and South Karnataka region. Efforts should be made to achieve better utilization of the existing irrigation potentials by the figure showed in the below table. In NKR 70% of the estimated costs have been already incurred, only 32% is utilized. Still a significant potential area is left in NKR to raise the utilization rate.

Table 2.2 : Status of Exploitation of Irrigation in NKR & SKR

Sl. No.	Particulars	Percentage of utilization (TMC)	Percentage of Irrigated area(Ha)	Percentage of Expenditure (Rs/lakh)
I.	Major Irrigation			
	(1) SKR	58.77	40.80	10.07
	(2) NKR	26.92	41.75	55.78
II.	Medium Irrigation			
	(1) SKR	09.00	08.54	19.27
	(2) NKR	05.31	08.91	14.88
III.	Total Major and Medium			
	(1) SKR	67.77	49.34	29.34
	(2) NKR	32.23	50.66	70.66

Source: Computed from *Nanjundappa Report on Regional Imbalance of Karnataka*, 2002, p.30.

Net Area Irrigated in Karnataka

There is serious problem with the irrigation schemes when it comes in implementation. Against the irrigation potentials created the actual utilization has been quite low as shown in Table 2.3. During the last three years there is a major progress in the irrigation front. As against the total area of 23.6 lakh hectares in 1997-98, there is a increase of 26.72 hectares, the net area irrigated in 2001. The share of irrigated land in NKR has been relatively improved. But the HKR lagging behind the state as well as SKR and NKRs i.e., only 37.86% net irrigated area to the total net area irrigated in NKR, it can be understood by the following table.

Table 2.3 : Net Area Irrigated in Karnataka (ha), 2006-07

Source of Irrigation	Karnataka	South Karnataka	North Karnataka	Hyderabad Karnataka
Canals	10,30,438	3,62,497	6,67,941	3,76,864
Tanks	1,91,691	2,11,194	49,702	14,373
Wells	3,72,236	1,02,814	2,69,422	69,141
Bore wells	9,55,216	5,19,462	4,35,754	1,23,539
Lift Irrigation	1,18,698	18,218	1,00,480	34,710
Other Sources	2,78,031	56,856	2,21,175	8,152
Total Net Irrigated Area	29,46,310	12,24,387	17,21,923	6,29,542

Source: *Karnataka at a Glance, 2007-08*, pp. 40-41.

It may be observed from the above table that the net irrigated area is higher in NKR than the SKR i.e., 57.98% of NK and 42.02% of SKR. Canals are the major source of irrigation in Karnataka; it has covered 36.57% land to total irrigated area, followed by bore wells i.e., 20.40%. Majority of land is irrigated from canals in SK and NKRs. When we compare between SK and NKRs, NKR has highest land irrigated through the canals than in SKR i.e., 39.32% in NK and 32.76% in SKR to the total net irrigated area, followed by tanks in NK and bore wells in SKR. Majority of land in HKR also irrigated through canals i.e., 62.23% it is highest from the state average and followed by wells i.e., 19% of the land irrigated to the total irrigated area of NKR.

Area Under Important Crops in Karnataka

Karnataka is having a variety of soil distribution and receiving normal rainfall, soils are suitable for growing many crops. The following table gives the details of cropping pattern in Karnataka.

Table 2.4 : Area Under Important Crops in Karnataka

(Hectares)

Name of the regions	Total Cereals & Minor Millets	Total Pulses	Commercial Crops
Karnataka	5078106	2315690	2039093
SKR	1965470	504984	735960
NKR	3112636	1810706	1303133
HKR	1091446	1123663	466192

Source: *Karnataka at a Glance, 2007-08,* pp. 43-44.

The above table shows that, the main feature of the area under crops in Karnataka is predominance of cereals and minor millets over other crops of the total cropped area of 97.04 lakh hectares, cereals and minor millets are grown in an area of 50.78 lakh hectares and also highest grown in NKR i.e., 31.26 lakh hectares to the total area of cereals and minor millets, 19.65 lakh hectares in SKR and 10.91 lakh hectares in HKR. Pulses and commercial crops are cultivated more in NKR (13.03 lakh hectares of pulses and 13.03 lakh hectares of commercial crops). But pulses are cultivated more in HKR(11.23 lakh hectares) compare to SKR i.e., 5.04 lakh hectares.

Production of Important Crops in Karnataka

Total production of agricultural produce reflects the combined effects of area and quantity in the state shown in Table 2.5.

Table 2.5 : Production of Important Crops in Karnataka, 2006-07

(In Metric Tonnes)

Name of the regions	Cereals & Minor Millets	Pulses	Commercial
Karnataka	8490157	838855	44004602
SKR	3995549	213358	11932224
NKR	4494608	625497	32072376
HKR	2034768	410469	3940366

Source: *Karnataka at a Glance*, 2007-08, pp. 47-48.

The above table reveals that, majority of cereals and minor millets (Paddy, Ragi, Jowar, Bajra, Maize, Wheat and minor millets) are highest output in NKR i.e., 44.94 lakh tones, similarly, majority of pulses (Gram, Tur and Other pulses) were highest output in NKR i.e., 62.54 lakh tones. The output of pulses in HKR is higher than the SKR to the total production of pulses in NKR. Commercial (Groundnut and Sugarcane) crops output is also highest in NKR i.e., 320.72 lakh tones. Regarding cotton output is also highest in NKR i.e., 6.56 lakh bales, but in HKR it is less if compare to NK and SKR.

Region-wise Classification of Agricultural Labourers in Karnataka

The agricultural laborers are the spring of an agrarian economy. Although all over the state, the conditions of agricultural laborers are simply appalling as they are miserably poor, and their level of living is too low than the riches. Most of them illiterates and some political factors also responsible in the rural areas, they are divided to lead a normal social life. The general indication is that, a major proportion of agricultural laborers are drawn from Scheduled Caste, Scheduled Tribe and Backward classes and they are confined by the caste structure in these backward regions. At present 62.09 lakhs people belong to these and their earnings or livelihood is depends on

Table 2.6 : Distribution of Agricultural Labour Force in Karnataka (1991 & 2001 Census)

Name of the regions	1991	2001
Karnataka	4999959	6226942
SKR	2094970	2664400
NKR	2904989	3562542
HKR	1420171	1673524

Source: *Karnataka at a Glance*, 2007-08, p. 27.

categories the development of irrigation in the state. Table 2.5 above indicates region wise distribution of agricultural labour force during the year 1991 and 2001 census.

The table also reveals that, distribution of agricultural labours in the State varies from region to another region, during 1991 and 2001 census. In the 1991 census, 20.94 lakhs in SKR and 29.04 lakhs of agricultural labours in NKR out of 49.99 lakhs of State total agricultural labours. But 48.88% of the agricultural labours in HKR to the total agricultural labours of NKR. In 2001 census, it is increased to 62.26 lakhs of State account, from this 26.64 lakhs in SK and 35.62 lakhs agricultural labourers in NKR to the total State agricultural labours. In HKR agricultural labours are increased to 16.73 lakhs from 14.20 lakh labourers compared to 1991 census.

Importance of Irrigation in Karnataka

In India and in Karnataka, agriculture is at the mercy of timely rains. But the rainfall in the country is highly irregular, uncertain and erratic. Consequently, droughts and floods have become most common. Supply of water from rivers, tanks, wells and canals to agricultural lands for cultivation is called irrigation. It is useful both in the areas of scanty rainfall and heavy rainfall. Thus, irrigation refers to the artificial supply of water for cultivation. In addition to the supply of water to agriculture, irrigation performs various others functions like flood control, storing of water, prevention of soil erosion, soil erosion, etc.

Both at national and State level, about 64 per cent of the cultivated land depends on rains. That is why, Indian agriculture is called 'a gamble in the monsoon'. In order to increase agricultural production and productivity, and to avoid all uncertainties, irrigation is a must. The important benefits of irrigation are as follows:

(*a*) To reduce dependence on rains,

(*b*) To increase agricultural productivity,

(*c*) To improve the possibility of multiple cropping,

(*d*) To implement new agricultural strategy,

(*e*) To bring more land under cultivation,

(*f*) To reduce instability in output levels,

(*g*) To create more job opportunities,

(*h*) To control floods and droughts and

(*i*) To improve transport and electricity generation, etc.

Problems of Irrigation Facilities in Karnataka

In India as well as in Karnataka State, 64% of agricultural land depends on rainfall. At present irrigation has vital role in the dry land agriculture, but it is facing lot of problems which are as follows:

1. Irrigation projects are not completed within the targeted period.
2. Irrigation potential rate is very low.
3. Low standard of irrigation projects.
4. Negligence of minor irrigation projects.
5. Inefficient utilization of Watershed Development Programmes, Ganga Kalyana Yojana and Million Wells Schemes.
6. Lack of political will.
7. Unscientific agricultural system adopted by neighboring state i.e. the Andhra Pradesh farmers.
8. Lack of formation of water users association.
9. Lack of knowledge in water harvesting system.
10. People participation in irrigation is very low.
11. North Karnataka and Hyderabad Karnataka regions are away from rain register instruments and
12. Less forest area in North Karnataka and Hyderabad Karnataka region when compared to South Karnataka region.

Suggestions

The following are important suggestions for efficient utilization of irrigation sources and potential in Karnataka State.

1. Full utilization of the major, medium and minor irrigation schemes and also ground water exploitation, for the development of irrigation sector in the sate during the coming eight years.
2. Water usage in the major, medium and minor irrigation areas are to be encouraged to form such co-operative associations with the responsibilities of collection of the irrigation charges collectively.
3. The lift irrigation scheme introduced in select districts of NKR is a glaring example. Almost 40% of the irrigation schemes implemented in the districts of Raichur, Gulbarga, Bidar, Bellary and Bijapur are not working satisfactorily. Even those working are providing just about 36% of potential water. A sum of Rs 17.59 crores invested in 9203 hectares for the development of irrigation.

4. To start the water users association in every Gram Panchayats.
5. To develop the reserve forest area.
6. Irrigation Projects should complete within the stipulated period.

Conclusion

Irrigation helps in reducing instability in crop production, changes the cropping pattern in favour of high valued crops, reduces inequality in income among various section farmers in the society. Simultaneously, some scholars pointed out that the inequity in sharing gains of development resulting from investment in irrigation and some drew attention to the increase instability of farm output. Irrigation is not certainly considered as blessings on the mankind. Its side effect in the shape of water logging and salinity within the large canal commands have been considered as one of the important negative impact on the farms output. Based on the theoretical framework, the financial, economic, social and environmental aspects of the project are analysed by applying the familiar cost-benefit analysis technique.

Irrigation is one of the most important inputs for enhancing the productivity of agricultural land. By irrigation we can make attempt to balance the different lands in agriculture. Irrigation can generate the both direct and indirect employment, like daily laborers, use of scientific technology can be applied through the irrigation facilities like tractors, high yielding variety of seeds and fertilizer etc. Good irrigation facilities can help to improve the output of the crop and seasoned crops throughout the year. As a matter of fact, irrigation increases the effective size of agricultural labour, otherwise the supply is in scares and inelastic. It is therefore, known as land augmentic factor. It displays its land augmentic capacity broadly. Hence, well irrigation is a very ancient method of irrigation in India. Tube wells are of recent origin. Tanks are an important and an ancient source of irrigation in India and in Karnataka. Canal irrigation is the most important form of irrigation in India accounting for nearly 31.6 per cent of the net irrigated area. The important benefits of canal irrigation are its cheapness, certainty, easy supply, control over supply etc. India has one of the world's largest canal systems stretching over more than one lakh km and serving more than 20 million hectares.

REFERENCES

Benjamin R.E., Hariharan S.V and Karunagaran. M (1989), *Economics of Agriculture*, S. Chand &Company Ltd, Delhi, p. 178.

Datta Ruddar and Sundaram. K.P.M (2002), *Indian Economy*. S. Chand & Company Ltd, Delhi, p. 522.

Karnataka at a Glance, 2007-08, Directorate of Economics and Statistics, Bangalore.

Nanjundappa Report (2002), *Regional Imbalance in Karnataka*, Government of Karnataka, Bangalore.

Nayak, Sanatan (2005), *Irrigation and Economic Development*, Abhijeet Publications, New Delhi, pp. 105-115.

Patel, Shah and Mello. D (1984), *Rural Economics* Himalaya Publishing House, Bombay, pp. 160-164.

Role of Government in Urban Development in Karnataka

—Prof. Sangappa Hosmani

ABSTRACT

Urban Development is a State subject. The Department of Urban Development assists Stat Governments in their programmes of urban development by way of formulating broad policy framework; providing legislative support by way of constitutional amendment, legislation or issue of guidelines; implementing a number of centrally sponsored schemes; processing and monitoring assistance from multilateral / bilateral institutions for State Government projects; and finally providing technical support and advice for promoting orderly urbanization., During the last few decades, India has undergone a dramatic demographic shift; its predominantly rural population has been rapidly urbanizing, and over 300million Indians now live in cities. India still has the world's largest rural population, but by 2040 or so, it will be home to the world's largest urban population. Karnataka has followed this national trajectory closely, led in particular by the spectacular growth of its capital city, Bangalore. During 1991-2001, urban Karnataka grew more than 2.5 times as fast as the rural areas. The future of Karnataka will increasingly be determined by the economic and social well-being of its cities. The urbanization of the state has thrown up a number of challenges. The redistribution of political power away from the villages, the migration of large numbers of people to cities (including from other States), the changing nature of the new economy, the threats to the environment and the character of old cities, are all issues that we must grapple with and overcome equitably and sustain ably. While some efforts, both at the Centre and the State level, have been made to meet these challenges, through legislation (primarily the 74th Constitutional Amendment and its several Schedules, and more recently the Jawaharlal Nehru National Urban Renewal Mission) as well as administration, there is much more that remains to be done.

Introduction

Constitution's call for decentralized governance by Urban Local Bodies (ULBs), and the consequent need to ensure that the ULBs have adequate administrative, financial, and technical capacities to manage themselves. Before setting out to achieve this, it is advisable to take a positive view of urbanization it self. In the past urbanization has been viewed primarily as a 'problem'. To overcome this, it is first important to accept that urbanization is a welcome phenomenon, and that it reflects the aspirations of millions of people in the state. What is needed is not to discourage urbanization, but to steer it correctly towards ends that are desirable.

Democratic Urban Governance

Despite the passage of the 74th Constitutional amendment almost two decades ago, most states, including Karnataka, have not fully devolved urban governance functions to the irrespective local bodies. Also, the full extent of citizen participation in urban governance that is envisioned in the Act has not yet taken place. The clear need on this front is to complete this transformation towards full, devolved, participatory governance, in line with the report of the Kasturirangan Committee (Expert Committee on Governance in Bangalore), and subsequent recommendations from other advisory bodies to the State government. The separation of powers between a deliberative, legislative council and an executive commissioner must be replaced by a system where political accountability and responsibility go together. To achieve this, executive powers must be vested in the elected representatives. A number of steps may be taken in this regard, including the institution of directly elected mayors in cities and towns, who along with a mayoral committee drawn from the councilors will exercise executive powers. Alternately, the mayor is drawn from among the councilors themselves, but with more powers than he currently holds, and also a meaningfully longer tenure in office (Mayor-in-Council). Such direct accountability is preferable, as it helps to build city leadership everywhere in the state. Alongside this, a system of elected ward committees, with members ideally drawn from different neighborhoods within a ward through elections, should also be introduced in all Class I cities (neighborhood committees themselves are needed in all municipal areas). The winners in each of the neighborhood area elections may be the member's of the ward committee, with the council as the chairman of the said committee. Further citizen engagement should also be taken up through the establishment of a system of grievance redress, and instituting 'time-bound' delivery of public services, along with monitoring and review. Citizens may also be brought into the budgeting process, so that the plans for various cities and towns reflect the priorities of the locals themselves. To complete this transformation, the delineation of powers to local bodies should be followed by providing the requisite financial autonomy to them, as also administrative freedom. The extent of these may vary according to the size of the urban area, but over a phased period all functions listed in the 12th schedule should be devolved. The various State government-level para-statals currently performing some of these functions should be brought under the authority of the municipal body itself. The legal framework around municipal governance will also need to be overhauled, with suitable revisions to laws governing planning, development and regulation in addition to the Karnataka Municipalities Act, 1964 and the Karnataka Municipal Corporations Act, 1976. Specific legislation is also needed to address the development of Bangalore, whose problems and needs are of a vastly different scale from those of other cities.

Urban Governance

There is a multiplicity of laws and institutions governing the urban areas in the State. There are 219 Urban Local Bodies or Municipalities which have elected representatives. Besides, there a number of parastatal organizations catering to ULBs specialized services like water supply, land development, housing, slum improvement etc. while the ULBs are governed by municipal laws, others are governed by separate statutes. The ULBs in the state suffer from several weaknesses such as shortage of financial resources, lack of adequate professional manpower and lack of autonomy. The 74th Constitution Amendment Act (CAA) envisages that the Municipalities would be developed into units of self government and the State Legislatures have been empowered to provide the ULBs with necessary authority and resources. The implementation of the provisions of the Amendment Act in Karnataka has been tardy. The State Government continues to exercise considerable control over the ULBs and there is little decentralization in the true sense of the term. The administrative system in our cities suffers from institutional weaknesses. Conflicts of jurisdiction and authority, inefficient planning systems, lack of transparency and accountability and poor management capacity characterize the urban institutions.

Impact of Government Policies and Programs

The programmes taken up for the improvement of our towns and cities and the various sectoral policies pertaining to housing, water, industry etc have impacted urban development in the state in the following manner:

(1) The investments made so far have provided certain basic infrastructure facilities in relation to water supply, sanitation, sewerage, solid waste management, roads and housing but they have not been adequate to meet the growing demands of the urban Population.

(2) The master plans prepared for various towns and cities have guided city development only partially. There is considerable unplanned development in all cities.

(3) Development in other sectors has contributed to urban development in a positive and negative manner. Industrial development has contributed substantially to the growth of cities, employment generation and urban prosperity as also to urban chaos and pollution. The lack of a policy focus to urban development has resulted in distorted development of our towns and cities. Government intervention has come in adhoc and piecemeal fashion in the form of certain legislations, sectoral policies and various projects and schemes as described above. It is essential to take a holistic view of urban growth in Karnataka and formulate a policy for urban development.

Democratic Urban Governance

The passage of 74th CAA has provided new opportunities for urban governance reforms in the country. The municipal bodies have for the first time been provided the constitutional status of the third tier of government. They have been vested with increased responsibilities as a result of the devolution of 18 functions through the 12th schedule to the Constitution. Clearly, the intention of the Constitution is to provide a democratic structure of governance at the local level. Local democracy is based on the principle of subsidiary i.e., functions which are local in nature should be performed by the local government. Thus, public health, water supply, sanitation, public works, public safety, welfare, recreation and regulation of construction, food and trade activities all come within the domain of the local bodies. Besides these traditional core functions of municipalities, the Constitution has included certain other functions like planning for economic development and social justice, urban poverty alleviation, and urban and town planning. However, while recognizing local governments and providing a list of functions which could be performed by them, the Constitution does not directly endow them with any functions, responsibilities and powers. They derive their powers and functions from the States through specific legislation. Thus, in practice, it is the state governments which determine the degree of autonomy of the local bodies. The reality of urban governance in Karnataka and in India general, in the context of a local government, stands in contrast to the philosophy of the Constitution. The colonial authoritarian structure of city governance continues to this day with resistance to sharing political power with local urban institutions. We, therefore, find a scenario where apart from urban local bodies, there is a host of parastatal and departmental agencies dealing with urban services. This is particularly so in metropolitan cities where there are separate government agencies dealing with water supply and sewerage, transport, land and infrastructure development etc. State level institutions such as the Karnataka Urban Water Supply and Drainage, Board, Karnataka Slum Clearance Board, Bangalore Water Supply and sewerage Board and Bangalore Development Authority, discharge some of the municipal functions. Even in the fiscal domain, the municipalities have very limited access to powers of taxation.

The argument for the State government or its agencies exercising some of what are generally municipal functions is that urban development requires depoliticized responses. The parastatals which enjoy greater functional autonomy than municipalities are said to be in a better position in terms of managerial efficiency and technical capacity to perform development functions. These arguments may appear valid only because the municipalities lack the autonomy to manage their affairs but if we are wedded to the policy of democratic governance, and decentralization, the answer actually lies in the empowerment of the urban local bodies which calls for redesigning of the local political institutions.

Conclusion

Efforts are underway to institutionalize the process of city development plan preparation to make it a living document, on a long term basis. The Ministry is planning to develop a framework and toolkit to enable the cities to do so. Such a framework shall seek to integrate the statutory planning process with perspective planning process. Capacity gap in the ULBs is well recognized as a key challenge for success of the Mission. To address the capacity constraint for implementation of projects and reforms and for addressing the human resource challenges in ULBs, the Mission Directorate is planning to establish a network of regional institutions across the country. Mechanisms are being put in place, at Centre, State and city levels, to ensure timely implementation of projects, and monitoring and evaluation. Platforms are being created to help the cities familiarize themselves with latest technological options and practices and build synergies with the private sector. Community Participation Fund is being created to enhance the citizen's ownership of community assets and take on responsibilities for community-based projects.

REFERENCES

Dempsey, N. and M. Jenks (2005). Future forms for city living? In *Future Forms and Design for Sustainable Cities*, M. Jenks And N. Dempsey eds. Elsevier, Oxford, U.K.

Government of India, Ministry of Environment and Forests, White Paper on Pollution in Delhi with an Action Plan. http://envfor.nic.in/

Government of India, Planning Commission (2008). *Eleventh Five Year Plan, 2007-2012 vol. III.* Oxford, India.

Hindustan Times, (2008). Death of the lakes. In *Hindustan Times*, August 5, New Delhi, Metro Edition.

Jenks, M. and N. Dempsey, (2005). The language and meaning of density In *Future Forms and Design for Sustainable Cities*, M. Jenks And N. Dempsey eds. Elsevier, Oxford, U.K.

Kenworthy J.and F.B. Laube (1999). *An International Sourcebook of Automobile Dependence in Cities* 1960-1990, University Press of Colorado, Boulder.

Kundu A. and S. Thakur (2006). Access to drinking water in urban India: An Analysis of emerging spatial pattern in the context of new system of governance In *Managing Water Resources: Policies, Institutions and Technologies*, V. Ratna Reddy and S. Mahendra Dev eds. Oxford, New Delhi.

National Commission on Urbanisation, (1988). *Report of the National Commission on Urbanisation* , Vol. II.

Opp. Susan M. (2008). Roles and realities. In *Local Sustainable Urban Development in a Globalised World,* Lauren C. Heberle and Susan M. Opp eds. Hampshire, Ashgate Publishing Limited, England.

Prud'homme R. and Lee, C. (1999). Size, Sprawl and the Efficiency of Cities. *Urban Studies*, 36 (11). 1849-1858.

Pucher, J., N. Korattyswaropam, N. Mittal, N. Ittyeraah (2005). Urban transport crisis in India. www.elsevier.com/locate/tranpol

Land-use Pattern and Forecasting of Carbon Sequestration in Madhya Pradesh Forests of India

—A K Singh
—Dr. V B Gupta
—Dr. Ram Kumar Jha

ABSTRACT

The present study estimates the net carbon sequestration/accumulation in Madhya Pradesh forests up to 2025 with the help of least squares method. The reported land use and forest data collected for 1991 to 2003 as a secondary in nature. Linear and log linear models used in calculation of land use and carbon accumulation changes. The carbon accumulation in MP forest was 3465.232 Mt in 1991 and it will be 3406.429 Mt in 2025. The downfall in carbon accumulation shows the significant change in forest cover area, inner conversion in geographical area, land use changes, and disproportionate variations in dense and open forests. This study will be helpful in understanding of inner land use shift and its impact on carbon.

Key words: *Forest, Carbon sequestration, Land-use, Forecasting, Biomass.*

Introduction

Managing forests having potential to sustain carbon, which will be helpful in mitigation of global climate change and stabilization of carbon dioxide on the earth. Third assessment of Inter-governmental Panel on Climate Change (IPCC) confirmed that the emissions avoidance and carbon sequestration in forest is only the key which can replace the global climate change. Brown *et al.,* (1996) and Kuuppi *et al.* (2001) suggested that forest keeps important means to sequestrate the Carbon in form of biomass.

Forests are natural store house for biomass and carbon. Several attempts have been made to estimate the Carbon storage in Indian forest ranges 23-175 Mg C (Sathay and Ravindranath, 1998). Ravindranath *et al.* (1997) studied the carbon sequestration/accumulation in Indian forest for reference year 1986 and framed current and future scenario for 2011. It shows that carbon sequestration in Indian forest accounts 9578.28 Mt Carbon for 1986 and 10503 Mt Carbon under business as usual scenario for 2011. Forests also act as source and sink of carbon. Net carbon sequestration and its release at global scale are highly uncertain, ranging from 0.4 to 1.6 Gt of C/Year (Detwiler and Hall, 1998) and from 1.1 to 3.6 Gt C/Year (Houghton, 1991). According to IPCC (1995) carbon emission from change in tropical land use is 1.6±1Gt. The net carbon emission estimates for India vary from 0.672×10^6 tons (Pachauri et al., 1992) to 41×10^6 tons (Houghton, 1991). These uncertainties in estimation are due to difficulties in obtaining the reliable data for the study area. The methods and definitions are also varies from study to study.

In India 20.64% area exists under forest of the total reported geographical area, whereas in MP, forest cover constitutes 26.26% of the total geographical area of state. MP contributes 9.4% geographical area of the country with 10.3% area under forest. The present study is important in reference to the carbon sequestration and land use change because carbon sequestration rate is directly proportional to the growth of the forest biomass, which will contribute to removing carbon from atmosphere. The specific objectives of the study are (i) to estimate annual rate of change and over the period of change for the nine land use pattern; and (ii) to evaluate and forecast the carbon sequestration in Madhya Pradesh forests.

Methodology

The present study is based on two-year time interval secondary information. The secondary information were collected for the 12 years i.e., from 1991 to 2003. The universe of the study is Madhya Pradesh one of the states of India. To examine the above objectives the following information are collected:

1. Reported area (R)
2. Forest (F)
3. Pasture and permanent grazing land (P)
4. Miscellaneous trees and groves (M)

5. Non-agricultural area (N)
6. Barren uncultivable land (B)
7. Uncultivable waste land (U)
8. Agriculture area (A)
9. Current fallows (F_c)
10. Other fallow (F_o)

Since, the total geographical area / total reported area is constant, the changes 'if any' occurs / occur these changes will be inner class shift.

Statistical/Econometrics Tools

To estimate annual growth rate and changes over the period, linear and log linear models have been used (Prakash and Jha, 2006).

Linear Model

$$Y = a + b * t + U_t$$

where,

Y = (F, P, M, N, U, B, A, F_c and F_o) i.e., 9 linear model separately.

t = time

a = intercept

b = coefficient (dy/dt = rate of change)

U_t = error term

Further the Annual growth rate in the linear trend has been defined as

$$\text{Annual Growth Rate} = \frac{b}{\bar{y}} * 100$$

Log Linear Model

$$\text{Ln } Y_t = \beta_1 + \beta_2 t + U_t$$

where,

Y = (F, P, M, N, U, B, A, F_c and F_o) i.e., 9 log linear model separately.

t = time period

β_1 = intercept

β_2 = instantaneous growth rate

U_t = error term

To work out over the period of change i.e.,

$$\text{Compound growth rate (C.G.R.)} = [\text{Antilog}(\hat{\beta}_2) - 1] \times 100$$

Data Source

The forest cover area (1991-2003) has taken from the various reports published by Forest Survey of India. The forests cover data gathered by using Landsat data of US satellite through visual interpretation technique. Forest cover area was divided into dense forest, open forest and scrub, but in this study scrubs are not considered in calculation because it cannot hold carbon for a long time. The required land use statistics has been compiled from Government of Madhya Pradesh compendium of Agricultural statistics 2003-2004, published by M.P. State Agricultural Marketing Board, Bhopal.

Biomass and Carbon Calculations

The forest cover area in state classified into dense cover (> 40% area covered by forest) and open (<40% are covered by forest). In the literatures it has described that dense and open forests area account nearly 96% of the total biomass, only 4% covered by scrubs and herbs (Pande, 2001). According to his study the conversion factor from dense and open forests area to biomass and biomass to carbon has been calculated.

Dense forest contains above biomass 92.66 t/ha and Open forest contains above biomass 37.12 t/ha. Carbon calculation made by using the conversion factor 0.48 multiplied to the biomass, the basic conversion formula taken from Chȃturvedi, 1994. Total accumulated carbon in the forest will be addition of carbon stored in dense and open forests.

$$\text{Carbon} = \text{Biomass} \times 0.48$$

Results and Discussion

Pattern and Growth Rates of Land-Use and Carbon Sequestration

The total geographical area of Madhya Pradesh is 307.34 million hectare (Mha) in 1990-91. The forest cover area in the state was 77.91 Mha (25.34%) of the total geographical area in 1990-91. This was declined to 306.45 Mha in 1996-97. During 1996-97 forest cover area also declined to 74.76 Mha (24.39%). In 1998-99 again the forest cover area elevated at 80.78 Mha (26.27% of total geographical area) (Table 4.1). MP forest area classified in Dense, Open forests and Scrubs. Scrubs area is not included in total forest cover area. Dense forest area constituted 61.71% in 1990-91 and decreased to 57.33% in 1996-97 and further it decreased up to 52.58% of total geographical area in 2002-03. Open forest constituted 38.29% in 1990-91 and increased up to 43.59% in 2002-03 of total forest cover area of the state (Table 4.1). Agriculture area was 148.65 Mha (48.36% of total geographical area) in 1990-91 and increases up to 151.3 Mha (49.21% of total geographical

Table 4.1 : Land-use Pattern in Madhya Pradesh (Unit: Million Hectares)

Years	Reported area (R)	Forest Area (F)			Permanent pastures & grazing land (P)	Land under miscellaneous tree crops & groves (M)	Non-agriculture Area (N)	Unculti-vable waste land (U)	Barren uncul-tivable land (B)	Agriculture Area (A)	Current fallow land (F_c)	Other fallow land (F_o)
		Dense (>40% covered area)	Open (<40% covered area)	Total forest area								
1990-91	307.34	48.08	29.83	77.91	18.69	0.23	17.41	16.74	12.68	148.65	5.26	5.97
1992-93	307.34	48.09	29.83	77.91	18.31	0.18	17.63	16.25	12.18	148.71	5.69	6.22
1994-95	307.48	47.78	29.99	77.75	17.77	0.24	17.39	14.55	11.65	149.37	5.97	5.68
1996-97	306.45	42.86	31.88	74.76	17.62	0.2	18.13	13.84	11.47	150.68	4.95	4.51
1998-99	307.45	47.95	32.83	80.78	16.99	0.17	18.45	13.47	11.75	151.3	4.99	5.41
2000-01	307.55	47.94	32.83	80.78	15.85	0.2	18.89	13.49	12.01	147.66	8.18	5.75
2002-03	307.55	41.73	34.59	79.36	14.81	0.18	18.6	13.95	12.18	149.62	6.04	6.36

Remarks: Scrub areas are not included in total forest area.

Sources: Government of Madhya Pradesh compendium of Agricultural statistics 2003-2004, published by M.P. State Agricultural Marketing Board, Bhopal

Unit: Million Hectares

area) in 1998-99. Again in 2000-01 agriculture area decreased, this is because increase in barren and current fallow land. Non agriculture area constituted 17.41 Mha (5.66% of total geographical area) in 1990-91 and increased up to 18.89 Mha (6.14% of total geographical area) in 2000-01.

Annual Growth Rate (AGR) and Compound Growth Rate (CGR) have been calculated for land use classes and carbon sequestration for dense, open and total forest area for year 1991-2003. The log linear model gives better result hence it is applied for estimation of carbon storage in MP up to year 2025. Permanents pasture and grazing land depleting significantly with 3.61 percent and uncultivable waste land depleting significantly with 3.5 percent at 1% level of significance. Open forest area and non agriculture area are increasing significantly with 2.62% and 1.42% respectively at 1% level of significance. Total carbon stored in forest is increasing over the period significantly with the growth of 5.9% (Table 2).

Forecasting of Forest Area and Carbon Sequestration

The present study is based on two year time interval secondary information. The secondary information were collected for the 12 years i.e., from 1991 to 2003. The forecasted values for Dense, Open forests area, biomass and Carbon have been calculated up to year 2025 (Table 4.3). The carbon accumulated/sequestration in MP forest was 3465.232 million tons (Mt) in 1991 and 3373.539 Mt in 2005. The carbon accumulation in MP forest decreased by 91.533 million tons in 2005 compared to 1991. The carbon sequestration forecasted up to 2025 with help of least squares method. Table 3 implies that carbon sequestration decreased by 46.06 Mt from 2015 to 1991. Carbon sequestration decreased by 65.252 Mt from 2025 to 1991. 2015 to 2005 carbon sequestration decreased by 19.192 Mt and 2025 to 2005 carbon sequestration decreased by 38.384 Mt. The change in forecasted forest area for 1991 to 2005 carried out to know exactly the forest cover area change. From 1991 to 2015 forest area decreased 1.036 Mha, whereas 1991 to 2025 forest area change observed negatively 1.467 Mha. Further from 2005 to 2015 the forest area decreased by 0.432 Mha and from 2005 to 2025 it decreased by 1.393 Mha. The change in total forest area shows the changes in dense and open forests area. It has been observed that the changes in dense forest area more in between 1991 to 2003, which was continuously up to 2025. Dense forest area has more capability to sequestrate carbon for a long time. Therefore, it is the significant responsible factor to reduce or to increase the carbon sequestration for the period.

Policy Implications and Benefits

Developing economy, rapid Industrialization, uncontrolled construction activities shows harmful effects on environment. Depleting dense forest,

Table 4.2 : Annual Growth Rate and Compound Growth Rates of Various Land-use Classes in Madhya Pradesh (1991 to 2003)

Sl.No.	Land-use Classes	Madhya Pradesh	
		CGR (Compound Growth Rate)	AGR (Annual Growth Rate)
1.	Reported Area (R)	0.0118	0.0120
2.	Dense Forest Area	-1.5160	-1.4779
3.	Open Forest Area	2.6278*	2.6061*
4.	Total Forest Area (F)	0.5940	0.5971
5.	Permanent Pasture & Grazing Land (P)	-3.6170*	-3.6112*
6.	Land Under Misc. Crop & Groves (M)	-3.0580	-3.2000
7.	Non-Agriculture Area (N)	1.4228*	1.4130*
8.	Uncultivable Waste Land (U)	-3.5000*	-3.6583*
9.	Barren Cultivable Land (B)	-0.5000	-0.5183
10.	Agriculture Area (A)	0.0649	0.0654
11.	Current Fallow Land (F_c)	3.4900	3.8580
12.	Other Fallow Land (F_O)	-0.6000	-0.0250
13.	Dense Forest Carbon Sequestration	-1.5100	-1.4720
14.	Open Forest Carbon Sequestration	2.6239*	2.6023*
15.	Total Carbon Sequestration in Forest	5.9070***	6.8327***

* Significant at 1% level of significance.

** Significant at 5% level of significance.

*** Significant at 10% level of significance.

Table 4.3 : Reported and Forecasted Values

Years	Reported Dense Forest Area	Biomass in reported Dense forest Area	Carbon in reported Dense forest Area	Fore-casted Dense Forest Area	Biomass in Fore-casted Dense forest Area	Carbon in Fore-casted Dense forest Area	Repor-ted Open Forest Area	Biomass in repor-ted Open Forest Area	Carbon in report-ed Open Forest Area	Fore-casted Open Forest Area	Biomass in Fore-casted Open Forest Area	Carbon in Fore-casted Open Forest Area	Repor-ted total Forest Area	Biomass in repor-ted total Forest Area	Carbon in repor-ted total Forest Area	Fore-casted Total Forest Area	Biomass in Fore-casted Total Forest Area	Carbon in Fore-casted Total Forest Area
1991	48.077	4454.815	2139.311	48.827	4524.310	2171.669	29.834	1107.438	531.570	29.229	1084.980	520.791	77.911	7219.233	3465.232	78.056	7232.669	3471.681
1993	48.078	4454.907	2138.356	47.926	4440.777	2131.573	29.834	1107.438	531.570	30.044	1115.241	535.316	77.912	7219.326	3465.276	77.970	7224.672	3467.843
1995	47.757	4425.164	2124.079	47.024	4357.244	2091.477	29.997	1113.489	534.475	30.859	1145.501	549.840	77.754	7204.686	3458.249	77.883	7216.676	3464.004
1997	42.855	3970.944	1906.053	46.123	4273.711	2051.381	31.876	1183.237	567.954	31.675	1175.761	564.365	74.731	6924.574	3323.796	77.797	7208.679	3460.166
1999	47.948	4442.862	2132.574	45.221	4190.178	2011.285	32.832	1218.724	584.987	32.490	1206.021	578.890	80.780	7485.075	3592.836	77.711	7200.683	3456.328
2001	47.948	4442.862	2132.574	44.320	4106.645	1971.190	32.832	1218.724	584.987	33.305	1236.282	593.415	80.780	7485.075	3592.836	77.625	7192.686	3452.489
2003	41.733	3866.980	1856.150	43.418	4023.112	1931.094	34.586	1283.832	616.240	34.120	1266.542	607.940	76.319	7071.719	3394.425	77.538	7184.690	3448.651
2005	40.982	3797.392	1822.748	42.517	3939.579	1890.998	34.871	1294.412	621.318	34.935	1296.802	622.465	75.853	7028.539	3373.699	77.452	7176.693	3444.813
2007	-	-	-	41.615	3856.046	1850.902	-	-	-	35.751	1327.062	636.990	-	-	-	77.366	7168.696	3440.974
2009	-	-	-	40.714	3772.513	1810.806	-	-	-	36.566	1357.322	651.515	-	-	-	77.279	7160.700	3437.136
2011	-	-	-	39.812	3688.980	1770.710	-	-	-	37.381	1387.583	666.040	-	-	-	77.193	7152.703	3433.298
2013	-	-	-	38.911	3605.447	1730.615	-	-	-	38.196	1417.843	680.565	-	-	-	77.107	7144.707	3429.459
2015	-	-	-	38.009	3521.914	1690.519	-	-	-	39.011	1448.103	695.090	-	-	-	77.020	7136.710	3425.621
2017	-	-	-	37.108	3438.381	1650.423	-	-	-	39.827	1478.363	709.614	-	-	-	76.934	7128.714	3421.783
2019	-	-	-	36.206	3354.848	1610.327	-	-	-	40.642	1508.624	724.139	-	-	-	76.848	7120.717	3417.944
2021	-	-	-	35.305	3271.315	1570.231	-	-	-	41.457	1538.884	738.664	-	-	-	76.762	7112.721	3414.106
2023	-	-	-	34.403	3187.782	1530.135	-	-	-	42.272	1569.144	753.189	-	-	-	76.675	7104.724	3410.268
2025	-	-	-	33.502	3104.249	1490.040	-	-	-	43.087	1599.404	767.714	-	-	-	76.589	7096.727	3406.429

Sources: Reported forest (Dense and Open forest) area from The *State of Forest* Report (1991-2005) *Forest Survey of India*, URL: www.fsi.co.in
Unit: Forest area in Million Hectare, Biomass and Carbon in Million Tons.

pasture and grazing land will show deteriorating affect in future. Dense forest area depleting shows that there is conversion from dense to open forest, which can majorly affect the flora and fauna (Table 4.2). Decreasing carbon sequestration in dense forest and total forest will impact negatively on local climate and weather. So, open forest area should be replaced by dense forest area in MP. Forest and agriculture area changing year to year shows improper management of land and underdevelopment of management information system for land. Managed information system will enhance the understanding and also helpful in sustainable policy development.

Forest expansion will conserve biodiversity and cooperate for micro climate. Forest development will be helpful in preventing soil erosion. That will be construct ecological balance in future. Forest will offer ecotourism. Forest expansion will execute carbon sequestration policy projected by Kyoto Protocol in 1997 under considerable amount of earned on carbon credits. Forest conservation and development will be a natural instrument to enhancing social and economic level of people and government.

REFERENCES

Brown, S., Sathay J., Cannell M., Kauppi P., (1996), "Management of forest for mitigation of green house gases emissions", *Climate Change 1995, Impact adaptation and mitigations of climate change, Scientific technical analysis* (ed. R.T.Watson, M.C. Zinyowera and R.H. (Moss) contributions of working group II to the second assessment report of IPCC on climate change, pp. 773-798, Cambridge University Press.

Chaturvedi, A.N., (1994), "Sequestration of Atmospheric Carbon in Indian forest", *Ambio.* 23, pp. 460-61.

Detwiler, R.P., and Hall, C.A., (1998), "Tropical forests and global carbon cycle", *Science* 239, 42-47.

Houghton, R.A., (1991), "Release to the carbon to the atmosphere from degradation of forest in tropical Asia", *Canadian Journal of Forest Research* 21, 132-142.

Pachauri, R.K., Gupta, S., and Mehra, M., (1992), "A reappraisal of WRI estimates of green house gas emissions", *Natural resource forum* 16, 33-38.

Pande, P.K., (2001), 'Carbon Budget for the Forest and Plantation of Madhya Pradesh', submitted to Oregon State University Corvallis OS, USA.

Prakash, Gyan and Ram Kumar Jha (2006), "Land Use Pattern and Ecological Implications: A Comparative Study of Uttar Pradesh and Madhya Pradesh", *International Journal of Environment and Development*, Vol. 3, No. 2, December, pp. 273-280.

Ravindranath, N.H., (1997), "Carbon Flow in India Forests", *Climate Change* 35, 297-320.

Sathay, J.A., and Ravindranath, N. H., (1998), "Climate change mitigation in the energy and forestry sector of developing countries", *Annual Review of Energy and Environment* 23, 387-437.

Impact of Pheasant Offtake on Populations of Game Birds in the Western Indian Himalaya

—Dr. Hilaluddin
—Dr. Naim Akthar
—Rashid Y. Naqash
—Dr. Faiza Abbasi

ABSTRACT

The present study tested the hypothesis that "game species are lost when forest areas are subjected to hunting and populations of already threatened species may become locally extinct from many forests of the Western Indian Himalaya". The study was designed to determine effects of vegetation structure and heterogeneity, and behaviour of animal species on their encounters in hunted and protected sites. The compared forest patches are similar in abundance of trees, herbs, and shrubs. Animal densities allowed the investigator to determine whether higher densities of pheasants in the protected areas are simply due to protection efforts accorded within this zone. The study provides scientific evidence that hunting seriously impacts populations of hunted species. The results show that cheer pheasant (Catreus wallichi), *kaleej pheasant* (Lophura leucomelanos), *koklass pheasant* (Pucrasia macrolopha) *and monal pheasant* (Lophophorus impejanus) *are seen more often in protected sites than in hunted sites. The locally common species are heavily impacted and at higher risk of local extinctions from forest patches in this landscape than the rare ones.*

Keywords. *Himalaya, pheasant, hunting and impact.*

Introduction

Wildmeat harvesting is posing serious threats to survival of species populations worldwide (Diamond and Case 1986, Reid 1992, Alvard *et al.* 1997, Wilkie and Carpenter 1999, Robinson and Bennett 2000, Barbusea 2001, Cullen *et al.* 2001, Brashares *et al.* 2001, Rosser and Mainka 2002, Peres and Palacios 2007) and heads the list of factors causing global and regional extinctions. (Martin and Steadman 1999). Most efforts investigating impacts of wild animal extractions and their ecological consequences on native wildlife primarily focus on mammals and such information on other equally important animal groups remains fragmentary across the world, while specifically lacking for game birds (Hilaluddin and Kaul 2007), in particular, across Asian Continent.

Certain top government wildlife officials (Pabla 2006) are lobbying for regulated hunting of wild animals in India to generate conservation money, arguing that since poaching happens anyway, why not legalise it partially and make the money legit? However, if we are to gain the critical conservation benefits that sustainable harvesting programme can provide then we must explicitly recognize and incorporate into our calculations, costs as well as benefits that such exploitations may bring. Therefore, the present study is designed to investigate impact(s) of pheasant offtake on their wild populations in and around Chamba district of the Western Indian Himalaya.

Methods

Study Area

Chamba is located in Himachal Pradesh, falls within India's bio-geographic province "2B Western Himalaya" (Rodgers and Panwar 1988) and forms part of "Western Himalaya Endemic Bird Area" (Satterfield *et al.* 1998). Evergreen Temperate Pine Forests dominated by chir pine (*Pinus roxburgii*), Evergreen Temperate Oak Forests dominated by ban oak (*Quercus leucotrichophora*) and Mixed Evergreen Temperate Forests with extensive Southwest facing grasslands occur in Chamba (Champion and Seth 1968). The associates of ban oak and chir pine are rhododendron (*Rhododendron arboretum*), deodar (*Cedrus deodara*), Himalayan blue pine (*Pinus wallichiana*), yew (*Taxus baccata*), and west Himalayan fir (*Abies pindrow*). The undergrowth is predominated by barberry (*Berberis* spp.) and hybrid berries (*Rubus* spp.) with some Rose (*Rosa* spp.), daphne (*Daphne* spp.), and cape myrtle (*Myrsine* spp.). These vegetation communities in Chamba district support over 200 bird species, including restricted range red-browed finch (*Callacanthis burtoni*) and globally threatened cheer pheasant and western tragopan (*Tragopan melanocephalus*) (BI 2004).

Hunting occurs mostly outside PAs in the Western Indian Himalaya to provide supplementary protein to an otherwise vegetarian staple mainly targeting large mammals and galliformes (Kaul *et al.* 2003, 2004). Effective community rules (restrictions on game extractions protecting sensitive and globally threatened species, breeding seasons, age-sex classes, bag limits) with regard to hunting are lacking and people are increasingly switching over to modern hunting devices (guns) at the cost of traditional ones. With methods varying from snaring to firearms three major types of hunting activities are prevalent: (1) Organized hunting targeting large bodied species with specific market; (2) regular snaring targeting galliformes in village vicinities, to provide food for family; (3) opportunistic hunting trips in forests for subsistence requirements.

Animal Census

Five forest fragments were studied in and adjoining Chamba within1410 and 3290 meters MSL during summer 2006. Forest fragments here are defined as continuous blocks of forests surrounded by agriculture fields and human settlements. In this study greatest distance between sites was <150 km and quantitative hunting pressures were not recorded. However, as an alternative, sites were selected from documented animal extraction rates and patterns in the forest fragments of Western Indian Himalaya in literature (Kaul *et al.* 2003, Hilaluddin and Naqash 2006) and focal discussions with hunters. These measures were used to define sites as "protected" and "hunted". The protected sites were located in Khajjayar-Kalatop and Kugti WLS; whereas, hunted sites were in Chamba and Kishtwar Territorial Forest Divisions (Table 5.1).

Pheasant populations were estimated using belt transect (pre-defined areas) surveys following sample count strategy (Sutherland 1996) identified on topo maps after discussing with concerned wildlife officials and local hunters. For verification, these were re-identified on the ground during reconnaissance surveys and starting and ending points were permanently marked on trees with paint for future reference. Transect length was measured using Hip-Chain Method (Chaturvedi and Khanna 1982). Covering all major vegetation types in two management units the, transects were spaced at a minimum distance of >1-km at a site to avoid double counts. Generally, for visibility, streams and prominent trails were utilized as sampling areas not withstanding bias in estimating natural densities as unconscious bias exists in route selection if landscapes differ, even subtly.

Table 5.1 : Locations and characteristics of the sampled transects

Transect name	Nearest village	Beat name	Forest division name	Transect characteristics		
				Length (km)	Area (km^2)	Altitude (MSL)
Burnar-Grad	Tyari	20 A^H	Kishtwar TRL	5.0	1.5	2600-3075 m
Top-Grad	-do-	20 B^H	-do-	4.5	1.35	2890-3290 m
Top-Pangi	Ishtiyari	19 A^H	Chamba & Kishtwar TRL	5.0	1.5	2600-3232 m
Namba Naal	Suendi	Sarah^H	Chamba TRL	4.5	1.35	2740-3210 m
Dramni Ki Bhurjee	-do-	-do-	-do-	3.7	1.11	2285-2440 m
Grad Bah	-do-	-do-	-do-	3.0	0.9	2020-2539 m
Haath Pav	Lagga	Kiri^H	-do-	4.5	1.35	1470-1820 m
Sukha Naala	-do-	-do-	-do-	4.5	2.02	1410-2400 m
Kalatop-Lakarmandi	Kalatop	Kalatop^P	Chamba WL	3.0	1.8	2590-2860 m
Kalatop-Khajrot Nala	-do-	Lakar Mandi^P	-do-	6.0	1.8	2040-2860 m
Khajrot Nala-Khajjyar	Khajjyar	Khajrot^P	-do-	5.0	1.5	1610-2040 m
Sunil Lodge-Kuringarh	Rakh	Krangda^P	-do-	4.0	1.2	1400-1800 m
Kalatop-RFC9	Lakar Mandi	Talai^P	-do-	5.0	1.5	1820-2480 m
RFC 11-15	-do-	Kalatop^P	-do-	4.0	1.2	1400-1860 m
Kangroo DPF	Kugti	Lower Kugti^P	Bharmor WL	4.0	1.2	2190-2840 m
Karog Dhar	-do-	Upper Kugti^P	-do-	5.0	1.5	2632-3210m

^{P}protected site & ^{H}hunted site. While TRL denotes Territorial Forest Division, WL means Wildlife Division.

Table 5.2: Pheasant Species seen and Number of Observations Recorded during Belt Transect Count Sampling in the Western Indian Himalaya

Species		Number of observations
Common name	Scientific name	
Cheer pheasant	*Catreus wallichi*	08
Kaleej pheasant	*Lophura leucomelanos*	23
Koklass pheasant	*Pucrasia macrolopha*	91
Monal pheasant	*Lophophorus impejanus*	28

However, vegetation characteristics of hunted and protected forests measured as part of present study did not show statistically significant variations (Table 5.3). Thus, homogeneity in vegetation between hunted and protected sites will outweigh variations in animal densities, if any occur, as a consequence of landscape heterogeneity across two management units.

Table 5.3 : Vegetation Characteristics (mean ± median) with Statistical Variations in Hunted and Protected Sites

Plant bio-morph type	Vegetation structural and compositional variables	Hunted site	Protected site	Statistical values Mann-Whitney U test	P
Tree	Density (# of plants/km^2)	307.4 ± 238.8	332.8 ± 302.54	U_{78} = 721.5	0.45
	Diversity (H')	0.6 ± 0.56	0.6 ± 0.56	U_{78} = 797.5	0.98
	Richness (N_0)	2.3 ± 2.0	2.3 ± 2.5	U_{78} = 765.5	0.73
	Tree cover (%)	36.0 ± 30.0	30.1 ± 30	U_{78} = 731.0	0.5
Shrub	Density (# of plants/km^2)	2226.4 ± 1783.45	4024.5 ± 2547.8	U_{78} = 570.5	0.03*
	Diversity (H')	0.5 ± 0.5	0.7 ± 0.68	U_{78} = 664.5	0.19
	Richness (N_0)	2.2 ± 2.0	2.9 ± 2.9	U_{78} = 663.0	0.18
	Shrub cover (%)	29.7 ± 25.0	24.1 ± 20.0	U_{78} = 730.0	0.5
Herb	Density (# of plants/km^2)	35540 ± 30500	39582 ± 32200	U_{78} = 751.5	0.64
	Diversity (H')	1.01 ± 1.01	1.3 ± 1.21	U_{78} = 603.5	0.06
	Richness (N_0)	4.6 ± 4.0	4.8 ± 4.0	U_{78} = 672.0	0.21
	Herb cover (%)	37.65 ± 30.0	31.3 ± 20.0	U_{78} = 735.0	0.53

*Denotes significant values.

Each transect was scanned them daily for pheasants, at least for three consecutive days following same census schedule. The animal counts in all transects within an area began simultaneously at sunrise and ended between 830 and 1000 hours depending upon transect length. Censuses involved walking slowly (approximately 1-1.5 km/ hour) and stopping briefly at every 50-100 meters interval (Emmons 1984) with the intention of flushing animals. A team of 5 observers trained previously in identifying galliformes with local names and walking transects scanned the 10-15 meter area on both sides of the transect depending upon the terrain and visibility. Maintaining a fixed distance of 20-30 meters from each other and silence for the calm of animals on transect, observers recorded total number of animals seen, sighting time, movement direction and activities in pilot surveys so that individuals evidently seen more than once by two different observers could be taken into account. Nawaz *et al.* (2000) used the Belt

Drive Count method for estimating pheasant populations in Pakistan Himalaya in winter in extremely steep and rocky terrain covered with snow and recommended its use with some limitations for the western Himalayas. As suggested downward pilot surveys were conducted from top to bottom of hill. However, the study area hardly received snowfall during summer and had snow-free peaks during the course of the study.

Vegetation Survey

The composition of trees, shrubs, and herbs within each belt transect was also assessed by selecting 5 sample points at 500 meters regular distances on 15 meters either side in order to avoid relatively disturbed vegetation due to trampling by cattle and humans. Circular plots (10 m radius) were established for estimating populations of trees (greater than 31 cm in basal girth) and shrubs (3 m radius), respectively; whereas, 1 m × 1 m square plots were established for quantifying populations of herbaceous vegetation. In addition, vegetation structure was also measured at each sample point. While Grid Mirror Method (Rodgers 1991) was adopted to quantify canopy cover of tree species, Line Intercept Method and Crown Diameter Method (Muller-Dombois and Ellenberg 1974) were used to estimate crown cover of herbs and shrubs, respectively.

Data Analysis

Animal densities per unit area at a given day were calculated as the total number of individuals of a species seen on a particular transect on a particular day divided by the total area of that transect. A non-parametric Man-Whitney U test was used to compare densities of each animal species in protected sites with their corresponding densities in the hunted sites to investigate impact(s) of hunting on their populations.

It was assumed, there might be differences in the vegetation characteristic between hunted and protected sites independent of hunting pressure, although all of the patches were once part of the same continuous forest and are of the same geological origin. Therefore, vegetation structural and compositional heterogeneity between hunted and protected sites was statistically compared using Man-Whitney U test. Vegetation densities of plant bio-morphs viz. trees, shrubs and herbs at each sampled point were calculated following Curtis and Mcltonish (1950). The general diversities (H') of bio-morphs were computed in accordance with Shannon-Wiener (1963), whereas species richness was calculated as total number of a species occurring in a sample unit (Ludwig and Reynolds 1988). All statistical tests were performed in following Sokal and Rohlf (1995).

Results

Sample Size and Survey Efforts

A total of 16 belt transects (8 each in protected and hunted sites) (Table 5.1) were actively scanned for searching pheasants. During three consecutive day census period, the census party travelled a total of 212.1 km (108 km in the protected site; 104.1 km in the hunted site) in 157.48 hours (77.11 hours in the protected site; 80.37 hours in the hunted site). All species were observed on more than 5 occasions (Table 5.2), ranging from 8 for cheer pheasant to 91 for koklass pheasant. The survey teams spent a mean of 9.65 hours/transect ± 0.69 CI in hunted site and an average of 10.01 hours/transect ± 0.88 CI in protected site actively searching game birds.

Vegetation Structure and Composition

With the exception of statistically significant higher shrub densities in protected site as compared to hunted one, the vegetation characteristics between the two management units showed statistically non-significant differences (Table 5.3), although densities, diversities, richness and covers of trees, shrubs, and herbs were generally higher in protected site.

Animal Abundance

The comparisons showed differences in game bird densities between hunted and protected sites (Table 5.4). In general, pheasants were more often seen in protected site than hunted one. *Koklass* pheasant and *kaleej* pheasant have shown statistically significant variations for their densities between hunted and protected sites. The densities of cheer pheasant and monal pheasant did not show significant difference. *Kaleej* pheasant, monal

Table 5.4 : Pheasant Densities (mean ± median) with Statistical Variations in Hunted and Protected Sites in the Western Indian Himalaya.

Species	Number of animals/km²			Statistical values	
	Hunted site	Protected site	Overall	Mann-Whitney U test	P
Cheer pheasant	1.2 ± 0	1.5 ± 0	1.4 ± 0 (0)	U_{14} = 29.0	0.6
Kaleej pheasant	1.2 ± 1.6	5.2 ± 4.2	3.6 ± 3.2 (0)	U_{14} = 4.0	0.003*
Koklass pheasant	4.7 ± 4.2	9.3 ± 5.4	6.1 ± 5.2 (0)	U_{14} = 8.0	0.01*
Monal pheasant	1.3 ± 0	3.5 ± 2.9	2.4 ± 0 (0)	U_{14} = 18.0	0.1

*Denotes significant values. Values in parentheses depicted in column 4 are quartiles.

pheasant, koklass pheasant and cheer pheasant are 77%, 62%, 49% and 20%, respectively, less common in hunted site when compared to protected site.

Discussion

Two types of sources of variations might affect animal abundance among different forest patches. First, vegetation structure and compositional heterogeneity, which independent of hunting, may cause changes in species abundance between the two sites. Second, hunting affects the behaviour of animals and makes hunted species difficult to sight than non-hunted ones. Animals in the protected site may be less wary and, therefore, easier to sight than the same species in hunted site (Hill *et al.* 1997). Comparisons of vegetation characteristics in hunted and protected sites showed that hunting pressures within the two forest types were independent of vegetation structure and composition as there is little detectable difference between the two units, at least on the basis of the vegetation heterogeneity measured as part of this study. Moreover, the studied forest fragments were once part of the same continuous forest, and are of the same geological origin. Further, it was quite unlikely to miss animals in narrow strips as taken in this study during the combing operation. Thus, animal densities between two management units are unlikely to be affected due to changed animal behaviour (more wary in protected site). However, the densities reported of certain species (e.g. cheer pheasant) here cannot be relied on for absolute comparisons with other sites, given the lack of control for differences in detectability. Such species are experts in hiding quietly without being spotted. This factor remained uniform across all transects and, therefore, made possible viable comparisons of bird abundances between two management units.

Thus, it could be concluded that hunting is resulting in decline of game birds in this landscape of the world, severely reducing the abundances of kaleej and koklass pheasant but with insignificant impact on the densities of monal pheasant. Compound effect of population statistics at 0.7 hectare per capita (Anon 2000), deforestation due to logging (FSI 2005), adoption of modern hunting devices and a community devoid of hunting regulations (Kaul *et al.* 2003) has increased the protein demand in this landscape and seems to exacerbate the hunting impact. This accentuated by logging, agriculture, and road network expansion may result in local extinctions of certain game species from several un-protected forest areas such as that of western tragopan from the hunted forest of Kiri Beat under Lower Chamba Range - one of the survey sites.

The present study has demonstrated the impact of game bird hunting on their wild populations in the Western Indian Himalaya. It, however, remains unclear how hunting is affecting the population dynamics of game species. Further, no information exists on population age structures and demographics of hunted versus protected sites, impact of hunting on game birds of different age classes, impact of hunting on vegetation characteristics and demographics of plant populations in hunted versus protected sites, and ecological sustainability of wildmeat from Asia, in general, and India in particular. These require immediate investigations.

Further, vertebrate animal harvesting theory suggests that a given level of harvest is more likely to be sustainable for a species with 'faster' life history, early maturity and high reproductive rate (Stokes *et al.* 1993, Kirkwood *et al.* 1994, Pope *et al.* 2001). Species response to over-exploitation is similar to that of other anthropogenic threats. Sustainable harvesting acts as selective agent of extinction, unless care is taken to make it otherwise (Law 2001); large slow species are expected to adapt to the new mortality regime by evolving smaller bodies and faster life histories. Either way some of the character diversity – an important aspect of biodiversity (Williams and Humphries 1996) is lost. It is probable that all significant use has biodiversity survival costs. Therefore, we must look for socially acceptable, economically equitable and morally agreeable ways of minimizing hunting pressures on wild animals and there is no escape from investing sustainably in their explicit protection.

Acknowledgements

We are grateful to the staff of the Wildlife Wing of Himachal Pradesh for their active participation in animal census exercises. We thank the graziers and the hunters for their open hearted discussions and suggestions during research design and becoming members of the census team. Last but not least, this study was funded by Oriental Bird Club, U.K. under its small grant programme.

REFERENCES

Alvard, M., Robinson, J.G., Redford, K.H. and Kaplan, H. (1997): "The sustainability of subsistence hunting in the Neotropics", *Conservation Biology*, 11:977-982.

Anon (2000): *Population and Forests: a report on India. United Nations Population Fund. 2000,* New Delhi, India.

Barbusea, A. (2001): "Hunting impacts on waders in Spain: effects of species protection measures", *Biodiversity & Conservation,* 10: 1703-1709.

BI (2004): *State of the World's Birds: Indicators of our Changing World*, Birdlife International, Cambridge, U.K.

Brashares, J.S., Arcese, P.S , Moses, K , Coppolillo, P.B., Sinclair, A.R.E and Balmford, A. (2004): "Bushmeat hunting, wildlife declines and fish supply in West Africa", *Science,* 306:1180-1183.

Champion, H.G. and Seth, S.K. (1968): *The Forests Types of India*, Government of India Press, New Delhi.

Chaturvedi, A.N. and Khanna, L.S. (1982): *Forest Mensuration*, International Book Distributors, Dehradun, India.

Cullen, L., Jr. Bodmer R.E. and Padua, C.V. (2001): "Ecological consequences of hunting in Atlantic forest patches, Sao Paulo, Brazil", *Oryx,* 35: 137-144.

Curtis, J.J. and Mcltonish, R.P. (1950): "The inter relationship of certain analytic synthetic phyto-sociological characters", *Ecology,* 31:434-455.

Diamond, J. and Case, T.J. (1986): "Overview, introduction, extinctions, exterminations and invasions" in Diamond, J. and T.J. Case, T.J.: *Community Ecology*. Harper & Row, New York, U.S.A., pp. 56-79.

FSI (2005): *The State of Forest 2003,* Forest Survey of India, Dehradun, India.

Hilaluddin and Kaul, R. (2007): "Galliformes hunting in India: the bigger picture" in Sathyakumar, S. and Sivakumar, *S.: Galliformes of India, ENVIS*. Wildlife Institute of India, DehraDun, India, pp. 163-167.

Hilaluddin, Kaul, R. and Ghose, D. (2005): Conservation implications of wild animal biomass extractions in northeast India. *Animal & Biodiversity Conservation* 28:169-179.

Hilaluddin and Naqash, R.Y. (2006): *Survey and Census of Kishtwar High Altitude National Park*, Department of Wildlife Protection, Kishtwar, India.

Hilaluddin, Kaul R., Pradhan S., Lachungpa U. and Taylor. J. (2006): "Wildmeat and its management in the eastern Indian Himalaya" in Yasmeen, S.: *Proceedings of the National Conference on Environment and Education for Sustainable Lifestyle*. Patna Women's College, Patna, India, pp. 19-36.

Hill, K., Padwe, J., Bejyvagi, C., Bepurangi, A., Jakugi, A., Tykuarangi, R. and Tykuarangi, T. (1997): "Impact of hunting on large vertebrates in the Mbaracayu Reserve, Paraguay", *Conservation Biology,* 6:1339-1353.

Kaul, R., Hilaluddin and Jandrotia, J.S. 2003. *Extraction of wild meat in the Western Indian Himalaya*: an assessment. U.K.: Oriental Bird Club. Technical Report.

Kaul, R., Hilaluddin, Jandrotia, J.S. and McGowan, P.J.K. (2004) "Hunting of large mammals and pheasants in the Western Indian Himalaya"' *Oryx,* 9:426-431.

Kirkwood, G.P., Beddington, J.R. and Rossonw, J.A. (1994): "Mammalian life histories and responses of populations to exploitation" in Edwards, P.J., May, R.M. and Webb, N.R.: *Large Scale Ecology and Conservation Biology*. Blackwell Scientific Publication, Oxford, U.K., pp. 169-189.

Law, R. (2001): "Phenotypic and genetic changes due to selective exploitation" in Reynolds, J.D., Mace, G.M., Redford, K.H. and Robinson, J.G.: *Conservation of Exploited Species*. Cambridge University Press, Cambridge, U.K., pp. 323-342.

Ludwig, A.J. and Reynolds, J.F. (1988): *Statistical Ecology: a Primer of Methods and Computing*, John Wiley & Sons, New York, U.S.A.

Martin, P.S. and Steadman, D.W. (1999): "Pre-historic extinctions on islands and continents" in Mocphee, R.D.E.: *Extinction in Near Time: Causes, Contexts and Consequences*. Kluwer/Plenum, New York, U.S.A., pp. 17-55.

Muller-Dombois, D. and Ellenberg, H. (1974): *Aims and Methods of Vegetation Ecology*, John Wiley & Sons, New York, U.S.A.

Nawaz, R. Garson, P.J. and Malik, M. (2000): "Monitoring pheasant populations in montane forests: some lessons learnt from Pakistan Galliformes project" in Woodburn, M., McGowan, P.J.K., Carroll, J. Musavi, A.H. and Zheng-wang, Z.: *Proceedings of 2nd International Galliformes Symposium*. World Pheasant Association-International, Fordingbridge, U.K., pp. 196-203.

Pabla, H.S. (2006): *Good Prospects for Community-based Conservation hunting in Madhya Pradesh, India*. Madhya Pradesh Wildlife & Forests Department, Bhopal, India.

Peres, C.A. and Palacios, E. (2007): "Basin-wide effects of game harvest of vertebrate population on densities in Amazonian forests: Implications for animal mediated seed dispersal", *Biotropica,* 39:304-315.

Pope J.G., McDonald, D.S., Dann, N., Reynolds, J.D. and Jennings, S. (2001): Gauging the vulnerability of non-target species to fishing'" ICES *Journal of Marine Science,* 57:689-696.

Robinson, J.G. and Bennett, E.L. (2000): *Hunting for Sustainability in Tropical Forests*. Columbia University Press, New York, U.S.A.

Rodgers, W.A. and Panwar, H.S. (1988): *Planning a Protected Area Network in India*. Volume 1 and 2. Wildlife Institute of India, DehraDun, India.

Rodgers, W.A. (1991): *Techniques for Wildlife Census in India: a Field Manual*. Wildlife Institute of India, DehraDun, India.

Rosser, A.M. and Manica, S.A. (2002): "Over-exploitation and species extinctions", *Conservation Biology,* 16:584-586.

Satterfield, A.J, Crosby M.J., Long, A.J. and Wege, D.C. (1998): *Endemic Bird Areas of the World: Priority Areas for Conservation*, Cambridge University Press, Cambridge, U.K.

Shannon, C.E. and Wiener, W. (1963): *The Mathematical Theory of Communication*, University Illinois Press, Urbana, U.S.A.

Sokal, R.R. and Rohlf, F.J. (1995): *Biometry: Principals and Practice of Statistics in Biological Research,* W. H. Freeman & Company, New York, U.S.A.

Stokes, T.K., McGlade, J.M. and Law, R. (1993): *The Exploitation of Evolving Resources*, Springer-Verlag, Berlin, Germany.

Sutherland, W.J. (1996): "Why census?" in Sutherland, W.J.: *Ecological Census Techniques: a Handbook*. Cambridge University Press, Cambridge, U.K., pp. 1-9.

Wilkie, D.S. and Carpenter, J.F. (1999): "Bushmeat hunting in the Congo Basin: an assessment of impacts and options for mitigations", *Biodiversity & Conservation,* 8:929-955.

Williams, P.H. and Humphries, C.J. (1996): "Comparing character diversity among biotas" in Gaston, K.J.: *Biodiversity: a Biology of Numbers and Difference*. Blackwell Science Ltd., Oxford, U.K., pp. 54-76.

Sustainable Development in India

—A.K. Biswas

Introduction

Once upon a time, 'nature' was considered by practically all civilizations as sacred for they ensured human survival and development. It was the duty of man to use the nature without jeopardizing its inherent regenerative capacity. Man's use of nature was circumscribed by its inherent capacity to recoup and regenerate or his won capacity to help nature recover its lost virginity. He used the land fertilizing it by enriching it with manures derived from plant and animal wastes; he used the water, without wasting and polluting it; he used the air without fouling it; he lived in small communities so that the waste generated was not too large for the nature to digest it; he cut the trees but planted them too. In fact, human behavior was so much in tune with nature that all that he turned out as a producer or consumer of goods and services was recycled in nature.

Modern era came in Europe in seventeenth century. Europeans spread over the whole world capturing both land and the people inhabiting it. They became the masters of all they surveyed. Both became the resources for exploitation; forest were cut, soils were destroyed, waters were polluted, air was poisoned, rivers were dammed – all this for increased production and consumption. A series of scientific discovers and technological developments strengthened man's hands to control nature in this era as a result of industrial revolution. As a result using energy resources like coal, petroleum, natural gases released green house gases in the atmosphere.

Our land water and air are no longer in their life supporting State. The result is: global warming and climate change that is threatening the very survival of life on planet earth.

In twenty-first century, we realize that something went drastically wrong with the way we tried to modernize ourselves; and that our fore fathers, who interfered with nature only with in the confines of the laws governing it on the one hand, and human craving for peace and harmony on the other, were perhaps right. This realization, even within a limited circle of people and institutions, has lead to a search for a paradigm of development that is devoid of violence against nature and fellow human beings. This search is, however, still with in the framework of the basic tenets of modern civilization, which gives priority to material advancement even if it means making nature inert and human beings less human. It is clear from the applied meaning of the new concept of sustainable development.

Concept of Sustainable Development

The term *'sustainability'* derived from the Latin root *'sustinere'*. The concept of sustainable development was first popularized by the words Conversation Strategy (UCN, 1980) and was very strongly promoted by the Brundlant Report, which define it as a "development that meets the needs of the present without compromising the ability of future generations to meet their own needs, improved living standard for all, better protected and managed ecosystem and a safer, more prosperous future". The World Conservation Strategy Report defined it as "the integration of conservation and development to ensure that modification to the planet do indeed secure the survival and well being of all people". Whatever the definition is, it carries the tenor of development that can be achieved without an undue exploitation of the natural resources. For long, it was taken for granted by the mankind that nature is bountiful and can be used unscrupulously. Accordingly, the resource exploitation continued unmindful of the consequences till it was realized that the resources are actually being over exploited. The international community called for a meet that aimed at bringing a halt to this menace and chalk out a programme to restore nature's capacity.

The first call to these environmental threats was given as early as 1960s. A new environmental movement emerged around this time that was sparked of by Rachel Carson's book *'Silent Spring'*. The book drew the attention of the world to the destruction of wildlife by the use of pesticide. She warned that this chemical contained the prospect of dying world in which spring time would no longer bring forth lease to new life but only silence. Carson revealed that our action could lead to seriously damaging environmental consequences when we interfered with the natural systems we fully did not understand. There were meetings from time to time addressing these issues including the Stockholm Conference of 1972; the United Nations General Assembly, in 1983, set up the World Commission on Environment and Development with the Norwegian Prime Minister Mrs. Gro Harlem Brundtland as the chairperson. The core theme of the report of this Commission was emphasized the importance of taking into consideration environmental resources limitation before deciding the economic policies of the State. Thus a need was felt into integrate environment and economics in a coordinated manner without having deter mental effects on both.

The market driven economics and globalization led's to over use of natural resources in the name of development. The developing countries are compelled to use their resources in an uneconomical manner; while the poverty levels remained as they are development eluded many a country. According this view the Brundtlant commission argued that in a world marked by extreme poverty, people are compelled to use resources in an erratic manner for meeting their immediate needs; these means of survivals result in an unhealthy environment.

Human needs are two dimensional; (1) the fulfilment of basic needs like food, clothing, shelter and clean environment; and (2) the option of pursuing a chosen lifestyle. The developed countries were successful, through early industrialization but the developing countries have not been able to secure the advanced technologies that would ensure a better lifestyle to their citizens. So they are in need of technical knowledge for not only good life but also an economically viable one. These countries have abundant natural resources but they take the know-how to convert them into environmentally sustainable technologies and tools. In this context, the second option is a subjective option. A good governance strategy promises a better standard of living and how this can be realized depends on the integrated approach adopted by the Government.

Gandhian Concept of Sustainable Development

Mahatma Gandhi is a perhaps the only great thinker of twenty century who could foresee the social and ecological consequences of the ruling model of development and offer an alternative model. Gandhi was not an academic theoretician, but a man of unparallel wisdom. He demonstrated how a very high level of culture and civilization could be evolved without destroying the environment, and without exploding the nature and fellow humans. But Indian leaders rejected his ideas. Gandhi was highly critical of modern civilization. He called it satanic. He says "this civilization is such that one has only to be patient it will be destroyed" and elsewhere he says, of "I ventured utterly to condemn modern civilization" because I hold that the spirit of it is evil. So after considerable amount of thinking and experimentation, Gandhi came to the conclusion that India had the potential of offering an alternative civilization model to the world, a model which can ensure human dignity, economic progress, ecological balance and interpersonal and interspatial equality. "We are inheritors of a rural civilization. The vastness of our country, the vastness of its population, its situation and climate of the country has in my opinion defined it for a rural civilization. Its defects are well known, but not one of them irremediable. To uproot it and substitute for it an urban civilization seems to me impossibility"

Gandhi advocated a new system of human settlements with cities subserving the interests of the villages. By village he meant a micro-Politian community consisting of approximately 1000-5000 people. It will have all the modern facilities of sanitation, housing, various infrastructures and community organizations which country at different stages of development would be able to afford. In his scheme of things much of the industrial activity would move back to the villages so that each village will be self-reliant in its basic needs like food, clothing, housing, education, health, recreation and community management. For other matters it will depend on the neighboring villages, the towns, the nation and the world as a whole. It will constitute the innermost circle in his theory of oceanic circle with man in the center. Gandhi was not against industrialization and machinery. According to Gandhi, "Mechanization is good when the hands are too few for the work intended to be accomplished. It is an evil when there are more hands than required for the work, as is the case in India". In other words, machinery must serve man, "it is good so long it is controlled by the human beings. But when it starts controlling human beings, it becomes evil."

Gandhi said, I believe that if India, and through India, the world is to achieve freedom then sooner or later we shall have to go and live in the village. In huts, not in palaces. Million of people can never live in cities and places in comfort and peace. We can have the vision of truth and nonviolence only in the simplicity of the villages. The sum and substance of what I want to say is that individual person should have control over the things that are necessary for the sustenance of life. My ideal village still exists only in my imagination. After all every human being lives in the world of his own imagination. In this village of my dreams, the villager will not be dull he will be all awareness. He will not live like an animal in filth and darkness. Men and women will live in freedom prepared to face the whole world. Granting all this, I can still envisage a number of things that will have to be organized on a large scale. I do not know what things there will be or will not be. Nor am I bothered about it. If I can make sure of the essential things, I give up everything. And this essential thing was the replacement of the ruling civilization.

Behind Gandhi's insistence on village economy was his grand design of the new civilization based on sustainable development in the real sense of the term. He wanted the human intrusion into the functioning of the biosphere to be minimized by closing men dominated systems such as cities, agricultural and industrial activities to the point where there net effects on the biosphere approximated those of the natural systems they have replaced. No other system of human settlement can achieve this except the village in the form of an urban centre.

Concept of Participatory Development

The objective of Economic and Social Development in developing countries is to set in motion a process of self-reliant and sustainable growth through which social justice can be achieved. Development with in a developing society aims, we believe, at building into society the mechanisms that will ultimately permit self-reliant growth without foreign assistance, at sustaining stable growth patterns for economic development in harmony with the environment, and at providing equal and appropriate opportunities to take part in development to overcome income gaps, regional disparities and in equalities between men and women.

For this to be possible, the central focus of development is not necessary to boost production of material goods; instead, it should be to foster and enhance people's capability to have a role in their society's development. To this end, people should be willingly involved in a wide range of development activities, as agents and beneficiaries of development. It is this participation that is important.

Participatory development as an approach to development that is designed to enhance sustainability and self-reliance and to achieve social justice through improvements in the quality of people's participation.The focal point of participatory development should be the qualitative enhancement of participation in local societies which can be defined as groups of rural communities and as administrative and developmental unit. Participatory development attempts to introduce a bottom up style of development in order to remedy the government – led approach's short comings, specifically by focusing on qualitative improvements in local society's participation. This participation must not be transient; it must entail the sustainable up grading of participation quality. For this to happen, the underlying conditions must be met to facilitate the long term process of participation and its self-reliant sustainability. The long term process of participation cited here is: rising the awareness local people, forming community groups, upgrading their requisite resource management abilities, and creating norms or internalizing their mechanisms, and improving capabilities for external negotiations. The shaping and planning of this participatory process requires both a long term vision and a willingness to selectively improve and bolster traditional community systems as tools of development.

To create the conditions for promoting sustainable participation, governments must create and adopt basic legislation and institutions that guarantee political and economic freedoms as well as strive to meet a broader range of basic human needs. Government also needs to relax regulations in order to remove obstacles to economic participation, improve financial management, builds infrastructure, and train business people and entrepreneurs. These are important components of good governance, which is the basis of participatory development.

Concept of Good Governance

Good Governance as such that should help countries to achieve sustainable and self-reliant development and social justice. Good governance can therefore be understood as comprising two concepts: the ideal orientation of a state that works best to achieve self-reliant and sustainable development and social justice; and the ideal functioning of government that operates most effectively and efficiency. The ideal orientation of a state, hinges on whether the state's basic attitudes are democratically oriented. Elements contributing to this include for example, the legitimacy and accountability of the government, the securing of human rights, local autonomy and devolution power, and civilian control of the military. The functioning of the government depends on whether a government has the requisite political and administrative structure and mechanisms and the capability to function effectively and efficiently. Elements contributing to the latter concept of good governance include the basic laws and institutions of a nation, the administrative competence and transparency, decentralization of its administration and the creation of an appropriate market environment; all of these are needed to support people's participation in every aspect of politics, the economy and society. These are therefore necessary components of good governance as "the government functioning as the basis for participatory development".

Relation between Participatory Development and Good Governance

Participatory development and good governance are related in the following way: Participatory development, with its central focus on raising the quality of participation by local societies and thus better achieving self-reliant and sustainable development and social justice, is one important form of people-oriented development. Good governance is the foundation of participatory development in as much as it provides the government functions needed to promote participation and create the environment in which participatory process take place.

Yet good governance as a function of government does not refer solely to support for participatory development: as participatory processes evolve, good governance develops into such functioning that supports wider and more mature people's participation. In this sense, participatory developments promote good governance in this tern. The projection of the concept of good governance on to the national system – an orientation of a state – then progressively boosts people's trust in their government, in as much as, through good governance, government service improve in effectiveness and efficiency. Thus in the long run, good governance evolves into stronger aspirations for further democratization. The strength of a state's desire for democracy also influences the process of formation of political and administrative structures and government's capability to translate this national stance into action. In turn, this, too, influences the evolution of participatory development. Participatory development and good governance are consequently interrelated, as are the two component elements of good governance, the ideal orientation of the state and the ideal functioning of government.

Relation between Sustainable Development and Good Governance

The National Human Development Report (2001) states that 'governance for human development relates to the management of all processes that, in any society, define the environment which permits and enables individuals to raise their capacity levels on one hand, and provide opportunities to realize their potential and enlarge the set of available choice, on the other'. The report also reiterates that the state is responsible for creating a favorable political, legal and economic environment for building individual capabilities and encouraging private initiative. Governance, therefore, requires the states to exercise their power through various designated bodies and pursue the said goals through an equitable, socially sensitive, non-discriminatory and participatory approach involving people at large. The most important factor is the accountability of the state in governance.

The governance for sustainable governance should include an integrated approach of economic and environmental concerns in the development strategy, keeping in view not only the quality of life that has to be offered to its citizens but also an equal distribution of it with 'social equity' as its goal.

Good governance should also safeguard of a citizen's right to develop, simultaneously holding the environmental concerns at a high pedestal. The Prerequisites towards achieving this goal include democracy, autonomy, fairness, interdependence, responsibility and accountability. A Government should incorporate these qualities before it formulates its policies and programmes for the betterment of a society. There are many virtues related to the above mentioned prerequisites: (*i*) A democratic government have various mechanisms and institutions that confer certain fundamental rights to the citizens to participate in the system. (*ii*) The development choices should be determined by the people and government together with a certain degree of autonomy. (*iii*) The resources of the planet need to be sustained and shared in an equitable manner. The disparities that are in vogue need to be reduced by taking up anti poverty measures and education people. A considerable degree of fairness should operate when the resources can be left un-utilized for the fortune generations; (*iv*) With an increasing level of globalization, there should be inter dependence between the nations in terms of technology transfer, providing assistance towards development projects and also extending co-operation. This should extend beyond local, regional and territorial borders so that the common problems are amicably settled; (*v*) It is the responsibility every citizen to preserve and protect the environment and to achieve development without harming the interests of fellow citizens. The government is also equally responsible for controlling the damage to the environment wherever necessary and impose stringent measures to prevent any loss to the natural habitant; (*vi*) Every nation is a stakeholder in the global environment and is entitled to sharing the common benefits. It is also accountable to the damages caused, intentional or un-intentional, and is liable to pay compensation in case of occurrence of such incidents. Therefore every nation is a custodian of the natural environment in its own capacity.

Challenges to Sustainable Development and Environment

After independence several development efforts in India created a lot of mess with misguided policies. The immediate task in front of us is it to cleanup this mess. According to the 2001 census, there are 6,38,365 villages in India and about 74% of Indian populations live in this village. The number of people living in such of the Indian villages also varies considerably. It is found that most of the Indian villages have a population less than 1000, while there are only a few villages where more than 10000 people live. Rural areas thus sustain fourth-fifths of the total labor force of the country. More than two thirds of the working population is engaged in agriculture and allied activities. These people live in mainly rain-fed areas.

The resources are limited for these people. 70% of populations are poor. Majority of the lands own by them are categorized as waste lands where yields are about 0.5 to 1 ton of grain per hectare. Forests and pastures have been highly degraded and the top soil has been eroded or deprived of nutrients. Usually one corps per year is cultivated in these areas due to inadequate irrigation facilities. On the whole the present natural resource endowment in this region appears quite bleak. Even through we talk about privatization, there is no real investment in agriculture, especially in these rain-fed areas that are outside the much hyped "Green Revolution" areas. That is why the theme of this talk is "turning the present crisis to an opportunity. In fact, by the combination of a scientific and participatory approach to land improvement and micro-watershed management a sufficiently large bio-mass surplus can be achieved in these areas. In fact it is possible to generate bio-mass surplus in the form of wood and processable material of 2 ton per household per year.

On the other hand India ranks 128 out of 177 countries in overall HDI, just below Morocco and Guinea, in life expectancy at birth India ranks 125. just below Pakistan and Comoros, in adult literacy rate in India rank 125 just below Rwanda and Malawi, in terms of primary and secondary education enrolment India ranks 122, just below Namibia and Vietnam and as far as GDP per capita India ranks 114, just below Syria and Nicaragua. Nearly 46% of the children below 5 years of age are underweight and only 33% of the population has uses to improved sanitation. So the question needs a detailed analysis and identification of the causes of underdevelopment of the rural areas and a search for an alternative remedy.

There are so many challengers to sustainable development in India. Many of these problems are caused due to insensitive use of natural resources. Governmental responsibility is also trifling in solving the critical issues. This deterioration of environment has direct impact on the life of individuals, affecting the longevity of life, which in turn, affects the development process on the whole. The degraded soil, depleted aquifer, diminishing forest cover, deteriorating urban environment and destroyed eco-systems can scarcely support better living standards and quality of life in future. The challengers are both natural and man-made and are enumerated as below.

(a) Deforestation: In the name of developmental projects, the felling of trees is being carried out leaving behind the goods of sustainable development and human progress. But forests provide environmental services such as hydrological regulation, arresting processes like top soil erosion, rapid siltation of water bodies global warming and maintaining bio-diversity. Forests provide resources for commercial use of industries and consumption. Also, forests meet local needs. According to one estimate about 35% of India's population directly depends upon forest resources for food, fodder, fuel, shelter and income for their subsistence. So the most serious problem of deforestation is the loss of bio-diversity which leads to not only the extinction of endangered animal species but also immense medicinal value of many plants.

(b) Threat to Biodiversity: The space and resources mean biodiversity and biodiversity is both opportunity and essential function in maintaining biosphere. The fair and equitable sharing of these resources is a prerequisite for a good life. The massive habitat destruction, pollution of the land, water and soil has a drastic effect on the survival of biodiversity. The biological resources, due to injudicious use, are on the verge of extinction.

(c) Effects of Climate Change: The drastic changes in the climatic variations resulted in poor health conditions of the human beings and earth resources. The climate change is likely to affect agriculture adversely and increase the risks of hunger and drinking water scarcity due to enhanced variability and more rapid melting of glaciers. The increasing temperature levels and carbon emissions had also severe effects like contagious disease, degradation of environment, increasing flood and so on. There is another fear that global warming might provoke large number of environmental refugees causing critical economic and social problems.

(d) Increasing Pollution Level: Half of the land of the world is partially or fully degraded. The degrading levels of air quality are widely recognized as a major factor of pollution. The sources of air pollution include industrial pollution, indoor and vehicular pollution. Air pollution is maiming millions of people through lung diseases of various kinds. Water pollution is now a mass killer. The urban regions are especially pron to water pollution as they are not equipped with adequate sewage treatment facilities. Many of the cities untreated municipal waste/ sewage is being discharged into the river, which is the most important cause of water pollution. The shrinking ground water levels have resulted in acute shortage of water across the nation, especially during the summer season.

(e) Poor Health: Right to health is a basic human right, which has been reflected in the directive principles of state policy. Health and education are recognized to be the two distinct influences, which can promote the freedom and capability of individuals to make use of available opportunities (Drez and Sen; 1995). Public health in India has been a subject of National attention. The UNDP Report to express its unhappiness over India's inability to provide health facilities to its pollution. The community health centers, responsible for ensuring the rural health care facilities are often under-staffed or comprise the staff that is unwilling to work in the rural areas.

30% of India's populations continue to live below poverty line. They are not getting clean water to drink; more than 60% people of India do not have appropriate sanitary facilities. New disease like AIDS is at our door steps and several of the diseases we thought we have conquered are on their come basic trail. 46% of the children below 5 years of age are underweight.

(f) Environmental Sustainability: Environment is essentially the resource – base, reflected in quality of land, water, energy, forests etc. the resource may be renewable or non-renewable. Their extraction, exploitation, management, conservation become important factors as they are harassed for material development. So long, the resources are in abundant supply, their utilization is progressive for the community and their use up scales development. Beyond a certain level extraction, the diseconomies of material development start reflecting themselves in various sectors of economy, society and regions. The environmental degradation as a result of use and miss-use of resources of remain a matter of grave concern since the middle of last century. The main causes of environmental degradation are: (*i*) Extra Human population; (*ii*) High resource consumption; (*iii*) Mismanagement of Natural resources; and (*iv*) Poverty.

Government Initiative for Sustainable Development

As per a report by UN Environment Programme, Global Trends in Sustainable Energy Investment 2010', India was ranked eight in the world in terms of investment in sustainable energy. The report further stated that India invested around US $2.7 billion in sustainable energy in 2009. Wind energy attracted 59% of financial investment in clean energy in India. India was placed fifth place in the world for installed wind power in 2010. Biomass and waste was the second largest sector recipient of investment, generating US $0.6 billion of new financial investment. India's sustained effort towards reducing greenhouse gasses will ensure that the countries per capita emission of greenhouse gas will continue to be low until 2030-2031. A new study suggests that the per capita greenhouse gas emissions would stay under four tonnes of CO_2 in 2031.

Major Achievements of sustainable development in India

There are many achievements for sustainable development in India. Such achievements are:

(*i*) India has been ranked ninth in the tree planting role of honour in 2009 in a campaign to plant a billion trees, which was launched by the United Nations Environment Programme in November

2006. The secretary of the Ministry of Environment and Forests, Mr. Vijay Sharma announced that India has joined the United Nations Environment Programmes plant for the planet: Billion tree campaign by planting two billion trees since 2007.

(*ii*) The number of carbon credits issued for emission reduction projects in India is set to triple over the next three years to 246 million by December 2012 from 72 million in November 2009, according to a CRISIL Research study. This will cement India's second position in the global carbon credits market. The growth in CER issuance will be driven by capacity additions in the renewable energy sector and by the eligibility of more renewable energy projects to issue CERS. Consequently, the share of renewable energy projects in India CERS will increase 31%. CRISIL Research expects India's renewable energy capacity to increase to 20,000 MW by December 2012, from the current 15,542 MW.

(*iii*) The contribution of renewable energy to the power business in India has now reached 70% Growth in use of green technologies has put India on the green building leader board with countries such as United States. About 2-3% of all construction in India is green and it will reached 10% in next two or three years.

(*iv*) India's first-ever 3MW solar photovoltaic power plant, developed by the Karnataka Power Corporation Limited, the State-owned power generation company, was dedicated to the nation at Yalesandra village in Kolar district on June 17, 2010. The plant, which uses modular crystalline technology to generate solar energy, has been set up at a cost of US $ 1.29 million. India is the fifth largest wind energy producer in the world, with installed capacity of nearly 10,500 MW and a target to scale up capacity to 14,000 MW by the end of 2011.

(*v*) The US $1.79 billion Indian lighting market is estimated to be growing at 18% annually and switching rapidly to energy-efficient systems. It value of terms, about US $425.58 million of the current market size belongs to the compact fluorescent lamp (CFL), according to Electrical Lamp and Component Manufactures, Association of India statistics.

(*vi*) Compressed natural gas-powered vehicles in India have increased 30% over 2009 to one million in 2010, according to NGV India, Advisor. The Society of Manufactures Electric vehicles expect more sellers of electric two-wheelers in current year.

(*vii*) Vijayawada will be one of the 60 cities in the countries that would be called solar cities, in very near future. The project, for which the centre has allocated over US $6.44 million with each city getting US $107,330 each, is part of the 11th five year plan. Geo-syndicate Power Pvt. Ltd, a Mumbai based energy company, plans to set up the countries first geothermal power plant of 25 Mega Walt (MW)in the Hama district of Andra Pradesh at an investment of US $ 64.7 million.

Government has an enormous responsibility in ensuring the conservation of resources in a sustainable manner a part from providing a decent standard of living. For development Government initiated the programmes like controlling urban pollution, minimization of deforestation measure, joint forest management, environmental management system, and water harvesting measures to control groundwater depletion, bio-diversity conservation measure and so on. The government even initiated a National Environmental Policy, which is under through scrutiny by various concerned bodies and organizations of the State. The Government has also given due importance to rural development programmes, development of indigenous systems and industries, enhancement of technical and ingenious know-how through social welfare and income generation scheme.

The role of panchayats is vital for the overall development and for pursuing development from the bottom to the top level. The 73rd Constitutional Amendment has vested the panchayats with constitutional status, more powers and functions including the financial matters. After 73rd Constitutional Amendment Act the panchayats have been taking an active interest in the local governance matters enabling an effective local participation. The areas that come under the panchayat development plans include agriculture, irrigation, watershed management, village farming, farms produce, dairy, poultry, animal husbandry, fisheries, rural development plans, housing, cottage industries, use of energy, social and family welfare, improvement of transport and communication and public distribution system, relief and rehabilitation, educational and training programmes, health and sanitation facilities and poverty alleviation programmes. As per the provisions of panchayats, the Gram Sabha and Gram Sansad is given power to control the institutions and functionaries in all social sectors, including activities like ownership of minor forest produce, selection of beneficiaries under various programmes, management of minor water bodies, minor mineral lease, MGNREGS also implemented and controlled by the Gram Panchayats.

The increasing pace of urbanization throughout the country is now posing enormous challenges to the management of urban environment.

Multi-centred settlements, sprawling shopping malls, multiplication of population, scare resources, poor urban infrastructure, inadequate housing facility, air, land and water pollution, problem of solid waste collection, access to safe drinking water have jeopardized the economy. Lack of careful design, planning and management further abated the existing environmental challenges. The Municipal bodies are directly responsible for safeguarding the urban atmosphere. This institution should promote environmental ethics and spread awareness among the general public to avoid such activities that directly or indirectly lead to environmental degradation.

Participatory management and techniques need to be adopted towards achieving development. The involvement of local communities, panchayats, cooperative societies and women is a must towards creating sustained and self reliant communities. The livelihoods of the local communities are dependent on the surrounding natural resources. So it is very necessary that they should be involved in the development schemes right from the beginning stage of the development plan, to the execution stage. This approach ensures their place and stakeholders and associates of the development course of the auctions and also enables and empowers them to classify, plan, sustain and share the common benefits.

Conclusion

Sustainable Development is the process of improving the quality of human life while living within the carrying capacity of supporting ecosystems. It carries the premise of development that can be achieved without an undue exploitation of the natural resources. It is the duty of the national, State and local government's, to meticulously work out the modalities of achieving the good of sustainable development in tandem with the National Policy. It is an ongoing process in India. The governance for sustainable development should include an integrated approach of economic and environmental concerns in the development strategy, keeping in view not only the quality of life that has to be offered to its citizens but also an equal distribution of it with 'Social equality' as its goods. Governance should also safeguard a citizen's right to develop simultaneously holding the environmental concerns at a high pedestal. There are various challenges to sustainable development in India such as loss of biodiversity, depleting natural resources, pollution of lands, water and air as also poor health, poor literacy rate, and environmental sustainability. The decentralized governance helps in promoting humans and environmental concerns by the helps of local participation.

REFERENCES

Datye, K.R. *Sustainable Development in India – How and why?*, http://www.clubs.psu.edu/up/aid/web/activities/talks/datye_2000.html.

Dutta, Prabhat (2003); *Towards Good Governance and Sustainable Development*, Dasgupta and Co. Pvt. Ltd. Kolkata

Mandal, Amal (2005): *Rural Development in West Bengal*, Northern Book Centre, New Delhi.

Ministry of Environment and Forests, Document and Data of Ministry of Environment and Forests (2006-07) in Panchayat, Environment and Related Issues, http://www.iesenvis.nic.in/data-base-panchayat-environment-and-related-issues.html.

Nangia, Sudesh, Jha Mrityunjay Mohan, Misra Suresh, Ramchandram R., Velayutham, M. (2010): *Development Concerns in the 21st Century*, Concept Publishing Company Pvt. Ltd.; New Delhi-110059

Narayana, S.K. (2006): Biodiversity conservation should be the Mantra of the century, *Kurukshetra*, Vol. 55, No. 2, December 2006.

Nayak, Krupasindhu (2008): Sustainable Development for vulnerable poor, *Kurukshetra*, Vol. 56, No. 5, March 2008.

Sen, Amartya, (2001): *Development as Freedom*, Oxford University Press, New Delhi.

Sustainable Development, http://www.ibef.org/india/sustainable development.aspx.

Vasudeva, S.P. (2010): Integrated and Sustainable Management of Natural Resources, *Kurukshetra*, vol.58, No.5, March 2010.

Industry Environment and Sustainable Development

An Overview

—Dr. Jagannath B. Kukkudi
—Veerendarakumar B.

Introduction

Environmentally Sustainable Development has been recongnised as the right goal of economic development. Building sustainability has to be approached as a threefold task – social, economic and ecological, simultaneously. The Environment and Sustainable Development visualize to restructure the traditional approach to development in a way that, the development activates are to be integrated with the environment policies. The increasing population, lopsided development activities and rapid industrialization all over the world have caused ecological imbalances at local as well as global level. Thus sustainable development without environmental considerations is ruining the human life by deteriorating the life support system. Sustainable development aims at reconciling Man, Nature and Development for a better future.

In the past two decades there has been increasing concern about the threat to the environment caused by economic growth and its more undesirable side effects. This concern was expressed much earlier in the developed countries. Rapid in industrialization, in spite of its positive effects on economic development of the world, has very seriously threatened the world's natural environmental balance. There is a growing pressure from environmentalists, government, society, customers, employees and competitors on business firms to be environment friendly. These days, protection of environment has become key issue of all over the world. Several factors and forces are responsible for destruction of environment. Of these growing hazardous industrialization is a major culprit. Through swift industrialization is an essential prerequisite for overall economic growth, yet it is damaging the environment drastically, water pollution, air pollution, solid and toxic waste pollution and other environment contamination are common in many production processes.

Environmental degradation and development are considered as two sides of the same coin. The environmental degradation, in fact, started with the propagation of human race. This process of environmental degradation was accelerated with the development of socio-economic activities, i.e agriculture, industrialization, drugs and pharmaceuticals, transport, civil construction including roads and buildings etc. with growing population the requirements of food grains and other consumer itmes increased greatly, leading to further degradation of environment.

In other words, rapid industrialization has created environmental disturbance of three types namely:

1. Depletion of non-renewable natural resources
2. Deforestation and
3. Degradation and destruction.

Thousand of years ago great Indian sages in *Prithvi Sukla* had stated the importance of keeping the earth free from pollution and any disturbance caused to its equilibrium. The message of environment protection is thus not new Environment as a term is very widely used and means different things to different people. It is used in management literature to refer to the external environment in which the organization functions. Ecologically, environment refers to the sum of all the external conditions and influences affecting the life and development of organism (Webster 1961). Two main aspects of the environment are biotic and abiotic (living and non-living).

Environment refers to all the surrounding the things, conditions, and influences affecting the growth or development of living things (World Bank Dictionary 1989). Environment as an area of study is thus conglomerate of all basic and applied sciences, engineering, socio-economic aspects, management, and law.

Environment as the United Nations Committee describes, is the sum total of identified and in identifiable natural resources, existing in finite quantities on earth and, of the quality of the environment of the milieu, which constitutes an important element of the quality of renewable resources. In the generic sense, it is aggregate of surrounding things, conditions, or influences. In specific sense, it is a thin layer of life supporting systems called biosphere, divided into physical and biological environment.

Three decades ago the international community gathered in Stockholm for the United Nations Conference on Human Environment to sound an alarm about the perilous state of Earth and its resources. That landmark event is widely credited with environment issues being placed on the international agenda, leading, in turn, to the establishment of environment ministries at the national level, and increased awareness of the impact that even local decisions can have, on the global environment. Every activity generates unavoidable environment impact of some kind or the other, but the ability of people and societies to adopt themselves to and cope with the change is varied. Environment degradation results in poor health and reduced quality of life:

(*a*) Poor environment quality is directly responsible for some 25% of preventable diseases.

(*b*) Air pollution is a major contributor to a number of diseases.

(*c*) Globally 7% of all deaths and diseases are due to water, and lack of sanitation and hygiene.

There are two basic reasons for our concern with environmental pollution, firstly, home, health and welfare, and secondly, sustenance and survival of mankind. While addressing the world conservation strategy on March 6. 1980, the Indian Prime Minster, Smt. Indira Gandhi, spoke that in India the interest in conservation is not a sentimental one, but the rediscovery of the truth well know to our ancient sages.

Concept of Sustainable Development

The term sustainable development was brought into common use by the World Commission on Environment and Development in its seminar report called "Our Common Future", despite a wide acceptance of the concept of sustainable development, no single definition is yet available which everybody accepts. Most of the definitions are built upon the view expressed by the Brundtland Commission which h defines sustainable le development as "Development that meets the needs of the present generation without compromising the ability of future generations to meet their own needs.

According to Mutofa K. Tolba (of UNEP) the concept of sustainable development implies:

1. Help for the very poor because they are left with no option other than to destroy their environment.
2. Idea of self-reliant development, within natural resource constraint

3. The idea of cost effective development, using differing economic criteria to the traditional approach, i.e. to say, development should not degrade environmental quality nor should it reduce e productivity in the long run.
4. The great issues of health control, appropriate technologies, food self reliance, clear water and shelter for all.
5. The nations that people centred initiatives are needed: human beings in other words are the resources in the concept.

The Brundtland definition emphasis on protecting the future generation. As emphasized by most environmentalists, we have a moral obligation to handover the planet in good order to future generation i.e. the present generation should bequeath a better environment to the future generation. The present generation should promote development that enhances the natural and built environment in ways that are compatible with:

(*a*) Conservation of natural assets, offsetting any unavoidable reduction by a compensating increase so that the 'stock' does not diminish.

(*b*) Preservation of the regenerative capacity of world's natural ecosystem.

(*c*) Achieving greater social equality.

(*d*) Avoiding the imposition of added costs or risks on succeeding generations.

David Pearce defines sustainable development as vector of desirable social objectives such as an increase in real income per capita, an improvement in health and nutrition, educational achievement, access to resource a fairer distribution of income and increase in basic freedom and adds that the elements to be included in the vector are open to ethical debate. "Sustainable Development is development which allow all future generations to have a potential average quality of life at least as high as the average quality of life of the current generation". In this definition quality of life is a measure of the average well being of the members of a generation and depends on traditional material consumption as well as on leisure environmental quality etc.

- Economic of sustainable development.
- A report from working group

"Sustainable development – development that is likely to achieve lasting satisfaction of human needs and improvement of the quality of human life."

Robert Allen "How to save the world."

Management Sustainable Development

There are three basic components of sustainable development: economic, social and environment component.

There are three basic goals of economic systems are:

(a) Increasing production of goods and service.

(b) Satisfying basic needs or reducing poverty.

(c) Improving equity.

The social goal are:

(a) Cultural diversity.

(b) Social justice.

(c) Gender equality.

(d) Public participation.

The environment component requires sustainable resource use, efficient sink function and maintenance of stock of natural capital i.e.; the environment should be able to perform its three functions efficiently and uninterrupted so that ecological stability and resistance are not affects.

In the 21st century, organizations are rapidly changing their structures, systems, work processes and activities. This changing environment calls for enterprising managers to manage and respond to the change in an appropriate manner. It is therefore, necessary for them to develop a clear focus and direction to facilities proper decision making process. The features of 21st century are:

1. As era if information revolution.
2. The traditional supply chains are fast disappearing, paving way to virtual supply chains.
3. The relationship among organizations, their customers, suppliers and government is also undergoing a drastic change.
4. Organisations are becoming extended enterprises.

Indicators of Sustainable Development

Pearce and Atkinson have developed a sustainability index or indicator of the form

$$Z = (S/Y) - (d_m K_m / y) - (d_n k_n / y)$$

Where 'S' is gross savings

Y is income

d_M is depreciation of man-made capital.

d_N is depreciation in natural capital

The above indicator assumes that $d_h = 0$, i.e. knowledge and skills do not depreciate. Sustainability condition is that the value of net change in total capital stock must be equal to or greater that Zero.

Net capital accumulation, k is expressed as

$K = S - d_k$

Assuming that $d_h = 0$ d_k is ex pressed in terms of d_M and d_N

Hence $k = S - d_M k_M - d_N k_N$

Dividing through by Y

$R/Y = (S/Y) - (d_M k_M/Y) - d_N k_M/Y)$

In terms of sustainability indicator Z

K/Y is replaced by Z

Hence, $Z = (S/Y) - (d_M k_M/y) - d_N k_N/y)$ and the value of $Z \geq 0$ to ensure sustainability. This is a weak sustainability indication.

The strong sustainability indicator based on strict complementarily of k_M and k_N takes the form.

DNdN /Y ≤ 0

i.e. stock of natural capital should be no declining.

To test sustainability over a time period, the criteria will have to be rewritten as;

$\Sigma Z \geq 0$

The strong sustainability index that requires constancy of natural capital stock i.e.; non-negative changes in the stock of natural resources and environmental quality, implies that environment should not be degraded further but improvements would be welcome. A similar conditionality is expressed in the Brundtland report, which he says: "If needs are to be met on a sustainable basis, the earth's natural resource base must be conserved and enhanced."

Important indicators of Sustainable Developement are:

1. GDP growth rate,
2. Population stability,
3. Human Resource Development Index,
4. Clear Air Index,
5. Energy Intensity,
6. Renewable energy proportion,

7. Material intensity,
8. Water use,
9. Soil degradation,
10. Forest average,
11. Recycling proportions,
12. Transport intensity.

To this one may also add proportion of urban population access to sewage and water facilities, government allocation for environmental protection, efficacy of policy tools, environmental awareness of the people etc.

Implications of Sustainable Developement

- The development work undertaken by State must be related not only to the present but also to the future. That is, the decision makers should keep it in their view that today's development does not become a disaster for tomorrow.
- Development work should be total or comprehensive. That is, while undertaking development in one direction; other directions must also to be taken into account.
- The development work of a state should keep in view its effect on other countries. Thus no state has the right to make its development at the cost of the interest of other countries.

The concept of sustainable development means good and sound economic growth that can be maintained with minimum environmental impact. The factors that can promote sustainable development are the following:

- Population stabilization and health care.
- Integrated land use planning and watershed management.
- Re-vegetating marginal land and greening the uncultivated area.
- Air pollution control in industrial pockets.
- Water pollution control in rivers.
- Use of non-polluting renewable energy.
- Waste recycling and reuse.
- Conservation of Biological diversity.
- Human settlement without congestion.
- Environmental education and awareness.

Industrial Response for Environment

Environment issues and concerns are common to all sectors and all activates. If the deterioration counties, the whole system of life will be thrown out of gear United Nations Environment (UNECP) programme was designed to be "the environment conscience of the United Nations". The major focus for UNECP has been the study of ways to encourage sustainable development– increasing standards of living without destroying the environment. A growing number of international agreements have been reached in an effort to improve the world's environment quality in most of the developed world. They are:

1. Ambient Environment quality standard
2. Effluent or emission standard
3. Technology based standard
4. Performance standard
5. Product standard
6. Process standard
7. Permits and license.

Industrial units are required to obtain from the concerned state pollution control board consented to operate the unit. Such consent is subject to the unit complying with the prescribed standards.

Challenge to Companies

Business enterprise involves the Darwiniam Maxim of "Survival of the fittest" to define their competitive action and their ecologically unfriendly method of production. To business enterprises, running a business with a conscience is like driving with breaks on. Green policies impose an extra cost on the firms. Companies investing on polluting control equipment will have less to spend on developing new products.

Management time spent on greening decisions regarding the firm's inputs, product and waste management is not available for corporate growth,. Growth of a business enterprise is measured in terms of scale and profits. Hence industries can become greened only slowly.

Industries when forced by regulation have to adopt a new technology with respect to what it takes, what it makes and what it wastes. Technology can be environmentally helped, finding substitutes for scarce natural resources and for allowing existing resource to be stretched further.

Ecological Marketing

Sustainable industrialization does not confine to production process and products alone but also calls for ecological marketing. Ecological marketing is developing consumption choices for the society that meets current needs without sacrificing the ability to meet its future needs. A new marketing approach promoting "reconsumption". The ability to use and reuse goods in whole or in parts in seen. Developing products that can be "re-consumed" over generation (life cycle usage) has become the task of the marketers. Consumer sensitivity to environment issues does not always turn into purchase behavior. Marketing strategies should achieve this. Eco marketing may focus on purchasing behavior alteration or non purchasing conservation activity. The four rules of corporate marketing strategy of consumer needs. Reconsumption, Reorientation of marketing mix and Reorganising are now oriented towards sustainable marketing.

Available resource to meet the standards are employed by the firms in successfully preventing and controlling pollution. Industries favour self-regulation and feel that the best from the regulation is "no regulation". But the environment record of may sectors of industry needs to improve and win public confidence on this.

The broad guidelines for sustainable industrial process are:

1. Use of low and non-waste technologies.
2. Transformation of as much material as possible into the marketable product.
3. Increasing the life of the products, i.e producing more durable products.
4. Up gradation of used products by making components available
5. Recovering components and recycling materials when products cease to be useful
6. Using toxic chemicals only as a last report.
7. Practicising a "Cradle to grave" approach to integrated waste management, i.e from acquiring raw materials to transforming them into manufactured usable goods and by managing wastes of every stage economically.

Measures to achieve sustainable industrialization

1. Protection of biosphere
2. Sustainable use of natural resources.
3. Reduction and disposal of wastes.
4. Wise use of energy
5. Risk reduction
6. Marketing of safe products and services
7. Damage compensation

Conclusion

Environmental protection is the best way for a nation to avoid the needs for costly environment regulations. The Environmental ethics is new and like the vital issues, it will undergo transformation as new data are made available and we are able to interpret rationally and live with nature. Education of the public to environment problems and solutions is of prime importance. Recognizing the environmental ethic alone is not enough; we must all live the environmental ethical way. We must also recognize the power of nature and feel humble in the realization that we are just a very small part in a wonderful and still mysterious system.

REFERENCES

Arora, Dinesh, "Sustainable Development" Third Concept, April 2004.

Banerjee, Dr. A, ''Issues in Environmental Accounting and Reporting'', *Indian Journal of Accounting*. June 1999.

Bose, B.C., *"Integrated Approach to Sustainable Developmet,* Rajat Publications 2001 New-Delhi.

Carroll, A.B., *"Business and Society: Ethics and Stakeholders Management"* South – Western: Cincinnati Ohio 1992.

Downs, A., Ups and downs with ecology: the issue attention Cycle the public interest, 1972.

Krishnamoorthy, Bala, "Environment Management", PHI private Ltd. New Delhi 2005.

Oza, Heera Sunil, "Environment Accounting Linkages with Management Control Systems". The Management Accountant June, 2005.

Passmore, J., *Man's Responsibility to Nature*, 2nd Ed., Duckworth, London, 1980.

Rathore, M.S., ''Environment and Development'', Ravat Publications 1996 Jaipur and New Delhi.

Rene, Dubos, "A Theology Ethics, Barbour, I.G Ed. Reading, Addison-Wesley, Mass, 1973.

Self-organizing complexity, *Conscious Purpose and Sustainable Development Ernest Garcia Environment and Global Modernity*.

Energy Consumption and Economic Growth in the South Asian Countries

—Md. Gazi Salah Uddin
—Dr. Phouphet Kyophilavong
—Dr. Watcharas Leelawath
—Mr. S. S. M. Sadrul Huda
—Manika Chakraborty

ABSTRACT

The chapter investigates the long run Granger Causality relationship between economic growth and energy consumption in South Asian countries. The chapter tries to access the impact of a change in energy consumption on income or vice versa in South Asian countries, namely Bangladesh, India, Pakistan and Sri Lanka. The ADF, DF-GLS, PP and KPSS test Granger Causality test and Co-integration Models are employed taking care of stochastic properties of the variables. The most interesting result is that there is long-run bidirectional causality between energy consumption to income growth in India, Pakistan and Sri Lanka. In Bangladesh, there is long-run unidirectional causality from energy consumption to growth. The estimated bivariate causality electricity consumption function for South Asian countries implies that South Asia is an energy-dependent country; thus, energy-saving policies may have an inverse effect on current and future economic development in South Asia.

Keywords: *Energy Consumption, Co-integration, Granger Causality, Error-correction Model, Economic Growth.*

JEL Classification: *Q43; Q53; Q56*

Introduction

In the post decades, the causality between energy consumption and economic growth has been an emerging area of investigation. While a positive interaction between energy and output is usually expected, findings in the existing literature do not necessarily conform to this stereotyped causality. Therefore, investigating the relationship between these variables on a country-by-country basis becomes important.

The South Asian region is currently experiencing a rapid growth in energy demand, concomitant with economic growth and industrialization. Adequate energy supply is, therefore, a major challenge facing the economies in the region. The total primary energy supply in South Asia, which is indicative of the total energy consumption, increased at the rate of 3.6% annually between 1990 and 1997[1]. In Bangladesh, oil (53 per cent) and natural gas (47 per cent) are the dominant fuels (the shares refer to the total energy consumption). The pattern is similar in Pakistan (oil constitutes 46 per cent and natural gas 38 per cent of the total energy consumption). Sri Lanka is largely dependent on oil (87 per cent). A significant change in the fuel structure in recent years has been the increase in the share of natural gas, because of the important gas discoveries made in India, Pakistan, and Bangladesh and the environmental considerations arising from the large quantities of coal consumed in the region. At present, gas accounts for only about eight per cent of the total energy consumption in India whereas it is the main source of energy in Bangladesh. Bangladesh has always been noted for its acute power shortage. Bangladesh's energy infrastructure is small, insufficient, and poorly managed[2]. The per capita energy use in Bangladesh is one of the lowest in the world. For a fact, only 32 per cent of Bangladesh's population has access to electricity. The quantity of primary energy produced in Sri Lanka is much lower compared to the energy demanded. During the period of 1980-2005, the primary energy production in Sri Lanka has fluctuated between 0.01-0.05 Quadrillion Btu, while the consumption of primary energy has increased steadily from 0.08 Quadrillion Btu in 1980.

With such a backdrop, this paper attempts to investigate the casual relationship between energy consumption and economic growth in South Asia, particularly in Bangladesh, India, Pakistan and Sri Lanka from a long-run Granger Causality perspective in bivariate framework. Nepal, Maldives and Bhutan are not taken into consideration owing to data availability. To deal with the investigation, this paper raises some research questions such as (*i*) does output growth foster energy efficiency in Bangladesh, India, Pakistan and Sri Lanka? (*ii*) does energy use play any significant role to output growth of the countries selected? (iii) is the policy of energy conservation warranted for the selected nations?

In answering the questions to facilitate the investigation, the analysis of this paper relies on recent time series technique. The most striking result of the investigation is that the long-run Granger Causality is running from energy consumption to economic growth in South Asia. This may have an important policy implication for the selected South Asian countries. However, this paper has limitations to address the additional questions such as (i) what other channels can be examined to explain the output effect on energy saving? (ii) how far is energy conservation policy sustainable in South Asia? The two issues are in fact intriguing, and thus left for future research.

Barring introduction that constitutes Section I, this chapter consists of five successive Sections: Section II: Literature Review, Section III: Data Priorities and the Empirical Model, Section IV: Results and Discussion, and Section V: Concluding Remarks.

Literature Review

There are a substantial number of studies that examine the casual relationship between energy consumption and economic growth in developed and industrialized countries. However, the empirical results are mixed and conflicting. Despite a large number of literature on energy and output, this chapter mainly focuses on the studies that examine the relationships between energy consumption and income growth, particularly in the developing countries. The actual causality between energy and output can be different due to different countries' characteristics such as different indigenous energy supplies, political and economic histories, cultures, and different institutional arrangements[3]. The results from earlier studies on the energy-output nexus fall into four broad categories: (*i*) no causality between energy and output, (*ii*) bidirectional causality between energy and output, (*iii*) unidirectional causality from energy to output, and finally, (*iv*) unidirectional causality from output to energy.

If unidirectional causality runs from energy consumption to economic growth, restrictions on the use of energy use could lead to a reduction in economic growth. If causality runs from GDP to energy use, energy conservation measures may be implemented with little or no adverse impacts on economic growth. A bidirectional causal relationship implies that energy use and economic growth are jointly determined and affected at the same time. If no causal relationships between the two variables are found, the "neutrality hypothesis"[4] holds. Therefore, the policy implications of these relationships can be significant depending upon what kind of causal relationship exists.

The findings of no causality between energy and output appear to mainly prevail in developed countries. For instance, various studies that finds no causality between energy consumption and income in the U.S.[5] There is no causality between these variables for New Zealand[6]. The same result is true for the U.K.[7] and France.[8] In contrast, the results of both bidirectional and unidirectional causality are prevalent particularly in developing nations. Numerous studies find bidirectional causality in countries like Argentina,[9] Canada,[10] Cyprus,[11] Greece,[12] Japan,[13] Malawi,[14] and Pakistan.[15]

Unidirectional causation from output to energy consumption is found in the countries such as Australia,[16] India,[17] Singapore,[18] South Korea,[19] and Taiwan.[20] The countries where the causality runs from energy consumption to output growth include China,[21] Fiji,[22] India,[23] Indonesia,[24] Philippines,[25] Sri Lanka,[26] Taiwan,[27] Turkey,[28] and Venezuela.[29]

Most studies, that find either unidirectional or bidirectional causality between energy and output, concentrate on developing countries, and more specifically the emerging economies of Asia. South Asia in particular has recently shown a complex pattern of higher output growth and energy expansion along with energy efficiency measures. Aqeel and Butt[30] investigate the causal relationship between energy consumption and economic growth and energy consumption and employment in Pakistan. They find that Economic growth also leads to growth in petroleum consumption, while on the other hand, neither economic growth nor gas consumption affect each other. A study (2007) on Bangladesh's energy and output,[31] over the period 1971 to 1999, attempts to find that per capita GDP causes per capita electricity consumption, but the reverse is not true. However, this paper uses total energy, which is inclusive of electricity. The (2009) study for India,[32] the nexus between electricity supply, employment and real GDP for India within a multivariate framework using autoregressive distributed lag (ARDL) bounds testing approach of co-integration. Long-run equilibrium relation ship has been established among these variables for the time span 1970-1971 to 2005-2006. The paper found a long-run and short-run Granger Causality running from real GDP and electricity supply to employment without any feedback effect. The absence of causality running from electricity supply to real GDP implies that electricity demand and supply side measures can be adopted to reduce the wastage of electricity, which would not affect future economic growth of India. The impacts of electricity supply have a significant impact on economic growth in Sri Lanka.[33] The findings from the Sri Lankan data imply that current as well as past changes in electricity supply have a significant impact on a change in real GDP in Sri Lanka.

Data Properties and the Empirical Model

This chapter uses annual data on energy consumption and income for four emerging countries in South Asia. It utilizes the annual data on real GDP(Y) (constant 2000US$) and energy consumption (E) (Kt of oil equivalent) data from World Development Indicator. The analysis is confined to the period 1972-2004 due to data availability. All data are used in natural logarithms.

The Basic Model

The relationship between energy consumption and the national income of a nation can be expressed in the following basic bivariate model:

$$Y_1 = \alpha + \beta E_1 + \varepsilon_1 \tag{1}$$

Where, Y_t is real gross domestic product (GDP) and E_t is the energy consumption and ε_t is white noise. Logarithmic transformation of the above equation and inclusion of a trend variable would leave the basic equation as follows:

$$LY_1 = \alpha_0 + \alpha_1 t + \beta LE_1 + \varepsilon_1 \tag{2}$$

Where, t is the trend variable.

The standard Granger Causality test[34] seeks to determine whether past values of a variable helps predict changes in another variable. In the context of this analysis the Granger method involves the estimation of the following equations:

$$LY_1 = \beta_0 + \sum_{i=1}^{q} \beta_{1i} LY_{t-i} + \sum_{i=1}^{q} \beta_{2t} LE_{t-i} + \varepsilon_{1t} \tag{3}$$

$$LE_t = \varphi_0 + \sum_{i=1}^{r} \varphi i_{1i} LE_{t-i} + \sum_{i=1}^{r} \varphi_{2i} LY_{t-i} + \varepsilon_{2t} \tag{4}$$

Where, LY_t and LE_t represent real GDP and energy consumption respectively, ε_{1t} and ε_{2t} are uncorrelated stationary random process, and subscript t denotes the time period. Failing to reject $H_0 : \beta_{21} = \beta_{22} = ... = \beta_{2q} = 0$ implies that energy consumption do not Granger cause real income activities. On the other hand, failing to reject $H_0 : \varphi_{21} = \varphi_{22} = ... = \varphi_{2r} = 0$ implies that real GDP do not Granger cause energy use.

Empirical works based on time series data assume that the underlying time series is stationary. However, many studies have shown that majority of time series variables are non-stationary[35] or integrated of order 1. The time series properties of the data at hand are therefore studied in the outset.

The above specification of the causality test assumes that the time series at hand are mean reverting process. However, it is highly likely that variables of this study are nonstationary. Formal tests will be carried out to find the time series properties of the variables. If the variables are integrated of order 1 i.e.; I (1), Engle and Granger (1987) assert that causality must exist in, at least, one direction. The Granger causality test is then augmented with an error correction term (ECT) as shown below:

$$\Delta LY_t = \beta_0 + \sum_{i=1}^{q}\beta_{1i}\Delta LY_{t-i} + \sum_{i=1}^{q}\beta_{2i}\Delta LE_{t-i} = \alpha_1 Z_{t-1} + \varepsilon_{1t} \quad (5)$$

$$\Delta LE_t = \varphi_0 + \sum_{i=1}^{r}\varphi i_{1t}\Delta LE_{t-i} + \sum_{i=1}^{r}\varphi_{2t}\Delta LY_{t-i} + \lambda_1 Z_{t-1} + \varepsilon_{2t} \quad (6)$$

Where Z_{t-1} is the ECT obtained from the long run co-integrating relationship between real GDP and energy consumption. The above error correction model (ECM) implies that possible sources of causality are two, lagged dynamic regressors and lagged co-integrating vector. Accordingly, by equation (5), energy use Granger causes real GDP, if the null of either $\sum_{t=1}^{q}\beta_{2t} = 0$ or $\alpha_1 = 0$ is rejected. On the other hand, by equation (6), real GDP Granger causes energy consumption, if λ_1 is significant or $\sum_{i=1}^{r}\varphi_{2i}$ are jointly significant.

Results and Discussion

Table 8.1: Descriptive Statistics on Real Income and Energy Consumption

	LYB	LEB	LYI	LEI	LYP	LEP	LYS	LES
Mean	5.656448	9.156437	5.707791	12.59584	2.331705	10.30347	2.331705	0.846456
Median	5.609445	9.192584	5.681223	12.65517	2.337750	10.35790	2.337750	0.849189
Maximum	6.030591	9.819562	6.302843	13.05381	2.396547	10.98517	2.396547	0.874029
Minimum	5.416923	8.524169	5.303465	12.05160	2.262173	9.603935	2.262173	0.816326
Std. Dev.	0.176219	0.392913	0.308490	0.313348	0.040040	0.410968	0.040040	0.017202
Skewness	0.579462	-0.004593	0.356655	-0.266983	-0.184854	-0.142462	-0.184854	-0.202974
Kurtosis	2.246536	1.758773	1.837395	1.714836	1.748587	1.741026	1.748587	1.753459
Jarque-Bera	2.627369	2.118502	2.5?8134	2.663053	2.341239	2.291019	2.341239	2.363156
Probability	0.268828	0.346715	0.278297	0.264074	0.310175	0.318062	0.310175	0.306794
Sum	186.6628	302.1624	188.3571	415.6628	76.94627	340.0144	76.94627	27.93306
Sum Sq. Dev.	0.993696	4.940173	3.045309	3.141976	0.051301	5.404624	0.051301	0.009469
Observations	33	33	33	33	33	33	33	33

Note: LY: Log of Real GDP; LE: Log of Energy Consumption

In order to obtain a better understanding of the behaviour of economic activity and energy consumption, a preliminary analysis of the data is first carried out. Table 8.1 presents summary of the logarithms of the income and energy consumption. Table 8.2 presents the pair-wise correlation is also calculated and the positive co-movements among the variables under investigation.

Table 8.2: Correlation Matrix

	LYB	LEB	LYI	LEI	LYP	LEP	LYS	LES
LYB	1.000	0.969	0.986	0.938	0.949	0.953	0.949	0.947
LEB	0.969	1.000	0.985	0.992	0.995	0.996	0.995	0.995
LYI	0.986	0.985	1.000	0.965	0.971	0.974	0.971	0.969
LEI	0.938	0.992	0.965	1.000	0.997	0.997	0.997	0.998
LYP	0.949	0.995	0.971	0.997	1.000	1.000	1.000	1.000
LEP	0.953	0.996	0.974	0.997	1.000	1.000	1.000	1.000
LYS	0.949	0.995	0.971	0.997	1.000	1.000	1.000	1.000
LES	0.947	0.995	0.969	0.998	1.000	1.000	1.000	1.000

Table 8.3: Unit root test results

		ADF	DF-GLS	PP	KPSS
		1	2	3	4
Levels intercept	LY_{BD}	1.760745	0.767349	7.299221	0.750068***
	LE_{BD}	0.678548	-0.217221	0.456510	0.666601**
	LY_{IN}	1.888623	1.306546	3.766755	0.657099**
	LE_{IN}	-2.112925	0.041020	1.892518	0.658529**
	LY_{PK}	-0.913134	0.890374	-0.913134	0.664961**
	LE_{PK}	-0.419699	0.924206	-0.411457	0.666035**
	LY_{SR}	-0.913134	0.890374	-0.913134	0.664961**
	LE_{SR}	-1.130649	0.876493	-1.130649	0.664460**
Levels intercept and trend	LY_{BD}	-0.723675	-2.789430	-0.056543	0.197811**
	LE_{BD}	-3.141368	-3.203634	-3.076049	0.081905***
	LY_{IN}	-1.728985	-1.501851	-1.528229	0.196528**
	LE_{IN}	-0.455793	-1.461020	-0.642524	0.180934**
	LY_{PK}	-1.389029	-1.334804	-1.570551	0.156983**

		1	2	3	4
	LE_{PK}	1.451944	-1.458877	-1.675084	0.141221*
	LY_{SR}	-1.389029	-1.334804	-1.570551	0.156983**
	LE_{SR}	-1.363445	-1.282139	-1.528302	0.162594**
First differences intercept	ΔLY_{BD}	-3.601083**	-3.660589***	-7.305984***	0.425454
	ΔLE_{BD}	-7.694960***	-6.996599***	-7.757603***	0.090561
	ΔLY_{IN}	-5.907657***	-5.796700***	-5.916656***	0.560209
	ΔLE_{IN}	-3.541951**	-3.451938***	-3.541951**	0.327421
	ΔLY_{PK}	-4.552144***	-4.425971***	-4.552144***	0.180752
	ΔLE_{PK}	-4.562160***	-4.511315***	-4.562160***	0.119827
	ΔLY_{SR}	-4.552144***	-4.425971***	-4.552144***	0.180752
	ΔLE_{SR}	-4.531901***	-4.369129***	-4.531901***	0.188086
First differences intercept and trend	ΔLY_{BD}	-8.850653***	-9.132724***	-15.92568***	0.500000
	ΔLE_{BD}	-7.686438***	-7.640083***	-7.768626***	0.073832
	ΔLY_{IN}	-6.825435***	-7.018990***	-10.09757***	0.109313
	ΔLE_{IN}	-4.027986**	-3.842115***	-4.098975**	0.103046
	ΔLY_{PK}	-4.496625***	-4.650998***	-4.483220***	0.113833
	ΔLE_{PK}	-4.467387***	-4.622993***	-4.453398***	0.101208
	ΔLY_{SR}	-4.496625***	-4.650998***	-4.483220***	0.113833
	ΔLE_{SR}	-4.509450***	-4.662978***	-4.496287***	0.112852

Notes: LY: Log of Real GDP; LE: Log of Energy Consumption. For ADF, the optimal lag length is selected using a testing down method and DF–GLS tests using SIC. For PP tests, bandwidth is selected based on the Newey-West procedure using Bartlett Kernel. The lag truncation parameter for the KPSS test is selected using the formula.* ,** and *** denote rejection of the null at 10%, 5% and 1% level of significance.

The estimation procedure begins with testing the time series properties of the data. Table 8.3 presents the unit root test results of the variables. As it is important to determine the order of integration among variables, four different types of tests are applied. The Augmented Dickey-Fuller (ADF)[36] test is widely used for unit root tests (Dickey and Fuller 1979, 1981) but it has poor power problem, the other two tests are more powerful in rejecting the null of nonstationarity. Between these two tests the DF–GLS tests performs well especially in the presence of unknown shifts in the mean and trend in the data. On the other hand, the PP test is more efficient in the presence of a single break in the data. In addition to augmented Dickey–Fuller (ADF), DF-GLS and PP test, another more powerful test, namely KPSS[37] test, is also applied. For ADF, DF-GLS and PP tests, both with constant and constant and trend, one is unable to reject the null at level, is able to reject when first differenced series is used. Similarly, for KPSS tests, again both with constant and constant and trend, the null (of stationarity) is rejected at levels but accepted when applied to first differenced data. In total, it emerges from the unit root test results that both the variables are integrated of order 1, *I (1)*.

Table 8.4 presents the long-run equation, which is derived by normalizing on output based on the estimated co-integration coefficient. As expected, all the signs are positive and significant indicating that energy consumption and positively contribute to GDP for Bangladesh, India, Pakistan and Sri Lanka.

Table 8.4: Output of Regression

Country	Model	Coefficient	Std. Error	t-Statistic	p-value	R^2	Adj R^2
Bangladesh	Constant	1.676869	0.182185	9.204224	0.0000	0.939	0.937
	Energy consumption	0.434621	0.019879	21.86315	0.0000		
India	Constant	-6.261717	0.582297	-10.75347	0.0000	0.931	0.929
	Energy consumption	0.950275	0.046215	20.56183	0.0000		
Pakistan	Constant	1.328003	0.003010	441.1936	0.0000	0.999	0.999
	Energy consumption	0.097414	0.000292	333.7101	0.0000		
Sri Lanka	Constant	0.361528	0.002531	142.8373	0.0000	0.999	0.999
	Energy consumption	2.327558	0.002990	778.5587	0.0000		

Therefore, standard Granger causality tests will be invalid and one needs to apply the ECM as explained before. Once it is established that variables are $I(1)$, the next step is to test for existence of any cointegrating relationship between income and energy consumption. The Johansen LR test[38] of cointegration is applied and results are showed in Table 8.3. The appropriate VAR lag length is selected using BIC. The λ-trace statistic rejects the null of $r \leq 0$ but cannot reject $r \geq 1$ and also, the λ-max statistic rejects the null of $r = 0$ but fails to reject $r = 1$ at 5% level. These Eigenvalue tests based on stochastic matrix indicate existence of the cointegrating relationship between income and energy consumption. So, the Granger causality tests will be modeled using ECM as explained in Eq. (5) and (6).

Table 8.5 : Co-integration Test Results

$X' = [LY, LE]$; [VAR lag $k = 2$]

	Null	Eigenvalues	Trace Test		Max Eigenvalue Test	
			λ-trace	p–value	λ-max	p–value
	1	2	3	4	5	6
Bangladesh	R ≤ 0	0.477714	20.42380*	0.0083	19.48622	0.0068
	R ≤ 1	0.030769	0.937584	0.3329	0.937584	0.3329
India	R≤0	0.434427	24.43814*	0.0125	17.09749	0.0322
	R≤1	0.217052	7.340656	0.1096	7.340656	0.1096
Pakistan	R≤0	0.423477	16.97708*	0.0297	16.52218	0.0216
	R≤1	0.015049	0.454902	0.5000	0.454902	0.5000
Srilanka	R≤0	0.432484	17.40765*	0.0255	16.99459	0.0181
	R≤1	0.013674	0.413060	0.5204	0.413060	0.5204

Note: (i) indicates Trace and states Maximum Eigen value unrestricted co-integration rank Test, (ii) One asterisk (*) denotes significance at 5% level, (iii) denotes the number of co-integrating vectors.

Table 8.6: Granger Causality Test Results

	Null Hypothesis	*F*–stat [*p*–value]	ECT_{t-1} [*t*–ratio]	Decision
Bangladesh	$LE \rightarrow LY$	3.180[.031]	.020[.269]	Accepted
	$LY \rightarrow LE$	3.543[.029]	-.613*[-3.244]	Rejected
India	$LE \rightarrow LY$	3.520[.030]	-.322 **[-2.074]	Rejected
	$LY \rightarrow LE$	11.256[.003]	-.250** [-4.393]	Rejected
Pakistan	$LE \rightarrow LY$	9.426[.001]	-.070** [2.181]	Rejected
	$LY \rightarrow LE$	9.272[.005]	-.080** [2.212]	Rejected
Srilanka	$LE \rightarrow LY$	4.979[.004]	-.073** [1.973]	Rejected
	$LY \rightarrow LE$	5.032[.011]	-.069** [1.963]	Rejected

Notes: Optimal lags are selected using Bayesian Information Criteria (BIC). *(**) denote rejection at 5% (10%) levels of significance. The Symbolmeans "does not Granger cause".

Table 8.5 presents the Granger Causality tests results. The *F* statistic on linear restriction on lagged values of *IY* rejects the null hypothesis that energy consumption do not Granger cause output *(IY)*. On the other hand, the coefficient of the lagged ECT has desirable negative sign and is also statistically significant reinforcing *F*-test results. It is found that energy consumption of India, Pakistan and Sri Lanka can explain movements in the income activity. Next, this paper considers the other null hypothesis that income does not Granger cause energy consumption. Again, it appears from *F* statistic that lagged *LY* terms are jointly significantly different from zero and lagged ECT term is carrying desirable negative sign and also significant: the null is hence rejected. It is also found that there is a long-run unidirectional causality between income and energy consumption of Bangladesh, as reflected by the coefficients of error-correction terms and the respective *t*-value. The results establish feedback or bidirectional causality between energy consumption and growth in India, Pakistan and Sri Lanka. In Bangladesh, the nexus is unidirectional.

Concluding Remarks

Following the global oil shocks of the early 1970s, the discussion of energy policy and its link with economic growth has been widespread in the economic literature. Developing countries that aspire to faster growth have been more interested in the role of energy in output performance than ever before. The major economies of South Asia in particular are experiencing spectacular growth on one hand, and confronting the challenges of energy expansion on the other hand. Hence, this paper notices a rise in the research on South Asian economies in the area of energy and output.

The chapter aims to examine the pattern of long run relationship between energy consumption and industrial activities in south Asia. It chooses to apply Granger causality tests to find the direction of causality between energy consumption and economic growth. Given that the variables are *I*(1) and are cointegrated, Granger causality tests incorporating an error correction model was selected. Results obtained reveal that the correction model (ECM) suggests that there is long–run bidirectional causality from energy consumption to economic growth and output growth to energy consumption in India, Pakistan and Sri Lanka. A bi-directional causal relationship implies that energy use and economic growth are jointly determined and affected at the same time. In Bangladesh, there is long–run unidirectional causality from energy consumption to income growth. It implies that restrictions on the use of energy use could lead to a reduction in economic growth in Bangladesh. The estimated bivariate causality electricity consumption function for South Asian countries implies that South Asia is an energy-dependent country; thus, energy-saving policies may have an inverse effect on current and future economic development in South Asia.

This chapter provides the possible policy implications. First, we find that uni-directional causality running from energy consumption to GDP exists in Bangladesh, suggesting that energy serves as an engine of economic growth. That is, current as well as earlier changes in energy consumption had a significant impact on income. It follows then that the cuts in energy consumption from the enactment of the Kyoto Protocol will actually harm the economy where this form of causality exists. Second, bi-directional causality between energy consumption and GDP exists in the India, Pakistan and Sri Lanka, which indicates the level of economic activity and energy consumption mutually influence each other in that a high level of economic growth leads to a high level of energy consumption and vice versa. This suggests that energy consumption and income are endogenous and, therefore, any single equation forecast of one or the other could be misleading. Furthermore, in order not to adversely affect economic growth, energy conservation policies that aim at curbing energy use must also, at the same time, find ways to reduce consumer consumption.

REFERENCES

Akarca, A.T. and Long, T.V., "On the relationship between energy and GNP: a reexamination", *Journal of Energy and Development*, Vol. 5, 1980, pp. 326–331.

Aqeel, A. and Butt, M. S., "The relationship between energy consumption and economic growth in Pakistan". *Asia-Pacific Development Journal*, Vol. 8 (2), 2001, pp.101-110.

Asafu-Adjaye, J. "The relationship between energy consumption, energy prices and economic growth; time series evidence from Asian developing countries", *Energy Economics*, Vol. 22, 2000, pp. 615–625.

Chang, Y. and Wong, J.F., "Poverty, energy and economic growth in Singapore". Working Paper, Department of Economics, National University of Singapore, 2001

Chen, S.T. Kuo, H.-I. & Chen, C.C., "The relationship between GDP and electricity consumption in 10 Asian Countries", *Energy Policy*, Vol. 35, 2007, pp. 2611–262

Cheng, B.S. "Causality between energy consumption and economic growth in India: an application of cointegration and error-correction modeling", *Indian Economic Review*, Vol.34, 1999, pp. 39–49.

Cheng, B.S. and Lai, T.W., "An investigation of cointegration and causality between energy consumption and economic activity in Taiwan", *Energy Economics*, Vol.19, 1997, pp. 435-444.

Cheng, B.S., "An investigation of cointegration and causality between energy consumption and economic Growth", *Journal of Energy and Development*, Vol. 21, 1995, pp. 73–84

Dickey, D., and Fuller, W.A., "Distribution of the Estimates for Autoregressive Time Series with a Unit Root" , *Journal of the American Statistical Association,* Vol. 74, 1979, pp. 427-431.

Dickey, D., and Fuller, W.A., "Likelihood Ratio Statistics for Autoregressive Time Series with a Unit Root". *Econometrica,*Vol.49, 1981, pp. 1057-1072.

Engle, R. and Granger, C., "Co integration and error correction representation: estimation and testing", *Econometrica*, Vol. 55, 1987, pp.251-276.

Erol, U. and Yu, E.S.H., " On the causal relationship between energy and income for industrialized countries", *Journal of Energy Development*, Vol. 13, 1988, pp. 113–122.

Erol, U. and Yu, E.S.H., "On the causal relationship between energy and income for industrialized countries", *Journal of Energy Development*, Vol. 13, 1988, pp. 113–122.

Fatai, K. and Oxley, L. & Scrimgeour, F., *"Energy Consumption and Employment in New Zealand: Searching for Causality"*. Paper presented at NZAE Conference, Wellington, 2002

Ghali, K. H., and El-Sakka, M. I. T., "Energy use and output growth in Canada: A multivariate cointegration analysis", *Energy Economics*, Vol. 26, 2004, pp. 225–238.

Ghosh, S., "Electricity supply, employment and real GDP in India: evidence from cointegration and Granger-causality tests", *Energy Policy*, 37 (8), 2009, 2926–2929.

Granger, C. W. J., "Some Recent Developments in the Concepts of Causality". *Journal of Econometrics*, Vol. 39, 1988, pp. 199-211

Hondroyiannis, G. Lolos, S. and Papapetrou, G., "Energy consumption and economic growth: assessing the evidence from Greece", *Energy Economics*, Vol. 24, 2002, pp. 319-336.

IEA, World Energy Outlook, International Energy Agency, 2009, France.

Johansen, S., "Estimation and hypothesis testing of cointegration vectors in Gaussian vector autoregressive models", *Econometrica,* Vol. 59 (6), 1991, pp. 1551-1580.

Jumbe, C. B. L., "Cointegration and Causality between Electricity Consumption and GDP: Empirical Evidence from Malawi", *Energy Economics*, Vol. 26, 2004, pp. 61-68.

Kwiatkowski, D. and Phillips, P. C. B. & Schmidt, P. & Shin, Y. "Testing the Null of Stationarity Against the Alternative of a Unit Root: How Sure Are We That Economic Time Series Have a Unit Root?", *Journal of Econometrics*, Vol. 54, 1992, pp. 159–178.

Masih, A.M.M. and Masih, R., "On the Temporal Causal Relationship between Energy Consumption, Real Income, and Prices: Some new Evidence from Asian-Energy Dependent NICs based on a Multivariate Cointegration/Vector Error-Correction Approach". *Journal of Policy Modeling*, Vol. 19(4), 1997, pp. 417-440.

Masih, A.M.M. and Masih, R., "On the Temporal Causal Relationship between Energy Consumption, Real Income, and Prices: Some new Evidence from Asian-Energy Dependent NICs based on a Multivariate Cointegration/Vector Error-Correction Approach". *Journal of Policy Modeling*, Vol.19(4), 1997, pp. 417-440.

Morimoto, R. and C. Hope, "The impact of electricity supply on economic growth in Sri Lanka" , *Energy Economics,* Vol. 26, 2004, pp. 77–85.

Morimoto, R. and Hope, C. "The impact of electricity supply on economic growth in Sri Lanka", *Energy Economics*, Vol. 26, 2004, pp. 77–85.

Mozumder, P. and Marathe, A., "Causality relationship between electricity consumption and GDP in Bangladesh", *Energy Policy*, Vol. 35, 2007,pp. 395-402

Narayan, P.K. and Singh, B., "The electricity consumption and GDP nexus for the Fiji Islands", *Energy Economics*, Vol. 29, 2007, pp. 1141–1150

Narayan, P.K. and Smyth, R., "Electricity consumption, employment and real income in Australia evidence from multivariate Granger causality tests", *Energy Policy*, Vol.33, 2005, pp.1109–1116.

Neutrality hypothesis means there is no causality runs from energy consumption to economic growth and economic growth to energy consumption. It would mean that energy conservation policies do not affect economic growth.

Shiu, A. and Lam, L.P., "Electricity consumption and economic growth in China". *Energy Policy*, Vol. 32, 2004, pp. 47–54.

Soytas, U. and Sari, R. "Energy consumption and GDP: causality relationship in G-7 countries and emerging markets", *Energy Economics*, Vol. 25, 2003, pp. 33-37.

Soytas, U. and Sari, R., "Energy consumption and GDP: causality relationship in G-7 countries and emerging markets", *Energy Economics*, Vol. 25, 2003, pp. 33-37.

Soytas, U. and Sari, R., "Energy consumption and GDP: causality relationship in G-7 countries and emerging markets", *Energy Economics*, Vol.25, 2003, pp. 33-37.

Squalli, J., "Electricity consumption and economic growth: bounds and causality analyses of OPEC members", *Energy Economics*, Vol. 29, 2007, pp. 1192-1205.

Stern, D., "Energy and Economic Growth in the USA, A Multivariate Approach". *Energy Economics*, Vol. 15, 1993, pp. 137-150

Temple, F., *Energy subsidies in Bangladesh: Magnitude and Beneficiaries.* Speech given at Dhaka Chamber of Commerce and Industries (DCCI), June 09, Bangladesh, 2002.

Unlike the ADF test, KPSS test has the null of stationarity against a nonstationary alternative. See, Kwiatkowski *et. al.* (1992)for details and critical values of the KPSS test.

Yang, H.Y., "A note on the causal relationship between energy and GDP in Taiwan", *Energy Economics*, Vol. 22, 2000, pp.309–317.

Yu, E.S.H. and Choi, J.Y., "The causal relationship between energy and GNP: an international comparison", *Journal of Energy Development*, Vol. 10, 1985, pp. 249–272.

Yu, E.S.H. and Choi, J.Y., "The causal relationship between energy and GNP: an international comparison", *Journal of Energy Development*, Vol.10, 1985, pp.249–272.

Yu, E.S.H. and Hwang, B.K., "The relationship between energy and economic growth in Korea", *Applied Energy*, Vol. 83, 1984, pp. 1181-1189

Yu, E.S.H. and Jin, J.C., "Cointegration tests of energy consumption, income and employment", *Resources and Energy*, Vol. 14, 1992, pp. 259–266

Zachariadis, T. and Pashourtidou, N., "An empirical analysis of electricity consumption in Cyprus", *Energy Economics*, Vol. 29, 2007, 183–198.

Causality Between Electricity Consumption and Economic Growth in Bangladesh

A Timeseries Approach

—Md. Gazi Salah Uddin
—Kohinoor Biswas
—Phouphet Kyophilavong

ABSTRACT

This chapter investigates the causality between electricity consumption and GDP growth for Bangladesh with special emphasis on the direction of causality and its impact on the short as well as long run. This study employs the co-integration and Granger causality tests to investigate long-run equilibrium relationship and the direction of causality between energy consumption and real income growth in Bangladesh. The estimation procedure also passes a battery of diagnostic tests indicating stability of the long and short run estimates. Analyses of 30 years' data since 1975 up to 2005 reveal some striking facts: the role of energy with respect to growth of Bangladesh is not 'neutral' rather' limiting'; unidirectional causality exists and directs from electricity generated from gas to growth in the long run where as bi-directional causality exists between them but only in the short run.

Key Words: *Cointegration, Granger Causality, Electricity Consumption, Economic Growth JEL Classification: C22, F51*

Introduction

The nature of causal relationships between energy consumption and income has been one of the most hotly debated issues in the past three decades

(Lee, 2005). For Bangladesh, an LDC, energy, indeed, lies at the core of development issue for some very clear reasons: low and less diversified natural endowment, dependency on import, hence burden on dollar reserve. Bangladesh with a consistent and modest growth of around 5 to 6% in the last decade is yet to reach her optimum potential of growth. This paper attempts to explore the causal relationship and direction between electricity consumption and economic growth for Bangladesh. Then, based on the outcome of analysis proposes some policy direction for the short as well as long-term.

The role of energy into the production function has been debated by two different schools of thoughts. The traditional economic view considers energy as a secondary factor of production. Few literatures support that notion since the cost of energy occupies a very small proportion of GDP. Beaudreau (2005) criticizes the conventional economic standing of energy as a secondary factor and points out that without the use of energy, production is not possible, from an engineering perspective. Beaudreau (2005), Ghali and El-Sakka (2204) and Stern (1997, 2000) supported the 'engineering' view of energy. Therefore, they incorporated energy consumption in a production function framework to analyze the relationship between energy consumption and output. Consequently, energy is a necessary requirement for economic and social development and so is potentially a "limiting factor to economic growth" (Ghali and El-Sakka, 2004; Kraft and Kraft, 1978; Jumbe, 2004; Masih and Masih, 1994; Stern 1993; Stern, 2000; Erol and Yu 1987; Shiu and Lam 2004)

In past times, the energy-income nexus has an obvious and unavoidable link with environmental issue since electricity generation has topped as a direct source of emission of GHG - the lethal contributor to greenhouse effect. (Sadorsky, 2009). Therefore, countries where energy is endogenous factor to growth are the probable targets of the environment watchdogs. The recent Copenhagen Summit voices out this concern and draws on attention of the global leaders to carry out a massive environmental campaign across the globe to fight global warming and reduce emission. This heightened concern about environment places a two-way pull, specially, on developing economies, to balance between environmental cleanliness and drive for growth.

In this chapter, we have investigated the relationship between energy consumption and economic growth in Bangladesh from a long run Granger causality perspective in multivariate framework. To extend our knowledge, there is available only a scanty number of studies that examine the Granger causality link between economic growth and energy consumption in South Asian countries, particularly for Bangladesh. Among the South Asian nations the case of India, though, has been substantially studied, the case of Bangladesh deserves some special attention in terms of holding a different geographical position in the world map which is the worst affected due to the effects of global warming. The most striking result may be noted that the long-term Granger Causality exists for Bangladesh, with direction running from energy consumption to economic growth. This particular finding has association with policy implication which hits the focal point that - growth with conservation or without conservation- which one is to suit to Bangladesh.

The remainder of the chapter has been organized as follows. Section 2 provides a brief summary of the literature review. Section 3 includes the data definitions and the times series properties of the variables. Section 4 deals with empirical results and relevant discussions. Section 5 provides ends with policy implication.

Literature Review

There are a considerable number of studies that have examined the link between energy consumption and economic growth in developed as well as developing countries. Earlier studies by Kraft and Kraft (1978) examined the Granger causality link between energy and income with mixed results (Akarca and Long, 1980; Yu and Hwang, 1984; Yu and Choi, 1985; Erol and Yu,1987; Hwang and Gum,1992; Bentzen and Engsted,1993; Glasure and lee,1997).

Following Stern (1993), numerous multivariate studies employed powerful time series techniques in the last decade (Stern,2000; Glasure, 2002; Sari and Soytas, 2003; Sari and Soytas, 2004; Lee, 2005, 2006). Further, in 2004, Stern examined the relationship between income, energy use, labor and capital stock in the US for the period of 1948-1994, using cointegration and vector error correction modeling. He found mutual causality between energy consumption and GDP in the US. A consensus of these studies is that employment is found to Granger cause electricity consumption in the long run. While in the short run, the causal effect is found to be 'neutral' between employment and electricity consumption, except in Taiwan (Chang *et al,* 2001). These studies also reveal that a country's population growth has a link with electricity consumption via the residential and commercial usage.The energy-growth 'neutrality' hypothesis has been widely studied and results are found to be conflicting. Wolde-Rufael (2005) found evidence to support the neutrality hypothesis of energy in connection with growth.

Al-Iriani (2006) for a group of six Gulf Cooperation countries found a unidirectional causality running from economic growth to energy consumption. Sari and Soytas (2006) in a trivariate model with energy, carbon emission and income failed to identify any significant Granger causality link between any of the variables. In case of Turkey, the relationship between carbon emissions and income was reported to be linear rather following EKC path (Lise, 2006). In 2006, Say and Yucel established energy as a function of three variables: income, population and emissions.

In 2007, Sari and Soytas conducted a study on six developing countries where energy was reported to be an important factor of production along with other conventional factors. In another study of bivariate relationship between energy consumption and economic growth on African countries, Ricci (2007), focused at the transmission mechanisms through which environmental policy and economic growth may interact. Ricci concluded that general environmental policies are deemed to have negative effects on growth. Chontanawat *et al.* (2008) compared the 'energy-growth' causality in the developed versus developing nations. The study reported that causality is more pronounced in the developed countries than in developing ones. 'Energy to growth' nexus was found in only 35% of the poorest nations, while it was 42% in the middle-income and 69% in the high-income countries. Another study, conducted by Huang et al. (2008) found congruency with Chontanawat et al; i.e 'energy-growth' causality was found insignificant in low-income nations while in middle-income and high-income countries the link was significant. Lee and Chiang (2008) found support for long-run causality from energy to growth. Further, for a group of 22 OECD countries Lee et al. (2008) found a bi-directional causality. In a panel study of G7 countries Narayan and Smyth (2008) proved that capital formation and energy consumption Granger cause real GDP positively in the long run. Sadorsky (2009) finds that real income and carbon dioxide emissions both are important drivers of renewable energy consumption.

Data and Model Specification

In this study, annual data of Real GDP, Total Electricity Consumption, Electricity production generated by Gas, Electricity production generated by Oil and Electricity production generated by Hydropower are taken from World Development Indicator 2007, covering the period 1975-2005 for the country of Bangladesh. All data are expressed in logarithms in order to include the proliferate effect of time series and reduce the problem of heteroscedasticity.[1]

In this study, the method of vector autoregressive model (VAR) is adopted to estimate the causal relationship between exports, imports and economic growth in following form:

$$LRY = f\,(LELC,\ LELCg,\ LELCo\ and\ LELCh\,) \tag{1}$$

Where: LRY = Log of Real Gross domestic product,

LELC = Log of Total Electricity Consumption

LELCg = Log of Electricity production generated by Gas

LELCo = Log of Electricity production generated by Oil

LELCh = Log of Electricity production generated by Hydropower

To check stationarity in data, this chapter has been investigated unit root test (Augmented Dickey Fuller and Phillips-Perron and Dickey Fuller-GLS). Usually time series analysis considers stationary time series in empirical studies. If the series is non-stationary, the relationship between the independent and dependent variables may exhibit misleading inferences leading to spurious regression. A series said to be stationary if the mean and auto covariance of the series do not depend on time. In order to examine whether each variable's time series is integrated and has a unit root, the study has considered three widely used popular unit root tests—ADF, PP and DF-GLS tests. Both the tests use the null hypothesis that the series does contain a unit root (non-stationary variable), against a stationary variable in the alternative hypothesis. If the calculated test statistics is higher than the critical value then one does not reject the null hypothesis and the concerned variable is non stationary, if not that is stationary. The test is based on the following regression equation:

$$\Delta y_1 = a_1 + a_{2t} + by_{t=1} + \sum_{t=1}^{m} p_1 \Delta y_{t-1} + \vartheta_t \tag{2}$$

Where, $\Delta y_t = Y_t - Y_{t-1}$ and Y is the variable under consideration, m is the number of lags in the dependent variable chosen by SIC and ϑ_t is the stochastic error term. The null hypothesis of a unit root implies that the coefficient of Y_{t-1} is zero. The ADF is widely used due to stability of its critical values as well as its power over different sampling experiment. Perron (1989, 1990) has shown that a structural change in the mean of a stationary variable tends to bias the standard ADF tests toward non-rejection of the hypothesis of a unit root. Therefore, this study has conducted Phillips Perron (PP) unit root test along with ADF test that all variables are integrated of order one (i.e. have one unit root).

Once the unit root test is accomplished, it is possible to carry out the co-integration test in order to examine the existence of a stable long-run relationship between electricity consumption and economic growth. To verify co-integrated relationship among the variables, Johansen Co-integration test (Johansen, 1988; Johansen and Juselius, 1990) has been performed only on integration of order one, i.e. I(1) according to unit root tests' variables.

The Johansen method applies maximum likelihood procedure to determine the presence of co-integrating vectors in non-stationary time series as a vector autoregressive (VAR) framework:

$$\Delta Y_t = C + \sum_{t=}^{K} \Gamma \Delta Y_{t-1} + \Pi Y_{t-1} + \eta_t \tag{3}$$

Where, Y_t is a vector of non-stationary variables and C is the constant term. The information on the coefficient matrix between the levels of the Π is decomposed as $\Pi = \alpha\beta$ where the relevant elements of the α matrix are adjustment coefficient and the β matrix contains co-integrating vectors. Johansen and Juselius (1990) specify two likelihood ratio test statistics to test for the number of co-integrating vectors. The first likelihood ratio statistics for the null hypothesis of exactly r co-integrating vectors against the alternative $r + 1$ vector is the maximum Eigen value statistic. The second statistic for the hypothesis of at most r co-integrating vectors against the alternative is the trace statistic. Critical values for both test statistics are tabulated in Johansen and Juselius (1990). It has been suggested that the above tests of cointegration rank are contingent upon the presence or absence of deterministic components in the dynamic model.

The next question is to investigate whether all the variables in the model should enter into a long-run equilibrium relationship. This can be done by testing linear restrictions on the long-run coefficients after they have been normalized. The hypothesis of long-run exclusion of each variable is tested using a likelihood ratio test, which is asymptotically distributed as X^2 with degrees of freedom equal to the number of restrictions tested. If the test statistic exceeds the 95% critical value then those coefficients are significant implying that the concerned variables should be present in the long-run equilibrium relationship. The number of cointegrating relationships found will result in a corresponding number of residual series, and hence error correction terms (ECTs), to be used in the subsequent vector error correction model (VECM). The systems we consider are equivalent to the following one, where the ECM must be seen as correcting towards an 'equilibrium subspace', which in this case is two-dimensional.

$$\Delta lry = \alpha_{11}\zeta_{1.t-1} + \alpha_{12}\zeta_{2.t-1} + \alpha_{13}\zeta_{3.t-1} + \sum_{t=1}^{m}\phi_{11.t}\Delta lry_{t-1} + \sum_{t=1}^{m}\phi_{12.t}\Delta lelc_{t-1} + \sum_{t=1}^{m}\phi_{13.t}\Delta lelcg_{t-1} + \sum_{t=1}^{m}\phi_{14.t}\Delta lelco_{t-1} + \sum_{t=1}^{m}\phi_{15.t}\Delta lelch_{t-1} + \mu_1 \tag{4}$$

$$\Delta lelc = \alpha_{21}\zeta_{1.t-1} + \alpha_{22}\zeta_{2.t-1} + \alpha_{23}\zeta_{3.t-1} + \sum_{t=1}^{m}\phi_{21.t}\Delta lry_{t-1} + \sum_{t=1}^{m}\phi_{22.t}\Delta lelc_{t-1} + \sum_{t=1}^{m}\phi_{23.t}\Delta lelcg_{t-1} + \sum_{t=1}^{m}\phi_{24.t}\Delta lelco_{t-1} + \sum_{t=1}^{m}\phi_{25.t}\Delta lelch_{t-1} + \mu_2 \tag{5}$$

$$\Delta lelcg = \alpha_{31}\zeta_{1.t-1} + \alpha_{32}\zeta_{2.t-1} + \alpha_{33}\zeta_{3.t-1} + \sum_{t=1}^{m}\phi_{31.t}\Delta lry_{t-1} + \sum_{t=1}^{m}\phi_{32.t}\Delta lelc_{t-1} + \sum_{t=1}^{m}\phi_{33.t}\Delta lelcg_{t-1} + \sum_{t=1}^{m}\phi_{34.t}\Delta lelco_{t-1} + \sum_{t=1}^{m}\phi_{35.t}\Delta lelch_{t-1} + \mu_3 \quad (6)$$

$$\Delta lelco = \alpha_{41}\zeta_{1.t-1} + \alpha_{42}\zeta_{2.t-1} + \alpha_{43}\zeta_{3.t-1} + \sum_{t=1}^{m}\phi_{41.t}\Delta lry_{t-1} + \sum_{t=1}^{m}\phi_{42.t}\Delta lelc_{t-1} + \sum_{t=1}^{m}\phi_{43.t}\Delta lelcg_{t-1} + \sum_{t=1}^{m}\phi_{44.t}\Delta lelco_{t-1} + \sum_{t=1}^{m}\phi_{45.t}\Delta lelch_{t-1} + \mu_4 \quad (7)$$

$$\Delta lelch = \alpha_{51}\zeta_{1.t-1} + \alpha_{52}\zeta_{2.t-1} + \alpha_{53}\zeta_{3.t-1} + \sum_{t=1}^{m}\phi_{51.t}\Delta lry_{t-1} + \sum_{t=1}^{m}\phi_{52.t}\Delta lelc_{t-1} + \sum_{t=1}^{m}\phi_{53.t}\Delta lelcg_{t-1} + \sum_{t=1}^{m}\phi_{54.t}\Delta lelco_{t-1} + \sum_{t=1}^{m}\phi_{55.t}\Delta lelch_{t-1} + \mu_4 \quad (8)$$

Results and Discussion

The estimation procedure begins with testing the time series properties of the data. Table 9.1 below presents the unit root test results of the variables. As it is important to determine the order of integration among variables, three different types of tests are applied. While the ADF is notorious for its poor power problem, the other two tests are more powerful in rejecting the null of nonstationarity. Between these two tests the DF–GLS tests performs well especially in the presence of unknown shifts in the mean and trend in the data. On the other hand, the PP test is more efficient in the presence of a single break in the data.

Table 9.1 demonstrates the unit root test results of time series data from 1975 to 2005 based on the Augmented Dickey Fuller (ADF), the Phillips-Perron (PP) and the DF-GLS tests - applied for both trend and constant. Both the level and first difference of the individual variables are reported under each test. The null hypothesis is that the variables have unit root (i.e. non-stationary) against the alternative hypothesis of no unit root (i.e. stationary).

In the ADF and PP test it is found that all the variables (LRY, LELC, LELCg, LELCo and LELCh) have one unit root i.e. these variables are integrated of order one or I(1) at the different level of significance (1% or

5%). On the other hand, in DF-GLS test it is found that except LELC (without trend), the other variables (LRY, LELC, LELCg, LELCo and LELCh) show integration of order one i.e. I(1) at the different level of significance (1% or 5%) .

Table 9.1: Unit root test results

Unit Root Tests (ADF, PP and DF-GLS) on LRY, LELC, LELCg, LELCo and LELCh

Variables	ADF Test		PP Test		DF-GLS	
	Without Trend	With Trend	Without Trend	With Trend	Without Trend	With Trend
LRY	2.713128 (0)	0.416209 (0)	3.079162 (2)	0.667862 (2)	-1.145945 (6)	-1.692153 (7)
"LRY	-1.255298 (2)***	-5.750834 (0) ***	-4.473107 (4)***	-5.854877 (3) ***	-5.958539 (2) ***	-4.721852(0) ***
LELC	-2.287568 (6)	-3.178904 (0)	0.020574 (7)	-3.178904 (0)	-1.181915 (5)	-3.166595 (0)
"LELC	-3.845993 (3) ***	-3.775878 (3) **	-7.860899 (10)***	-8.015510 (10) ***	-0.810523 (6)	-3.249203 (2) **
LELCg	-2.078857 (0)	-0.658140 (0)	-2.078857 (0)	-0.658140(0)	0.083459 (2)	-0.825209 (0)
"LELCg	-4.970810 (0) ***	-5.986689 (0) ***	-5.008403 (2)***	-5.955044 (1) ***	-4.697041 (0) ***	-5.691701 (0)* **
LELCo	-1.310444 (0)	-1.962937 (0)	-1.221626 (1)	-1.962937 (0)	-1.249459 (0)	-2.104984 (0)
"LELCo	-6.127258 (0) ***	-6.094223 (0) ***	-6.107266 (3)***	-6.087711 (3) ***	-6.217973 (0) ***	-6.321292 (0)* **
LELCh	-2.516277 (0)	-4.039573 (0)	-2.344586 (3)	-3.932484 (5)	-2.184335 (0)	-4.148385 (0)
"LELCh	-7.972594 (0) ***	-7.831485 (0) ***	-18.40172 (27)***	-19.16091 (27) ***	-7.940257 (0) ***	-8.092681 (0)* **

Notes: (i) Figures in Parentheses ( ) indicate Lag Length, (ii) Figures in parentheses [ ] are MacKinnon's p-values, (iii) Figures in parentheses { } are order of integration, and (iv) ***, ** and * indicate rejection of the unit root hypothesis at the 1%, 5% and 10% level respectively.

To qualify for co-integration test, the time series variables should have same order of integration. ADF, the optimal lag length is selected using a testing down method and DF-GLS tests using SIC. For PP tests, bandwidth is selected based on the Newey–West procedure using Bartlett Kernel. Since the variables are integrated of order 1, i.e. **I(1)**, we can test whether they are cointegrated or not (Engel and Granger, 1987). We test for the number of cointegrating relationships using the approach proposed by Johansen (1988) and Johansen and Juselius (1990). The optimal lag length of the level VAR system is determined using the Akaike's Information Criterion (AIC), Hernan-Quinn criterion (HQ) and Schwartz criterion (SC). Table 9.3 below report the number of cointegrating relationships among the variables under consideration.

The Johanson test statistics show rejection for the null hypothesis of no cointegrating vectors under both the trace and maximal eigenvalue forms of the test. I The λ-trace statistic rejects the null of $r \leq 0$ but cannot reject $r \geq 1$ and also, the λ-max statistic rejects the null of $r = 0$ but fails to reject $r = 1$ at 5% level. These Eigenvalue tests based on stochastic matrix indicate

Table 9.2 : Cointegration test Results

Null	Eigenvalues	Trace Test		Max Eigenvalue Test	
		λ – trace	p–value	λ – max	p–value
$r \leq 0$	0.974085	174.8322	0.0000	98.62923	0.0000
$r \leq 1$	0.800693	76.20297	0.0000	43.54855	0.0002
$r \leq 2$	0.521667	32.65442	0.0228	19.91109	0.0734
$r \leq 3$	0.346782	12.74333	0.1246	11.49782	0.1310

Note: (i) λ_{Trace} indicates Trace and λ_{Max} states Maximum Eigen value unrestricted co-integration rank Test,

(ii) One asterisk (*) denotes significance at 5% level,

(iii) r denotes the number of co-integrating vectors

existence of the cointegrating relationship between income and energy consumption. In case of the trace test, the null of no cointegrating vectors is rejected since the test statistic of 174.83 is greater than the 5% critical value of 33.87. Moving on to test the null of at most 1 cointegrating vectors, the trace statistic is 76.20, while the 5% critical value is 47.85, so the null hypothesis is just rejected at 5%. Moving on to test the null of at most 2 cointegrating vectors, the trace statistic is 32.65, while the 5% critical value is 29.79, so the null hypothesis is just rejected at 5% (Table 9.2). Finally, this implies that the series under consideration are driven by at least three common trends. We save the residuals from the first three equations of the VAR, which are used as the error-correction term in the subsequent tests for Granger causality. Results indicate the existence of at least three cointegrating relationship among the variables in the series. So, the Granger causality tests will be modeled using VECM as explained in Equations (4), (5), (6), (7) and (8) above.

Table 9.3 reports the Granger non-causality statistics for the variables ΔLRY, ΔLELC, ΔLELCg, ΔLELCo and ΔLELCh with error-correction terms-$\xi_{1,t-1}$, $\xi_{2,t-1}$ and $\xi_{3,t-1}$. The error-correction terms are adjustment term toward equilibrium sub-space and also indicate to long-run causality. Results indicate ΔLELCg, ΔLELCo Granger cause GDP growth in the short-run while the growth of electricity consumption and change of electricity production from gas has effect on the income growth in the long run. Empirical results presented in Table 9.3 also indicates GDP growth and growth of electricity consumption Granger cause change of electricity production generated by gas in the short-run while the growth of electricity production generated by gas has further effect on the income growth in the long run. There is a bidirectional relationship between change of electricity production generated by gas and income growth in the short run and growth of electricity consumption and change of electricity production generated by

Table 9.3 : Granger Causality Test

	ΔLRY	ΔLETC	ΔLETCg	ΔLETCo	ΔLETCh	$\xi_{1,t-1}$	$\xi_{2,t-1}$	$\xi_{3,t-1}$
ΔLRY		0.0790116 [0.7786]	13.0428 [0.0003]**	4.35316 [0.0369]*	0.105156 [0.7457]	12.4431 [0.0004]**	5.90481 [0.0151]*	4.63628 [0.0313]*
ΔLETC	5.51218 [0.0189]*		1.9079 [0.1672]	0.00378525 [0.9509]	0.00981536 [0.9211]	0.0126071 [0.9106]	1.34912 [0.2454]	9.745 [0.0018]**
ΔLETCg	0.748464 [0.3870]	8.23314 [0.0041]**		0.274412 [0.6004]	2.95698 [0.0855]	0.0124585 [0.9111]	0.544478 [0.4606]	12.1068 [0.0005]**
ΔLETCo	0.932058 [0.3343]	1.99576 [0.1577]	3.19007 [0.0741]		2.13356 [0.1441]	0.01258 [0.9231]	0.679888 [0.4096]	3.49443 [0.0616]]
ΔLETCh	0.159843 [0.6893]	0.133761 [0.7146]	3.43295 [0.0639]	0.413054 [0.5204]		0.645326 [0.4218]	0.645326 [0.4218]	2.23956 [0.1345]

Note: *(**) denote rejection at 5% (10%) levels of significance.

gas. Furthermore, the causal nexus is unidirectional between the income growth and electricity production generated by oil. There is no causal nexus amongst ELCh and GDP. The estimation procedure also passes a battery of diagnostic tests indicating stability of long-run and short-run estimates.

Conclusion and Policy Implication

Bangladesh with her natural endowment of gas reserve is at a critical juncture with respect to energy issue since the existing reserve is about to run dry in near future. This chapter clearly states the significance of electricity to growth for Bangladesh, specially, from gas source. Electricity consumption from gas has been found to have effect on income growth in the short as well as long-term. In this particular connection, the case of Bangladesh fits into the minor 35% cases of the poorest nations, which appear to be energy dependent - a typical developed world phenomenon. (Chontanawat and Hunt, 2006). Mutual causality has been found between electricity consumption from gas and income growth in the short-run, which is, again, contrary to the average tendency of a very poor nation. According to Jumbe (2004) the causality from GDP to energy appears to be generally weak for the very poor nations.

Therefore, the role of energy turns out endogenous for the economic growth of Bangladesh, indicating that energy conservation would likely to stall the growth accounting of the country. Since the economy appears to rely primarily on natural gas which is non-thermal, cleaner and less carbon-intensive, momentum of growth in Bangladesh would not likely to cause environmental degradation, substantially reasonable to term it as 'green growth' (Shrestha R. M. *et al.,* 2009). However, non-existence of causality between electricity from hydro-power and GDP could be supported by the fact that the amount of electricity generated from hydro-power source constitutes an insignificant proportion of the total energy production in Bangladesh. The only hydro-power project in Bangladesh has increased power generation by merely three fold in last three decades implying that Bangladesh can rarely embark on the potential of hydro-power for her future economic growth.

Though result shows unidirectional relationship from electricity generated from oil to GDP in the short run; for Bangladesh, relying on oil would probably not be feasible, given the fact that Bangladesh is entirely dependent on foreign source for oil. Hence, to depend on imported oil for electricity generation leading to economic growth for a weak economy like Bangladesh is difficult to be sustainable. This paper attaches emphatic importance on electricity generation by commenting that lighting up Bangladesh could potentially gear up the economic engine of the country.

REFERENCES

Akarca, A.T., Long, T.V. 1980. "On the relationship between energy and GNP: a re-examination." *Journal of Energy and Development 5*, 326-331.

Al-Iriani, M., 2006. Energy–GDP relationship revisited: an example from GCC countries using panel causality. *Energy Policy*, 34, 3342–3350.

Beaudreau, B. C. 1995. The Impact of Electric Power on Productivity: The Case of US Manufacturing 1958- 1984. *Energy Economics*, 22, 615-625

Bentzen, J. and Engsted, T., 1993. Short- and long-run elasticities in energy demand. *Energy Economics* 15, 9–16.

Chang, T., Fang, W. and Wen, L.F. 2001, "Energy consumption, employment, output, and temporal causality: evidence from Taiwan based on cointegration and error-correction modelling techniques", *Applied Economics*, Vol. 33 No. 8, pp. 1045-56.

Chontanawat. J., Hunt C. L. 2006, Causality between Energy Consumption and GDP:Evidence from 30 OECD and 78 Non-OECD Countries Surrey Energy Economics, *Discussion paper Series 113*. ISSN 1749-8384. University of Surrey

Engle, R.F., Granger, C.W.J., 1987. Cointegration and error correction: representation, estimation, and testing. *Econometrica 55*, 251–276.

Erol, U. and Yu, E.S.H. 1987. "Time series analysis of the causal relationships between US energy and employment.", *Resources Energy* 9: 75-89.

Erol, U. and Yu, E.S.H., 1987. On the causal relationship between energy and income for industrialized countries. *Journal of Energy and Development* 13, 113–122.

Ghali, K. H., and El-Sakka, M. I. T. 2004. Energy use and output growth in Canada: A multivariate cointegration analysis. *Energy Economics* 26, 225–238.

Glasure, Y.U. and Lee, A.R., 1997. Cointegration, error-correction, and the relationship between GDP and energy: the case of South Korea and Singapore. *Resource and Energy Economics* 20, 17–25.

Huang, Bwo-Nung., Hwangc, M.J., Yangd, C.W. 2 0 0 8 Causal relationship between energy consumption and GDP growth revisited: A dynamic panel data approach, *Ecological Economics* 67, 41 – 54

Hwang, D.B.K. and Gum, B., 1992. The causal relationship between energy and GNP: the case of Taiwan. *The Journal of Energy and Development* 16, 219–226.

Johansen, S. 1988. "Statistical analysis of cointegrated vectors", *Journal of Economic Dynamics and Control*, Vol. 12, pp.131–154.

Johansen, S., and Juselius, K. 1990. Maximum likelihood estimation and inference on cointegration: With an application to demand for money, *Oxford Bulletin of Economics and Statistics*, Vol.52, pp.169–210.

Jumbe, C. B. L. 2004, Cointegration and Causality between Electricity Consumption and GDP: Empirical Evidence from Malawi. *Energy Economics* 26: 61-68.

Kraft, J. and Kraft, A. 1978. "On the relationship between energy and GNP." *Journal of Energy and Development* 3, 401-403.

Lee, C. C. 2005. "The causality relationship between energy consumption and GDP in G-11 countries revisited." *Energy Economics*, 34 pp. 1086–1093

Lee, C.-C., 2006. The causality relationship between energy consumption and GDP in G 11 countries revisited. *Energy Policy* 34, 1086–1093.

Lee, C.C., Chang C.P. and Chen, P.F., 2008. Energy–income causality in OECD countries revisited: the key role of capital stock. *Energy Economics*, 30, 2359–2373.

Lee, C.C. and Chiang, C., 2008. Energy consumption and economic growth in Asian countries: a more comprehensive analysis using panel data, *Resource and Energy Economics* 30, 50–65.

Lise, W., 2006. Decomposition of CO2 emissions over 1980–2003 in Turkey. *Energy Policy* 34, 1841–1852.

Mahadevan, R., and Asafu-Adjaye, J., 2007. Energy consumption, economic growth and prices: a reassessment using panel VECM for developed and developing countries. *Energy Policy*, 35, 2481–2490.

Masih, A. M. M., and Masih, R. 1997., On the Temporal Causal Relationship between Energy Consumption, Real Income, and Prices: Some new Evidence from Asian-Energy Dependent NICs based on a Multivariate Cointegration/Vector Error-Correction Approach. *Journal of Policy Modelling* 19(4): 417-440.

Narayan, P.K., and Smyth, R., 2008. Energy consumption and real GDP in G7 countries, new growth? Evidence from systematic study of over 100 countries. *Journal of Policy Modelling* 30, 209–220.

Perron, P. 1989., "The Great Vrash, the Oil Price Shock and the Unit Root hypothesis", *Econometrica*, 57, pp. 1361-1401

Perron, P. 1990., "Testing for a Unit Root in a Time Series with a Changing Mean", *Journal of Business and Economic Statistics* 8, pp. 153-162.

Ricci, F., 2007. Channels of transmission of environmental policy to economic growth: a survey of the theory. *Ecological Economics* 60, 688–699.

Sadorsky, P .2009. , "Renewable energy consumption, CO2 emissions and oil prices in the G7 countries", *Energy Economics* 31, pp. 456-461.

Sadorsky, P., 2009. Renewableenergyconsumption,CO2 emissions and oil prices in the G7countries. *Energy Economics* 31, 456–462.

Say, N.P., Yucel, M., 2006. Energy consumption and CO2 emissions in Turkey: empirical analysis and future projection based on an economic growth. *Energy Policy* 34, 3870–3876.

Shiu, A.L. and Lam, P.L. 2004. "Electricity consumption and economic growth in China." *Energy Policy* 32, 47-54.

Shrestha, M.R. *et al.,* 2009. "Factors affecting CO_2 emission from power sector of selected countries in Asia and the Pacific." *Energy Policy*, Vol. 37, Issue. 6, pp.2375-2384.

Soytas, U., Sari, R., 2003. Energy consumption and GDP: causality relationship in G-7 countries and emerging markets. *Energy Economics* 25, 33–37.

Soytas, U., and Sari, R., 2006. Energy consumption, economic growth, and carbon emissions in Turkey. *International Conference in Economics–Turkish Economic* Association Sept. 11–13, Ankara, Turkey.

Stern, D. 1993, Energy and Economic Growth in the USA, A Multivariate Approach. *Energy Economics* 15: 137-150.

Stern, D. 2000. A Multivariate Cointegration Analysis of the Role of Energy in the US economy. *Energy Economics* 22: 267-283.

Stern, D.I. 1997., Limits to substitution and irreversibility in production and consumption: A neoclassical interpretation of ecological economics, 21, 197-215.

Wolde-Rufael, Y., 2005. Energy demand and economic growth: the African experience 19 countries, *Journal of Policy Modelling*, 27 (8), 891–903.

Yu, E.S.H. and Choi, J.Y. 1985. "The causal relationship between energy and GNP: an international comparison." *Journal of Energy and Development 10*, 249-272.

Yu, E.S.H. and Hwang, B.K. 1984. The relationship between energy and economic growth in Korea. *Applied Energy* 83, 1181-1189.

FOOTNOTE

1. Gujrati, D., *Basic Econometrics,* 3rd Edition 1995, McGraw-Hill.

Environment in the Era of Globalization in Rural Economy

A Study of Bhutan

— Komol Singha

ABSTRACT

As the economic development processes pick up, the environmental condition is also affected aggressively at the same time. This poses a great threat to sustainable development, human society and to the natural world. On the other side of the coin, the policy of economic development without sound environment is short-lived. The issue of environmental degradation and climate change is not only the concern for the giant nations, like United States of America and China but also the tiny Himalayan Kingdom of Bhutan. This tiny Kingdom has also felt the impact of climate change and environmental degradation in the recent years. In this context, the present paper portrays the stock of environmental condition of Bhutan in the age of globalisation. How does it degrade and in what magnitude? Can the nation sustain development without sacrificing its natural resources?

Key Words*: Environment; Industrialisation; Economic Development; Forest; Middle Path*

> *"Throughout the centuries, the Bhutanese have treasured their natural environment and have looked upon it as the source of all life. This traditional reverence for nature has delivered us into the twentieth century with our environment still richly intact. We wish to continue living in harmony with nature and to pass on this rich heritage to our future generations."*
>
> —His Majesty, the fourth King of Bhutan

Introduction

With the growth of development processes (when left unmanaged), the environmental condition deteriorates aggressively (WDR 2010). This poses a great threat to sustainable development, human society and to the natural world. The policy of economic development without sound environment is short-lived. But, issue is quite contradictory, and will be discussed in detail in the following sections of this paper. In this front, National Environment Commission (2006) of Bhutan has also recognised that the modern development brings many improvements in the quality of life in this tiny nation and at the same time it invites some negative impacts to the environment, which is considered as one of the top priorities in country's development agenda.

It is also realised that environment is a priceless and irreplaceable property for all living beings. World Rainforest Management (2002) has identified that the environmental degradation or climate change is a man-made disaster. The loss of environment due to human misconduct and ignorance impoverishes the world. In the opinion of Aggarwal (2005), it is only a result of institutional failure. Societies have always depended on the climate but are only now coming to grips with the fact that the climate depends on their actions (WDR 2010: 37). So, the protection or preservation of environment becomes need of the hour. And, it is indeed the work of all inhabitants of our planet earth if we are to have adequate enjoyment of the vast resources at our disposal. This, in return, will prolong our life-span and maintain the resources for generations yet unborn to experience and emulate.

To reconcile the two conflicting goals of rapid development process on one hand and environmental conservation on the other, the United Nations instituted a commission called "World Commission on Environment and Development". The commission's report "*Our Common Future*" published in 1983, articulated the concept of *Sustainable Development*, which implies as "development that meets the needs of the present without compromising the ability of future generations to meet their own needs" (Brundtland 1987; NEC 2006; WDR 2010). The tenet of sustainable development is to bridge the gap between economic growth and environmental preservation. Development of a nation is likely to be sustainable only when it improves the quality of human life and it conserves the earth's vitality and diversity (NEC 2006). It is nothing but an approach of "Middle Path" adopted for the sustainable development in the Himalayan Kingdom - Bhutan.

With the help of secondary data collected from the published works, the present paper portrays the stock of environmental condition of Bhutan.

How does it degrade with the growth of economy and in what magnitude are also discussed. The chapter further analyses that - can Bhutan balance these two conflicting issues in the age of globalisation and what steps are to be followed.

In order to provide a concrete view point, the entire study is divided into six sections, including introduction and conclusion. The Section II shows the growth trend of Bhutan's economy in the recent past. The Section III portrays the stock of environment and the issue of its conservation in the country is discussed in Section IV, and the Section V explains the paradox of globalisation and the conservation of environment in the country. Finally, the Section VI wraps up with the some suggestions to balance these two conflicting issues.

Economic Growth in Bhutan

The economy of Bhutan is one of the smallest and least developed economies in the world, and is based on agriculture and forestry, which provide the main livelihood for more than 60% of the population. Agriculture consists largely of subsistence farming and animal husbandry. The country's economy is closely aligned with Indian economy through strong trade and monetary links, dependence on India's financial assistance.

Table 10.1 : GDP Growth Rate and Sectoral Share from 2003-07 (at 2000 price)

(Percent in Nu./Rs.)

GDP/Sector	2003	2004	2005	2006	2007
GDP Growth Rate	7.2	6.8	6.5	6.3	21.4
GDP	29385.5 (100.0)	32320.0 (100.0)	36462.6 (100.0)	40494.8 (100.0)	51521.5 (100.0)
Primary Sector	7873.0 (26.8)	8303.7 (25.7)	8805.3 (24.1)	9783.5 (24.2)	10467.6 (20.3)
Secondary Sector	10500.8 (35.7)	11187.2 (34.6)	12417.3 (34.1)	13896.5 (34.3)	22298.9 (43.3)
Tertiary Sector	11011.7 (37.5)	12829.1 (39.7)	15240.0 (41.8)	16814.8 (41.5)	18755.0 (36.4)

Source: National Statistics Bureau (2008:138)

Note: Figures in the parentheses are the percentage of the total in the same column.

Despite of the weaknesses, the country's economy (GDP Growth rate) has been growing very rapidly from 7.70% in 2003 to 22.40% and 21.40% in 2008 and 2009 respectively (NSB 2008; Dahal 2009). GDP Growth rate in Ninth Five-year Plan (2002-07) at current price in Bhutan was 15.8%, and construction and electricity sector's percentage share to nation's GDP at the end of the plan were 17.8% and 14.6% respectively (IMF 2004). Bhutan's GDP per capita income (at current prices) is $ 2,218.69 in 2009 (Dahal 2009), making it the highest in South Asia. The secondary sector contributes the highest percent of GDP share, i.e. 43.3% (at 2000 prices) in the country in 2007 (NSB 2008). Manufacturing, electricity, and construction showed a marginal increase from 33.6% in 2000 to 39.1% in 2008 (Dahal 2009). Electricity, gas and water supply registered a quantum jump in the sectoral GDP share from 1.3% in 1981 to 46.6% in 1989. During 1990s, the average share of this sub-sector to the nation's GDP was 36% (Mehta 2009), and still it is maintaining the same trend even after 2000. It is also identified that the industrial sector has grown by more than 200% over a 5 year period, that is, from 1997 to 2002 (ADB 2006), which is mainly due to the growth of power sector. The sectoral growth rate of electricity alone contributed to national GDP were 34.6% and 120.8% in 2006 and 2007 respectively, and occupies highest position in the national economy (Choden 2007).

As shown in Table 10.1, sectoral GDP composition is concerned; agricultural/primary sector's contribution had been declining from 26.8% to 20.3% in 2003 and 2007 respectively. At present, the agriculture contributes 17.6% (it is expected to be much lower in future too), and industry and service sector contribute 45% and 37% respectively. On the other hand, the involvement of labour force by occupation is quite opposite. In agriculture, 63% of the total workforce of the country is being involved now. Whereas the involvement of labour force in the sector of industry and service stand at 6% and 31% respectively[1]

Stock of Environment in Bhutan

On the environmental front, Bhutan maintains a conservation-based policy in regard to its natural assets. With almost 72 per cent of the country's total area under forest cover against the minimum of 60% requirement of the legislation (NEC 2007). Bhutan has the largest forest coverage in proportion to its land mass in Asia, and the environmental degradation in Bhutan is minimal or negligible compared to the neighbouring nations like, Nepal, India and other part of the Himalaya (Karan 1987; TFYP 2008-13). The air and water quality in Bhutan are still relatively good compared to the neighbouring nations (TFYP 2008-13).

The climate change, global warming, global financial crisis and economic downturn have had a limited impact on Bhutan as the economy is driven largely by construction of hydropower sector (Choden 2007), and restrictive tourism policy. In 2007, the total electricity generation was 6422.5 MU. Domestic consumption has been marginal approximately 9% of the total generation and rest exported to India (Choden 2007; NSB 2008).

Unlike other countries, the growth of power sector has negligible impact on environment, but generates high economic benefits in Bhutan (Choden 2007). The answer is - no big destruction of forest has been made to tap electricity in the country. Minimum destruction of forest is made while installing power transmission lines/wires. Besides, no big reservoir has been created for power plants because Bhutan is blessed with good rainfalls and most of the rivers are on steep gradient hills that allow the run-off to go to the hydro-electric plant. Water is diverted and run through a hydroelectric plant and back to the river. Almost all the power plants are underground in Bhutan (Choden 2007).

With the emergence of globalisation, the country is changing from a rural society based on subsistence farming to a society with a growing services sector that increasingly relies on tourism and the export of hydro-energy for economic growth (Rinzin *et al.* 2007). Bhutan is a unique tourist destination being the last Buddhist Kingdom in the world. Tourism provides the opportunity for Bhutan to earn significant foreign exchange. However, ever since the country opened up to tourism in 1974, Bhutan has taken a cautious approach to tourism and it is carefully regulated. This is done in order to minimise negative impacts that tourism have on the national socio-cultural and ecological heritage.

Environment and its Conservation

Coming to the conservation of environment, the Royal Government of Bhutan's (RGoB) policy "Middle Path" emphasises the equal priority of economic development and environmental conservation. The philosophy has been put in place from time immemorial in this country, and has benefited directly or indirectly, not just the country alone but the region and world at large (TFYP 2008-13). The RGoB has impressive achievements in developing national policy and regulatory frameworks for the environment, and in the conservation of its forests, biodiversity, and renewable natural resources. The need for conservation and environmental management are rooted in the rich traditions of the Bhutanese people for which the nation has received international recognitions. For this noble effort of environmental conservation, Bhutan was conferred the United Nations Environment Programme "UNEP Champions of the Earth Award" in 2005 (Bhutan Strategy Paper 2007-12) and being a leader of environmental protection in Bhutan, His Majesty the Fourth King was honoured the "J. Paul Getty Conservation Leadership Award" in 2006 by the World Wildlife Fund (NEPA 2007).

The key environmental issues basically include the need to reduce land degradation, preserve biodiversity, protect water resources and manage/ mitigate the environmental effects of urbanisation and industrial development (ADB 2004). On the other hand, economic development in a nation is basically enhanced by the growth of secondary and tertiary sectors, which includes trade, tourism, banking and services, etc. (Singha 2009). The major concern of environment during the process of industrialisation in a nation is what economists called it '*externality*',[2] which does not command price in the market (Bezbaruah et al. 2009). So, market fails to provide for social optimality. Here, the question arises is- can Bhutan internalise "the externalities" created by the industrialisation or economic growth?

On the one hand, some scientists, scholars, and economists argue that growing economic activities (production and consumption) require increased extraction of natural resources and accumulation of waste, so a transition to a steady-state economy is required to save the environment (Meadows *et al.* 1972; Daly 1991). On the other hand, there are those who argue that economic growth leads to an increased demand for less material intensive goods and services and improved environmental quality, so more attention will be paid to environmental protective measures (Beckerman 1992; Barlett 1994). Others have hypothesised an inverted-U relationship between economic growth and environmental degradation, which is known as the "Environmental Kuznets Curve" (Kuznets 1966; Halkos 2006). The underlying hypothesis is that at the early stages of economic growth, pollution and degradation of natural resources increase rapidly, but beyond a certain threshold of growth, the relationship reverts and pollution declines (Brooks and Borgerhooff 2008).

Yet some other scholars (like, Hawken 1993; Jerasakanon 2007) opine that economic development and environment can go hand in hand if community, people are educated, couple with the development of technology. Still, market forces will not automatically lead to socially optimal level of output and pollution (Bezbaruah *et al.* 2009), which implies that zero pollution may not be consistent with socially optimal level because any type of economic activity involves some amount of pollution. Environmental policy failures or "Tragedy of Commons" occur when there is lack of political will and commitment to environmental protection, especially lack community's participation, limited financing for environmental improvement, etc.

Hence, one area of environmental economics focuses on the method of "environmental conservation". Grossly, the method of environmental conservation can be divided into two categories (Bezbaruah *et al.* 2009), viz., (1) Command and control measures, and (2) Incentive-based measures, which include Hicks-Kaldor compensation principle- compensating the victim by the polluter, Pigovian tax as pollution fee etc. In this context, which measure does Bhutan follow?

Globalisation and Environment Nexus

The most significant environmental problems in Bhutan are soil erosion and water pollution. The erosion of the soil occurs because 50% of the land in Bhutan is situated on mountainous slopes which are subject to landslides during the monsoon season. Other contributing factors are overcutting of timber, road construction, and the building of irrigation channels. Annual precipitation ranges widely in various parts of the country. Other scholars (Dey 2003; ADB 2004; Rinzin *et al.* 2007; 2009; NEC 2007 etc.) have opined that animal-man conflict, overgrazing, over consumption of fuel-wood are the major threats to forest conservation and environment. To Roder (2002), cattle grazing are also harmful to the environment. Tenth Five Year Plan (2008-13) document also emphasises that over grazing by livestock, inefficient use of forest resources, high levels of fuel-wood consumption and the loss of prime agricultural lands to urbanisation and development, and landslide due to excessive rain are the main factors to environmental degradation in Bhutan.

As far as air pollution is concerned, *Bhutan Environment Outlook (2009)* reported that the industry sector is the largest source of emission of CO_2 in the country. The industry sector contributed 133.69 million kg of CO_2 emission until 2002, making up more than 58% of the total CO_2 emission. Unlike its neighbouring countries in the South Asia region and with the rest of Asia, air pollution is still not a major problem in Bhutan but it is an emerging concern (NEC 2006).

In the severe climate of the north, there is only about forty millimetres of annual precipitation, primarily, the snow. In the temperate central regions, a yearly average of around 1,000 millimeters is more common, and 7,800 millimeters per year has been registered at some locations in the humid, subtropical south, ensuring the thick tropical forest, or savanna. Thimphu (the capital city) experiences dry winter months (December through February) and almost no precipitation until March, when rainfall averages 20 millimeters a month and increases steadily thereafter to a high of 220 millimeters in August for a total annual rainfall of nearly 650 millimetres.

Environmental conservation is concerned, according to Chitra (2003), success of environmental preservation depends basically on the awareness and consciousness of the people. An integrated effort is required in environmental planning management and action. Interdisciplinary understanding, cooperation and coordination and increased public participation and support are important components in the process towards sustainable development. Research by Das (2010) found that the environmental problem in India is due to its weak legal and institutional frameworks. He further suggested for reinforcing institutional settings if India wants better environmental condition. In the finding of BIDS (2010), the main threats to the environment could be rapid population growth, uncontrolled industrialisation, deforestation and unsustainable cultivation methods in agriculture.

On the other side of the coin, Bhutan is undergoing rapid industrialisation and urbanisation and the secondary sector doubled its contribution to the GDP within the last one-decade (refer to Table 10.1). At present, only about 16% of the population now lives in urban areas compared to around only 5% ten years ago (*Thimphu City Corporation*), and its growth rate is almost 220% within the decade. In urban areas, the number of vehicles and industries has been increasing at a rapid pace. Although air pollution is not yet a severe problem in Bhutan, incidences of urban air pollution are becoming more evident. Urban air pollution is mainly due to pollution from heating appliances including *bukharis*[3] and vehicle emissions. In the study of Kim (2002), the air pollution is primarily a result of emissions from vehicles and airplanes. The number of vehicle registered in Bhutan was 22, 527 in 2001 and it had increased to 35,703 in 2007 and 45, 819 in 2009 (NSB 2008; 2009). This was an increase of 23, 315 vehicles or 103.4% over a period of nine years. The increase in construction activities—and associated increases in haphazard stockpiling—is leading to deterioration in the air quality (ADB 2006). Besides these, the congestion of footpath, rubbish created by vegetable hawkers on the footpath of Thimphu city is an emerging issue of environmental degradation in Bhutan. Is this a sign of development or environment degradation?

Conclusion

Till date, in Bhutan, the environmental problem is not as serious as what other developed and developing nations (like USA, China, India, etc.) confront. To maintain environmental stock of the country, the RGoB has been following the noble *Middle Path approach* and it should not be loosen. But, with the emergence of globalisation, this balance between the two seems to be unequal. Despite of the determined philosophy of Middle Path, country's economic growth rate is much higher than the environmental regeneration rate.

So, the country's environmental resources are not just to be preserved. They are an immense asset to be utilised to address the development priority of poverty reduction, and to achieve economic growth, social development, and the overarching objective of Gross National Happiness. The imperative is that such utilisation of the country's environmental resources must be done wisely and sustainably. In order to facilitate this, the Fifth Ministerial Conference on Environment and Development in Asia and the Pacific (2005), embraced the "Green Growth" approach. It is a policy-focused strategy to create a win-win situation between the environment and the economy by improving eco-efficiency of production and consumption and promoting effective decision-making (Hawken 1993).

The effective utilisation of these opportunities requires strong political will for policy integration, i.e., the creation of institutions, resources, and policy tools that allow economic actors to respond positively to pressure for enhanced environmental performance at lower economic and social costs. The need for people's commitment and respect towards the country's rule and regulation is very essential on the other. Both these institutional settings are to be made more effective and stronger in Bhutan.

REFERENCES

Aggarwal R. M. (2005): *Globalisation, Local Ecosystems, and the Rural Poor*. UNU-WIDER, Research Paper No. 2005/28 (June)

ADB (2004): *Bhutan Country Environmental Analysis (Draft, November)*. New Zealand: Asian Development Bank

ADB (2006): *Country Synthesis Report on Urban Air Quality Management- Bhutan, Discussion Draft (December)*. Philippines: Asian Development Bank and the Clean Air Initiative for Asian Cities (CAI-Asia) Centre

Barlett, B. (1994): The High Cost of Turning Green. *The Wall Street Journal*: 14 September

Brooks, J. and Borgerhoff, M. M. (2008): *Testing Bhutan's attempt to Balance conservation and Development- the Little Country that Could*. Paper presented at the annual meeting of the International Congress for Conservation Biology, Convention Center, Chattanooga, TN

Bangladesh Institute of Development Studies (2010): *Protecting Environment and Reducing Vulnerability of the LDCs*. Draft Discussion Paper (January), Ministry of Finance, Government of Bangladesh, 2010.

Brundtland, G. H. (1987): *Our Common Future- World Commission on Environment and Development*. New York: Oxford University Press

Beckerman, W. (1992): Economic Growth and the Environment- Whose Growth? Whose Environment? *World Development* 20: 481-486.

Bezbaruah, M.P. *et al.* (2009): *An Overview of Environmental Economics*. Paper presented in a National Seminar at K. C. Das Commerce College, Guwahati (India) 28-29 January.

Bhutan Country Strategy Paper (2007-13): Bhutan [accessed on 24/03/10 http://ec.europa.eu/external_relations/bhutan/csp/07_13_en.pdf]

Chitra, A. (2003): *Role of NGO's in Protecting Environment and Health*, In Martin J. B., et al. (eds.), *Proceedings of the Third International Conference on "Environment and Health"*, Chennai, India, 15-17 December, Department of Geography, University of Madras and Faculty of Environmental Studies, York University, pp. 105-112

Choden, T. (2007): *Bhutan- Balancing Growth and Environment Conservation through Hydro Power*, Manila: Asian Development Bank Publication

Daly, H. (1991): *Steady-State Economics*. Washington, DC: Island Press

Dahal, R.C (2009): *Real GDP Growth Increases*. Bhutan Observer (27th December)

Das, S. (2010): *The Strange Valuation of Forest in India*, Economic and Political Weekly. XLV (9): 16-18

Dey, D. (2003): *Community Forest in Bhutan Himalayas- Sustaining Life and Environment through Participation*. Paper presented at the XII Wold Forestry Congress, Quebec City, Canada

Hawken, P. (1993): *The Ecology of Commerce: A Declaration of Sustainability*. New York: Harper Collins

Halkos, G. E. (2006): *Economic development and environmental degradation: Testing the existence of an Environmental Kuznets Curve at regional level*. Greece: Department of Economics, University of Thessaly

Jerasakanon, F. (2007): *The Alternative Solution- Economic Growth and Environmental Conservation for Sustainable Development*.

Kaznets, S. (1966): *Economic Growth and Structural Change and Modern Economic Growth*. New Haven: Yale University Press

Kim, K. (2002): *The Effects of Tourism Impacts upon Quality of Life of Residents in the Community*, PhD thesis submitted to the Deptt. of Hospitality and Tourism Management, Virginia: Virginia Polytechnic Institute and State University.

Karan, P.P. (1987): *Environment and Development in Bhutan*. Human Geography: 69(1): 15-26

Meadows, D. H., et al. (1972): *The Limits to Growth*. London: Earth Island Limited

Mehta, S. (2009): *Nature and Structure of Bhutanese Economy*. Thimphu: KMT Publishers

National Environment Commission (2006): *Reference Manual for Environmental Impact Assessment Training in Bhutan*. Thimphu: National Environment Commission of Bhutan (RGoB)

National Environment Commission (2007): *Reference Manual for Environmental Impact Assessment Training in Bhutan*. Thimphu: National Environment Commission of Bhutan (RGoB).

National Environment Protection Act (2007): *National Environment Protection Act of Bhutan*. RGoB: Thimphu

National Statistics Bureau (2008): *Statistical Handbook of Bhutan 2008*, Thimphu: RGoB

National Statistics Bureau (2009): *Statistical Handbook of Bhutan 2008*, Thimphu: RGoB

Rinzin, C. *et al.* (2007): Ecotourism as a Mechanism for Sustainable Development: The Case of Bhutan. *Environmental Sciences*, 4(2): 109-125

Rinzin, C. et al. (2009): Nature Conservation and Human Well-being in Bhutan- An Assessment of Local Community Perceptions. *The Journal of Environment and Development*: 18 (2): 177- 202

Roder, W. et al. (2002): Cattle Grazing in the Conifer Forests of Bhutan, *Mountain Research and Development*. 22(4): 368-74

Singha, K. (2009): *Indo-ASEAN* Economic Integration, *South Asian Journal,* Issue No. 25, pp. 139-153 (July 1)

TFYP (2008-13): *Tenth Five Year Plan- Vol. 1 Main Document*. RGoB: Gross National Happiness Commission

World Rainforest Management (2002): *Community Forest Management- A Feasible and Necessary Alternative.* WRM's bulletin N° 61, August

World Development Report (2010): *Development and Climate Change*. Washington DC, The World Bank.

FOOTNOTES

1. These figures are retrieved from "Bhutan Economy 2011" accessed on 02/03/2011 and available at http://www.theodora.com/wfbcurrent/bhutan/bhutan_economy.html
2. Externalities are the effects of production, especially industrial or consumption by one on production and/or consumption opportunity of another which is not captured price in market transaction.
3. Bhutanese fire-wood room heater

Globalization and Environmental Qualities

The Tribal Ethics from Arunachal Pradesh, India

—Prof. Dipak Kr. Mandal
—Bappa Ghosh

ABSTRACT

Globalization in the sense of present chapter is a process of economic activities that cuts the barrier across the boundaries of the nations, cultures and societies, which moves toward a larger integration of the world and facilitates interdependence, directing an en route for a single global patio. Environmental qualities, on the other hand, are being used and affected in the process of production. The trade-off relationship between the environmental sustainability and development has given rise the concept of 'sustainable development' and the very obvious question to raise again, what should be the limit of 'trade-off'? The tribal people of different age groups in Arunachal Pradesh have different views on these dimensions. The present paper deals with the concepts of the indigenous tribal people of Arunachal Pradesh, who do hitherto have a culturally rich bio-diversity heritage to provide a healthy living for future generations of the region as well as for the country as a whole.

Introduction

Globalization, whatever the dictionary writes, we mean it's an aggregate of economic activities that takes place all over the world, which also has a time dimension that the event is more or less contemptuous in different societies.

Hence, the process of globalization encompasses a force to the barrier across the boundaries of nations, societies and cultures; '*Thanda matlob, Coca-cola*' is also known to the remote villages of India's north east extremity, Arunachal Pradesh. The process of commoditization clutched the tribal livelihood too. It might be termed as 'economic development' rather the aged ones in the study area say, *"Tis modernity"*. ***Gale* and *Galuk* have been replaced by Jeans and Tops!**

In their good yesterdays, the *Kebang*, headed by the *Kebang Abu* allocated land to the different families for *Adiavik*, and the entire family devoted its *wear and tears* to accrue its just needs for the rest of the year and no surplus at all. They did not have money nor did they bother about market. Rather they had their own state, own society, own law and order. They had two types of forests — somewhere they used to produce; somewhere they believed, the deity and divinity lived. **An institution of their own, which protected them for generations!!**

In the days, when market forces were absent, the tribal people had produced their bare needs from the abundant forest resources. Although production took place in various modes vis-à-vis, farming, rearing, hunting and other subsistence ones, the outer world did not have to give any baffled look for the territory and her resources, which hitherto provides the first shine to pronounce, "*Good Morning India*". By the wave of globalization, the same Jhumia has had to reduce his jhum cycle by ten or twenty folds. The mode of production has also been changed. **It is not only 'paddy for rice' and 'millet for *apong*' rather 'ginger for money' and 'money for car'!!!**

It is therefore, to gavel that the changing consumption pattern, which has reshuffled the age-old traditional livelihood vector of the tribesmen and thereby they have been reincarnated as modernity impels them to do so; as market forces have indulged them to have a global identity; as globalization has wigwagged them to move forward (?) by evacuating the mountains mile after miles.

Study Area

The study area, Arunachal Pradesh (lies between the 26° 28′ N and 29° 30′N latitudinal and 91°30′E and 97°30′E longitudinal extents), erstwhile known as Northeast Frontier Agency (NEFA) was indeed a hidden land until the Ahom rulers came into contact them sometimes in the Fifteenth Century, had established a trade relation with the tribesmen. However, it was to wait till the British advent of the territory that we have come to know about them. The indigenous tribal people originated with Tibeto-Burmese genealogy are believed to be migrated into the territory in search

Fig. 11.1. Arunachal Pradesh: The North-East Extremity of Indian Union

of agricultural land. The art of cultivation was known to them and they had led their livelihood basically on abundant forest resources. Apart from grazing, hunting, gathering, fishing and weaving, they used to practice shifting cultivation, a very much crud form of agriculture, which is also known as *slash and burn* method. On the other hand, the territory was blessed with rich natural resources. Even at the present figure, **62.5%** of the total geographical area has forest coverage. The most sparsely populated territory of the country is the abode of a number of flora and fauna that provides a flourishing bio-diversity heritage for the region as well as for the country as a whole.

The Tribal Ethics on Environmental Qualities

The tribal economy in general was defined by its primitiveness. In the absence of any market force, the traditional institutional framework provided them a subsistence type of economy, where production relation was established on basis of the interactions between man and nature. People evolved the nature for their own shake. Man extracted the nature for producing his bare needs in the forms of gathering, hunting, rearing and later in agriculture but to every extent he was limited by the concept of provisions; neither had he produced for the market nor did he buy the needs from there. Money economy was virtually absent until the very yesterday. Although static, but a self-sufficient and self-reliant economy was prevailing under the guidance of a traditional framework. However, the recent scenario in this respect is very much different from its original version.

Fig. 11.2 : High-hill Jhum Tillage

The Nehruvian philosophy paved the path of development in the socio-economic dimensions of the tribal society and thereby market forces gradually have come into operation. In the days of market mechanism, the mode of production has also got a drastic change in respect to the functional relationship of various inputs involved in the production process as well as in its distributional aspects. From a mere subsistence level of mode of production, the economy as a whole has been reorganized for the market shake. Thus, generation of personal income has achieved priority among the tribesmen. As revealed from the field investigation (Table 11.1), nearly 50% of the respondents have been vertically shifted their profession i.e. from the traditional agricultural practice to secondary and tertiary sector. The rising literacy level alone is not the only cause of shifting the choice of profession of the tribesmen in the study area as found in the field investigation rather this vertical mobility is a spontaneous result of modernity.

APPENDICES

Appendix 1 (Vernacular/ Glossary)

1. *Thanda* (Hindi) = Cold/ Chilled
2. *Mat lob* (Hindi) = Meaning

3. *Gale* (Adi) = the traditional Adi Gown
4. *Galuk* (Adi) = the traditional Adi Coat
5. *Kebang* (Adi) = the traditional Adi Administrative body at village or any unit level Administrative body
6. *Kebang Abu* (Adi) = The Head man or the Village Chief
7. *Adiavik* (Adi) = the practice of shifting cultivation

Appendix-2 (Field Survey)

Table 11.1: Age Group, Literacy Level and Family Size of the sample Households

Age Group of the Respondents (Year)		Literacy Level		Family Size	
Age Group	No. of Respondents	Literacy Level	No. of Respondents	No. of Family Members	No. of Family
Below 40	30	Illiterate	52	02-05	2
41-50	21	Fundamentally Literate	16	06-07	93
51-60	17	Up to Class V	19	08-09	19
61-70	33	VI- VIII	21		
71-80	9	IX- X	9	10-11	5
81-90	3	XI – Graduation	2	12 and above	1
Above 90	7	Post Graduation	1		
Total	120	Total	120	Total	120

(Field Survey)

Materials and Method

The present chapter is a by-product of another UGC funded Research Project, where interview was taken from the various age groups of people to analyze their perceptions towards environment and its future usages. The randomly selected samples were questioned on different relevant aspects like production, income, consumption and others. On basis of the data obtained from field were crossed checked with the available secondary sources. Hence, data related to production, consumption and other economic activities have arranged into the Tabular Forms; some simple statistical applications discover the facts that the drastic change of the physical environment of the study area is a spontaneous result of the changing consumption pattern, which is again acquired a faster rate of change in the days of Globalization and

Consumerism. For the shake of study, interview was taken from the various age groups of people with sample size of 120 covering 24 villages of 8 districts of the state in order to sketch out their varied perceptions towards the environment and its qualities.

Fig. 11.3 : Gamburas: They were the Ultimate Village Guardians

Result and Discussion

It is revealed from the field study that the people of the age groups 50 and less have a different view about agriculture, environment and the economy as a whole than that of the people of age groups of more than 50 years. The former group wants to bring a change into the traditional agricultural practice by replacing with a viable alternative source of income because they feel traditional agriculture is too much labour intensive as well as it courts ruin to their rich bio-diversity; while the later groups do not bother much about the environment and want a continuity of their traditional going. Although the aged people (of age group 50 years and more) believe that there is environmental degradation of some degrees, they do not like to mention that the traditional agricultural practice is the main culprit for this situation. Rather the people are vocal to blame the developmental activities undertaken in and around the locality along with expansion of population size are the major factors to be considered for the present situation. These people strongly believe that their traditional institutions were sufficient enough to protect the environment in their old golden days. The newly introduced civil codes are not sufficient for the same, which on the other hand, makes the people greedy and selfish in nature towards the environment.

Fig. 11.4 : Farm surplus generates some disposable money at village markets

Table 11.2 : Occupational Structure of the sample Households

Name of the occupation	No. of Respondents	% of the respondents
Landless agricultural Labour	9	7.5
Landless non-agricultural labour	4	3.33
Marginal Cultivators	7	5.83
Small Cultivators	13	10.83
Medium Cultivators	29	24.16
Large Cultivators	9	7.5
Business and Supply (including Govt. Contractors)	19	15.83
Service	28	23.33
Other (not mentioned)	2	1.66
Total	**120**	**100**

(Field Survey)

The aged generation enjoys putting labour in the *jhum* field and merry making, whilst the younger generations, who are otherwise being qualified want to gash their age old traditional practice (*jhum* cultivation) and want to work more in number in the secondary and tertiary occupation.

Table 11.3 (Family Income of the sample Households) shows a clear cut distinction of the income generating groups, which categorizes into two broadly divided income groups *vis-a-vis,* High Income Group and Low Income Group and the virtual absence of Middle Income Group polarizes the society in the study area. Out of the 120 households, it is found that a total of 17 households (14.16%) have yearly income less than Rs 50,000, which is considered as the basic requirement of maintaining livelihood of a five members family at the present market price. Again, amongst this lower income group, 11 households (9.17%) households do hardly able to earn their daily requirement from their present structure of occupation. Interestingly, this group of people comprises mainly from the occupational groups (permanent occupation) of 'agricultural labour' and 'non-agricultural labour', whom we found living below the poverty line. However, it is also revealed from the household level study that the people of this category are being engaging themselves in other subsistence activities like gathering, rearing, and fishing etc based on the local forest resources. However, 'hunting' is a practice, persisting into the society irrespective of any economic group.

Table 11.3: Family Income of the sample Households (Rs. /Year)

Income level	No. of respondents	% of the Respondents
Less than 25,000	11	9.16
25001- 50,000	6	5.00
50,001-75,000	7	5.83
75,001-100,000	6	5.00
100,001-125,000	5	4.16
125,001-150,000	17	14.16
150,001-175,000	19	15.83
175,001-200,000	18	15.00
More than 200,00	31	25.83
Total	**120**	

(Field Survey)

It is however, to note that the present study has revealed the fact that at around 90% of the people in the study area are living with middle and high income, contrary to the general perception that the tribal people are generally backward and living below the poverty line. Poverty persists there rather in very shadow form. Apart from their known sources of income, easy money flow as injected into the economy has been revealed from the field study results a vertical mobility of the occupational structure of tribesmen as well as their consumption pattern.

The tribal society in the study area has shown the tendency of a steady rise of income level, when the collected field data has been compared with the available secondary data. Out of the 120 samples, 90 (75%) families were found to have an annual income of Rs 100,000 or above; surely belong to the 'High Middle Class to Higher Income Group' categories. Thus, consumption pattern of the tribesmen as found from the field survey (Table 11.4) has also been evolved likewise.

It is however, to note the fact that very small amount of the total income (3%), the average households do spend on food. This is because of the fact that the tribesmen do produce there all the necessary requirements for food from their farms and merely the items, which could not be produced in the farm sector, are bought from the market; these includes salt, sugar, muster oil and so on.

Apart from food, they do spend a very trivial amount on their shelter. Construction of house is not a regular phenomenon for the tribesmen in the study area. At an average, the local people build their house at every 10 years; moreover, the materials for construction are collected from local forests too. Apart from these, the required labour is gathered from the community jargon; so that the cost of constructing houses is nominal as compared to the other components of total expenditure.

Education is an emerging phenomenon of the totality of tribal livelihood. As because of the family size is not fringed by the norm of two children, the average tribal family spends a considerable portion of the total income on education of their wards in the form of school/ college tuition fees, hostel fees, cost of dresses and educational stationers, tuition fees for the private tutors etc. As it is revealed from the field survey that the wards of a bit well-to-do families are accommodated in the school hostels in the far flanged urban centres and because of lesser density of higher educational institutions, the students have to stay in the hostels and other self-arranged rental houses during their study in colleges and institution of higher studies. As we found from the sample universe, at an average of 10% of the total income is spent for education.

Another noteworthy component of the total expenditure of the sample households has been revealed from the field study that the villagers have had to spend 12% of their total income in an average as their expenditure on medicine and other health related problems – a very much uncommon component in the totality of the tribal livelihood in the study area. It was even some decades ago, that the local *miris* (village medicine man) had taken care of the physiological problems by means of traditional system of medicine, which radically disappeared because of the active presence of modern form of allopathic medicine and Medicare. Although the rugged topographical features retard the adequate growth of infrastructural facilities in the study area, the people of remote villages still prefer to go to the health centres of modern medicine and sometime they do prefer to be present in the luxurious nursing homes located outside the State. Thus, expenditure on medicine has risen considerably in the study area.

Expenditures on cosmetics and recreation are other new dimensions of the tribal livelihood as it is found from the field study that the younger generation uses imported cosmetics of high price. And the expenditure on recreation has been raised rapidly in the form of television and other electronic media of entertainment; although living in the remote villages, the facilities have an active presence in the study area.

Since the field survey was conducted among the villagers, who are basically attached to the agricultural activities directly or indirectly, do have an expenditure in the form of purchasing farm input; although very insignificant rather the medium and large cultivators are investing a considerable amount of their total income to purchase modernized farm inputs such as fertilizer, insecticides, pesticides, fungicides, HYV seeds and sometime they do employ mechanized farm equipments like tractor, power tiller, sprayer etc. hired from the Department of Agriculture and other organizations. As found from the field report that in an average, about 4%

Table 11.4: Distribution of Consumption Expenditure of the Sample Households (As percentage of Total Income)

Expenditure Heads	Expenditureas % of total income
Food	3%
Clothing	25%
Shelter	1.2%
Education	10%
Medicine	12%
Cosmetics	16%
Recreation	20%
Farm inputs	4.0%
Total	**91.2**

(Field Survey)

of the total income is spent in this head. No doubt, an emerging phenomenon in the way of modernization of agriculture as revealed in the different dimensions of the present study.

From the analysis of the distribution of consumption expenditure (Table 11.4) it reveals that the high percentage of consumption expenditure (91.2%) of the sample households implies their marginal propensity to save (MPS) is automatically low. These may be the reason that the tribal communities in the study area have taken the first generation test of liquid money that too in the era of globalization and consumerization.

Fig. 11.5 : The way consumerism grasps the tribal livelihood too!

Conclusion

From the analysis of field data it is clear that the tribal society in the study area and all its societal are in transition. But the changes are not synonymous when compared to the other parts of the country or the world. Changes are rapid and sometimes jumbling to the heights without obeying any established theory of social transition. Impelled from the way of the modern living, the tribesmen are now running after cheap money easily available at their surroundings in the form of abundant natural resources, which they are exploiting without giving any future look therein. The faster rate of degradation of natural resources in the study area thus claims an inside look for further studies. The moral limitations, by which the tribesmen were once guided to protect their environment within the traditional framework and had a deep belief on the mother nature, has been detracted to a large extent due to the outrageous presence of so-called market forces, which are more prominent in the days of globalization and consumerization.

REFERENCES

Banerjee, A.C. (1912): *The Eastern Frontier of North East India,* Third Edition, Calcutta, Reprinted in 1964.

Baruah, U., T. Bhattacharya (1996): 'Degradation Hazards in Arunachal Pradesh' in *Hill Geographer,* xii (1 & 2), pp. 48-53.

Bhattacharjee, Dr.R.P. (2000): *Economic Development of Arunachal Pradesh,* Himalayan Publishers, Itanagar.

Bower, U.G. (1953): *The Hidden Land,* John Hurry, London.

Butler, J. (1947): *A Sketch of Assam,* Smith Elder & Co. London.

Choudhury, D.P. (1978): *The North East Frontier of India, 1865-1914,* the Asiatic Society, Calcutta.

Choudhury, J. N (1985): *Arunachal Through the Ages,* Mrs. J.N. Choudhury, Shillong.

Dalton, E.T. (1973): *Tribal History of Eastern India,* Cosmo Publications, Delhi.

Das, J.N. (1989): *Land System of Arunachal Pradesh,* Law Research Institute, Guwahati.

Das, S. (2002): 'Changing Economy of the Nyishings: A Case Study of a Nyishing Village under Papumpare District of A.P.' in the *RESARUN,* Vol. 28, Department of Cultural Affairs, Government of Arunachal Pradesh, Itanagar.

Das, S.T. (1986): *Tribal Life of North East India,* Giyan Publishing House, Delhi.

Datta, P.S. (1985): *Economic Development of Arunachal Pradesh (A Case Study in NEC Role),* Vikash Publishing House Pvt. Ltd., New Delhi.

Director of Economics and Statistics (2000): *Statistical Abstract of Arunachal Pradesh,* Government of Arunachal Pradesh, Itanagar.

Director of Economics and Statistics (2001): *Economic Review of Arunachal Pradesh,* Government of Arunachal Pradesh, Itanagar.

Director of Economics and Statistics (2001): *Statistical Abstract of Arunachal Pradesh,* Government of Arunachal Pradesh, Itanagar.

Director of Economics and Statistics (2003): *Statistical Abstract of Arunachal Pradesh,* Government of Arunachal Pradesh, Itanagar.

Dutta Roy, B. (Ed 1989): *Tribal Identity and Tensions in North East India,* Cosmo Publications, Delhi.

Dutta Roy, B. and Agarwal, S.P. (ends 1986): *Reorganigation of North East science 1947,* Concept Publishing Company, New Delhi.

Dutta, D.K. and Duarah, D.K. (2002): 'Impacts of Arts and Crafts in the Economy of the Monpas of Arunachal Pradesh' in the *RESARUN*, Vol. 28, Department of Cultural Affairs, Government of Arunachal Pradesh, Itanagar.

Dutta, P.S. (1985): *Economic Development of Arunachal Pradesh (A Case Study of NEC's Role)*, Vikas Publishing House, New Delhi. .

Dutta, S. (2000): *Studies in the History, Economy and Culture of Arunachal Pradesh*, Himalayan Publishers, Itanagar.

Elwin, V. (1953): *India's North East Frontier in the Nineteenth Century*, Oxford University Press, Bombay.

Elwin, V. (1964): *The Tribal World of Verrier Elwin*, Oxford University Press, Bombay.

Elwin, V. (1980): *A Philosophy of NEFA*, Director of Research, Government of Arunachal Pradesh, Itanagar.

Elwin, V. (1988): *Democracy in NEFA*, Director of Research, Government of Arunachal Pradesh, Itanagar. Ess, Charles (Ed) (2001): Culture, Technology, Communication: Towards an Intercultural Global Village, SUNY Press, New York.

Fisk, E.K. and Shand, R.T. (1970): 'The Early Stages of Economic Development in a Primitive Economy' in C.R. Wharton (Ed book) *Subsistence Agriculture and Economic Development*, Frank Cass, London.

Ghosh, B. and Ali, N (2006): 'Changing Dimensions of Shifting Cultivation: The Story from an Adi Village of Arunachal Pradesh' in N. Ali (Ed) *Natural Resources and Tribals in North East India*, Mittal Publications, New Delhi.

Hamilton, A. (1912): *In Abor Jungles of North East India*, Mittal Publications, New Delhi.

Husain, Z. (2000): 'Land Management in the Hill Eco-System': A Case Study of Yangse Valley in the Kameng Himalayas' in *Hill Geographer*, xvi (1 & 2), pp. 50-58.

Mackenzie, A. (1883): *History of Relations of the Government with the Hill Tribes of North East Frontier of Bengal*, Mittal Publications, New Delhi.

Panda, D. (2000): 'Changing Human Perspectives towards Shifting Cultivation ---- A Case Study of Poma Village, Arunachal Pradesh' in *Hill Geographer*, xvi (1 & 2). Sachchidananda (1989): *Shifting Cultivation in India*, Concept Publishing Company, New Delhi.

Sukla, A.P (1982): 'Spatio-Temporal Organizational Dimensions of Agriculture in Siang Region, Arunachal Pradesh' in *Hill Geographer*, I (1 & 2), pp. 14-22.

Contract Farming: A Necessity for Sustainable Rural Development in Developing Countries

An Indian Perspective

—Krishna Murari
—Pooja Kumari

ABSTRACT

Contract farming has opened new vistas of life for poor farmer. Now they can manage there food portfolio according to the market demand. Due to rapid industrialization the land for cultivation is decreasing day by day. Secondly, globalization has created new markets for agricultural products. This has necessitated organized farming practice in India. The role of Contract Farming in Indian Rural Economy involves government and private participation along with the rural workers. The farmer agrees to provide established quantities of a specific agricultural product, meeting the quality standards and delivery schedule set by the purchaser. In turn, the buyer commits to purchase the product, often at a pre-determined price. This kind of practice is beneficial for both the parties. Farmers get good remuneration for their farm products. The private sector has made great strides in bringing poorer farmers into the larger agricultural picture through including them in contract farming structures. Though there are some problems in running contract farming but this system is inevitable in globalised world.

Introduction

Contract Farming in Indian Rural Economy is a new concept. Contract farming involves cultivating and harvesting for and on behalf of big business establishments or Government agencies and forwarding the produce at a pre-determined price. In return, the contracted farmers are offered high price against their farm produce. The role of contract farming in Indian rural economy is becoming more and more important, since organized farming practice has become the need of the hour in the world of rapid industrialization. The rapid industrialization process in India has created shortage of farmland, which in turn has necessitated organized farming practice in India

The process of contract farming in India involves scientific and optimum use of land and farm resources for maximum output of agriculture produce. Small time farmers practicing primitive agricultural methods for cultivation and harvesting of crops dominate the Indian agriculture sector. But, with the liberalization of India economy, there has been a sudden spurt in contract farming in India. Moreover, today more and more established business houses are taking interest in the business of contract farming in India. This has happened as a result of rapid growth of retail industry in India. The growth of retail industry in India has propelled the growth of farm retail in India, which caters fresh vegetables and fruits from the farms to the Indian mass.

Contract farming is Agricultural production carried out according to an agreement between a buyer and farmers, which establishes conditions for the production and marketing of a farm product or products. Typically, the farmer agrees to provide established quantities of a specific agricultural product, meeting the quality standards and delivery schedule set by the purchaser. In turn, the buyer commits to purchase the product, often at a pre-determined price. In some cases the buyer also commits to support production through, for example, supplying farm inputs, land preparation, providing technical advice and arranging transport of produce to the buyer's premises. Another term often used to refer to contract farming operations is 'out-grower schemes", whereby farmers are linked with a large farm or processing plant which supports production planning, input supply, extension advice and transport. Contract farming is used for a wide variety of agricultural products.

Advantages for Farmers

Access to credit

The majority of smallholder producers experience difficulties in obtaining credit for production inputs. The collapse or restructuring of many agricultural development banks and the closure of many export crop marketing boards (particularly in Africa), in which the past supplied farmers with inputs on credit; difficulties have increased rather than decreasing. Contract farming usually allows farmers access to some form of credit to finance production inputs

Introduction of appropriate technology

New techniques are often required to upgrade agricultural commodities for markets that demand high quality standards. New production techniques are often necessary to increase productivity as well as to ensure that the commodity meets market demands. However, small scale farmers are frequently reluctant to adopt new technologies because of the possible risks and costs involved. They are more likely to accept new practices when they can rely on external resources for material and technological inputs.

Skill transfer

The skills the farmer learns through contract farming may include record keeping, the efficient use of farm resources, improved methods of applying chemicals and fertilizers, knowledge of the importance of quality and the characteristics and demands of export markets. Farmers can gain experience in carrying out field activities following a strict timetable imposed by the extension service

Guaranteed and fixed pricing structures

The returns farmers receive for their crops on the open market depend on the prevailing market prices as well as on their ability to negotiate with buyers. This can create considerable uncertainty which, to a certain extent, contract farming can overcome. Frequently, sponsors indicate in advance the price(s) to be paid and these are specified in the agreement. On the other hand, some contracts are not based on fixed prices but are related to the market prices at the time of delivery.

Problems Faced by Farmers

Increased risk

Farmers entering new contract farming ventures should be prepared to balance the prospect of higher returns with the possibility of greater risk. Such risk is more likely when the agribusiness venture is introducing a new crop to the area. There may be production risks, particularly where prior field tests are inadequate, resulting in lower-than-expected yields for the farmers

Unsuitable technology and crop incompatibility

The introduction of a new crop to be grown under conditions rigorously controlled by the sponsor can cause disruption to the existing farming system. Harvesting of the contracted crop may fall at the same time as the harvesting of food crops, thus causing competition for scarce labour resources. Particular problems may be experienced when contract farming is related to resettlement programmers.

Manipulation of quotas and quality specifications

Inefficient management can lead to production exceeding original targets. Sponsors may have unrealistic expectations of the market for their product or the market may collapse unexpectedly owing to transport problems, civil unrest, change in government policy or the arrival of a competitor. Such occurrences can lead managers to reduce farmers' quotas. Few contracts specify penalties in such circumstances.

Corruption

Problems occur when staff responsible for issuing contracts and buying crops exploits their position. Such practices result in a collapse of trust and communication between the contracted parties and soon undermine any contract. Management needs to ensure that corruption in any form does not occur. On a larger scale, the sponsors can themselves be dishonest or corrupt.

Domination by monopolies

The monopoly of a single crop by a sponsor can have a negative effect. Allowing only one purchaser encourages monopolistic tendencies, particularly where farmers are locked into a fairly sizeable investment, such as with tree crops, and cannot easily change to other crops. On the other hand, large-scale investments, such as for nucleus estates, often require a monopoly in order to be viable. In order to protect farmers when there is only a single buyer for one commodity, the government should have some role in determining the prices paid.

Advantages for Sponsors

Political acceptability

It can be more politically expedient for a sponsor to involve smallholder farmers in production rather than to operate plantations. Many governments are reluctant to have large plantations and some are actively involved in closing down such estates and redistributing their land. Contract farming, particularly when the farmer is not a tenant of the sponsor, is less likely to be subject to political criticism.

Production reliability and shared risk

The failure to supply agreed contracts could seriously jeopardize future sales. Plantation agriculture and contract farming both offer reasonable supply reliability. Sponsors of contract farming, even with the best management, always run the risk that farmers will fail to honor agreements.

Quality consistency

Markets for fresh and processed agricultural produce require consistent quality standards. Moreover, these markets are moving increasingly to a situation where the supplier must also conform to regulatory controls regarding production techniques, particularly the use of pesticides. For fresh produce there is a growing requirement for "traceability", i.e. suppliers to major markets increasingly need to be confident of identifying the source of production if problems related to food safety arise

Problems Faced by Sponsors

Land availability constraints

Farmers must have suitable land on which to cultivate their contracted crops. Problems can arise when farmers have minimal or no security of tenure as there is a danger of the sponsor's investment being wasted as a result of farmer landlord disputes. Difficulties are also common when sponsors lease land to farmers. Such arrangements normally have eviction clauses included as part of the conditions.

Social and cultural constraints

Problems can arise when management chooses farmers who are unable to comply with strict timetables and regulations because of social obligations. Promoting agriculture through contracts is also a cultural issue. In communities where custom and tradition play an important role, difficulties may arise when farming innovations are introduced. Before introducing new cropping schedules, sponsors must consider the social attitudes and the traditional farming practices of the community and assess how a new crop could be introduced.

Extra-contractual marketing

The sale of produce by farmers to a third party, outside the conditions of a contract, can be a major problem. Extra-contractual sales are always possible and are not easily controlled when an alternative market exists. Unfortunately members often sold their vegetables to traders at higher prices than the cooperative had contracted.

Acts and Rules in Contract Farming

- Agricultural Produce (Grading and Marking) Act, 1937 as amended in 1986.
- Agricultural Produce Grading and Marking Act, 1937
- Schedule Appended to AP (G&M) Act 1937
- General Grading and Marking Rules, 1988
- Commodity Grading and Marking Rules
- List of commodities whose Agmark Grade Standards have been covered under AP (G&M) Act 1937
- Manual on Standards of Paddy
- Manual on Standards of Wheat
- Manual on Standards of Maize
- Manual on Standards of Mustard and Rapeseed

Agricultural Product under Contract Farming

The main agricultural products of India under the process of contract farming are as follows -

- **Food Grains** - Rice, Wheat, Pulses, Cereals, Corn, Maize, Rice Bran Extractions, Sorghum, Soy meal, Suji, Parmal, Lentils, Jowar, Bajra, Chick pea,
- **Fruits & Nuts** - Cashew Kernels, Cashew Nut, Cashews, Almonds, Roasted Dry Fruits, Peanuts, Groundnut, Walnut Kernels, Walnuts, Indian Peanuts, HPS Groundnuts
- **Fruits** - Bananas, Beans, Cherry, Cucumbers, Dried Fruits, Dried Truffles, Carrots, Lemon, Mandarins, Mango, Meslin, Shallots, Apples, Asparagus, Grapes, Oranges, Gherkins, Turnips, Oranges, Papaya, Pineapple,
- **Vegetables** – Potatoes, Bitter gourd, Stripe Gourd, Pumpkin, cauliflower, Cabbage, Tomato, Onion, Green Pepper, Drum Sticks, Lady's finger, Banana, Papaya, Spinach, Cucumber, Mushroom, Mushroom Spawn, Radiata, Seeds, Buds, Plantation & Related Products - Basil Seed, Cumin seeds, Dill Seed, Buds, Celery Seed, Hybrid Seeds, Sesame Seeds, Sesbania Seed, Sunflower Seeds,

Mustard Seeds, Oil Seeds, Plant Products, Plantation, Plants, Psyllium Seed, Fennel Seed, Fenugreek Seed, Herb Seeds, Tamarind Seed, Vegetable Seeds

- **Spices** - Black Pepper, Chilly, Cinnamon, Cloves, Coriander Powder, Cumin, Dry Ginger, Dry Red Chilly, Cardamom, Anise, Salt, Pepper, Fenugreek, Clove, Ginger, Turmeric, Turmeric Powder,
- **Tea & Coffee** - Black Tea, Coffee, Coffee Beans, Darjeeling Teas, Assam Teas, Instant Coffee, Leaf Coffee, Leaf Tea, Packaged Tea, Green Tea, CTC Teas,
- **Tobacco & Tobacco Products** - Betel nut Leaves, Betel nut, Bidi Leaves, Chewing Tobacco, Arecanut, Snuff, Opium, Pan, Jute, Tobacco, Rubber etc.

The Indian institutes engaged for marketing agricultural products under contract marketing

- Karnataka State Agricultural Marketing Board
- Krishi Maratavahini
- Madhya Pradesh State Agricultural Marketing Board
- Maharashtra State Agricultural Marketing Board, Pune
- Meghalaya State Agricultural Marketing Board
- Orissa State Agricultural Marketing Board, Bhubaneswar
- Punjab State Marketing Board
- Rajasthan State Marketing Board
- AP Agricultural Marketing Board
- Domestic & Export Market Intelligence Cell
- Tamil Nadu Agricultural University and Agri Marketing Board
- HP State Agricultural Marketing Board.

Table 12.1 : Agri-export zones recently established in India

State	Products
1	2
Andhra Pradesh	Mango pulp, fresh vegetables, grapes
Assam	Fresh and processed ginger
Bihar	Litchi
Himachal Pradesh	Apple

1	2
Jammu and Kashmir	Apple, walnut
Jharkhand	Vegetables
Karnataka	Gherkins, flowers
Kerala	Horticultural products
Madhya Pradesh	Potato, onion, garlic, seed spices
Maharashtra	Mango, grape, onion, flowers, orange
Orissa	Ginger, turmeric
Sikkim	Flowers (orchids), cherry, pepper, ginger
Uttar Pradesh	Mango, potato, vegetables
Uttarakhand	Litchi, flowers, medicinal and aromatic plants
West Bengal	Litchi, pineapple, potato, mango, vegetables

Source: Science, Vol. 93, No. 12, 25 December, 2007

Table 12.2: Progress of self-help groups and bank loans

Year	No of self-help groups	Loan availed (Rs in million)
1992–93	255	3
1993–94	620	7
1994–95	2,122	24
1995–96	4,757	61
1996–97	8,598	118
1997–98	14,317	238
1998–99	32,995	571
1999–2000	114,775	1,930
2000–01	263,825	4,809
2001–02	461,478	10,263

Source: NABARD, New Delhi, Current Science, Vol. 9 3, No. 12, 25 December 2007

Table 12.3: States-wise Contract Farming Initiatives by Private Sectors

State	Crop	Company/Corporate	Area(ha)
1	2	3	4
Karnataka	Ashwagandha	Himalaya Health Care Ltd	700
Karnataka	Dhavana	Mysore S N C Oil Company	400-500
Karnataka	Marigold & Caprica Chili	AVT natural Product Ltd.	4000

1	2	3	4
Karnataka	Coleus	Natural Remedies Ltd.	150
Karnataka	Gherkins	Global Green Company Ltd.	8000(inc of TM & AP)
Maharashtra	Soybean	Tinna Oil & Chemicals	134800
Maharashtra	Fruits,Vegetables, Cereals, Spices & Pulses	Ion Exchange Enviro Farm Ltd.	800
Madhya Pradesh	Wheat, Maize and Soybean	Cargil India Ltd.	NA
Madhya Pradesh	Wheat	Hindusthan Lever Ltd.	15000
Madhya Pradesh	Fruits,Vegetables, Cereals,Spices & Pulses	Ion Exchange Enviro Farm Ltd.(IEEFL)	NA
Madhya Pradesh	Soybean	ITC_IBD	1200
Punjab	Tomato & Chilly	Nijjer Agro Food Ltd.	250
Punjab	Barley	United Breweries Ltd.	2270
Punjab	Basmati & Rice	Mahindra Shubhlabh Services Ltd.	4000
Punjab	Basmati	Satnam overseas, Amira Food India Ltd.	14700
Punjab	Basmati,Groundnut, Tomato,Chilli,Potato	Pepsico India Ltd.	Around 6000
Punjab	Milk	Nestel India Ltd.	134800
Tamil Nadu	Cotton	Super Spinning Mill	570
Tamil Nadu	Maize	Bhuvi Care Pvt. Ltd.	800
Tamil Nadu	Paddy	Bhuvi Care Pvt.Ltd.	200
Tamil Nadu	Cotton	Appachi Cotton Co.	260

***Source:** NIAM (2003), *The Times Agriculture Journal* (2003) and (FICCI-IFPRI-ICRISAT: 2003)

Conclusion

The combined effects of globalization, the rising demand for high-value crops, and the development of transport infrastructure in rural areas has opened up new opportunities for the rural poor to participate in the global marketplace, though including the poor in the market has some challenges. The public sector traditionally has not involved the poor enough in agriculture production and marketing efforts. The private sector has made great strides in bringing poorer farmers into the larger agricultural picture through including them in contract farming structures. Contract farming appears to be a promising institutional arrangement to facilitate farmers' access to an array of agricultural services from which they are typically excluded. Contract farming enhances the agricultural productivity and efficiency of poor farmers by introducing improved farming practices through the provision of inputs, transportation, extension services, and, most importantly, market access. It also brings investments and technical expertise to rural areas, facilitates cross-border quality control, contributes to employment, and fosters sustainable cooperation within the region. Though this review focused primarily on GMS transition economies, the potential benefits of contract farming are relevant in the broader context of other developing countries.

REFERENCES

Agarwal, I. (2005): "Contract Farming Venture in Cotton: A Case Study in Tamilnadu", *Indian Journal of Agricultural Marketing*, 19(2)153-161.

Bhavani, T.A. (2007): Structure of the Indian Food Processing Industry: Towards Scaling Up and Consolidation. International Food Policy Research Institute, New Delhi.

Gahukar, R.T. (2007): Contract farming for organic crop production in India, *Current Science*, Vol. 93, No. 12, 25 Dec. 2007.

Kumar, P. (2006): "Contract Farming through Agribusiness Firms and State Corporation: A case study in Punjab", *Economic and Political Weekly*, 52(30), Dec.30, A5367-5375.

Rustagi, P. (2002): Girl child labour: regional dimensions and motivations. The Indian *Journal of Labour Economics*, 45 (3): 465-477.

Saravanan, V. (2002): Women's employment and reduction of child labour – beedi workers in rural Tamilnadu. *Economic and Political Weekly*, 37 (52): December 28, 5205 – 5214.

Setboonsarng, Sununtar (2008): Global Partnership in Poverty Reduction: Contract Farming and Regional Cooperation, *ADB Institute Discussion Paper No. 89.*

Sundaram, K. (2001): Employment-unemployment situation in the nineties: some results from NSS 55th Round Survey. *Economic and Political Weekly*, 36(11): March 17, 931-940.

Tripathi, R S, R Singh and S Singh (2005): "Contract Farming in Potato Production: An Alternative for Managing Risk and Uncertainty", *Agricultural Economics Research Review*, 18, 47-60.

Trivedi, Divya (2008): *Food for thought. Business Line*. New Delhi, 15 May 2008.

Sustainable Agricultural Development from Soil and Water Management

A Case Study on Jhansi Division of Uttar Pradesh

—Ram Kumar Jha

ABSTRACT

Sustainable agriculture refers to the ability of a farm to produce sufficient food, without causing irreversible damage to ecosystem health. The issue is two-fold. One aspect is biophysical that relates to the long-term effects of various practices on soil properties and processes essential for crop productivity. The other is socio-economic that relates to the long-term ability of farmers to obtain inputs and manage resources such as land, labour and capital. The study focuses on the following objectives: (1) to know the opinion of farmers on reasons of increasing agricultural productivity; (2) to know the framers knowledge about soil management; (3) to know the awareness of farmers about water management; and (4) to check the sustainable impact of different selected variables on total per acre output. In all the selected regions, majority of marginal, small and large farmers answered that with the use of farm yard manure, fertilizers and insecticides and pesticides the agricultural productivity has increased.

Key Words: *Sustainable Agricultural Development, Water Management, Soil Erosion, Knowledge.*

JEL Classification: *Q110, Q120, Q150*

Introduction

Agricultural sector, besides being a prime source of food is a source of raw material for the expanding industry. Agricultural development would lead to an increase in the purchasing power of the rural poor and will help the growth of non-agricultural sector by providing a market for increasing production of industries. Agricultural sector carries the double obligation to increase production, and to provide capital for other sectors in order to promote economic growth, while at the same time, it must provide for the welfare of the farmers and their families. The farm sector also provides welfare for other sectors of the economy. Thus it is agriculture which must provide greater employment, either within itself or by providing capital to non-farm jobs.

Sustainable agriculture refers to the ability of a farm to produce sufficient food, without causing irreversible damage to ecosystem health. The issue is two-fold. One aspect is biophysical that relates to the long-term effects of various practices on soil properties and processes essential for crop productivity. The other is socio-economic that relates to the long-term ability of farmers to obtain inputs and manage resources such as land, labour and capital.

During the past few decades, the pattern of agricultural production has changed dramatically due to use of new technologies, mechanization, increased chemical use, specialization and government policies that favoured maximizing production. These changes have had significant costs such as, top soil depletion, groundwater contamination and the disintegration of economic and social conditions in rural communities. A growing movement has emerged during the past two decades to question the role of the agricultural establishment in promoting practices that contribute to these environmental and social problems. Today, this movement for sustainable agriculture integrates three main goals: environmental health, economic profitability, and social and economic equity. A variety of philosophies, policies and practices have contributed to these goals. People in many different capacities, from farmers to consumers, have shared this vision and contributed to them. Not only does sustainable agriculture address many environmental and social concerns, but also it offers innovative and economically viable opportunities for growers, labourers, consumers, policymakers and many others in the entire food production and consumption system.

Productivity which is outcome of combined contribution of different technological factors such as seeds, manures, fertilizers, pesticides, soil, water, etc., are the real indicators to judge the economic viability and profitability of a crop and serves as the basis for ultimate solution for increasing the existing level of production to a desired level. Misra and Rao (2003) have mentioned in their study that the yield, total production, income and profit of crops increased under organic farming system as compared to inorganic system. Further, authors describes about organic inputs for organic farming and sustainable agriculture system in India. At present, in addition to food grains output of above 200 million tonnes, more than 350 million tonnes of organic matter in the form of biological wastes of cereal and legume plants such as straw and stubbles and another more than one billion tones of annual and perennial crop plants are produced per annum. These biological wastes considered as a bane can be a boon to increase soil fertility for sustainable agriculture.

As measures of sustainability, Campbell *et al.,* (1997) have been chosen three indicators, each of which falls in the stability category. These are soil organic matter, soil erosion and crop yield. Taylor *et al.,* (1999) have developed a composite farmer sustainability index, which is, designed to measure the degree of sustainability of individual farm management practices followed in the production of cabbage in Malaysia. The included resources in their study are: use of integrated pest management for controlling insects, employing crop rotations, intercropping and relay cropping to enhance soil fertility, control weeds and maximize use of space and time, soil incorporation of livestock wastes, crop residues and green manures to enhance fertility and good physical properties, promoting nitrogen use efficiency by sequestering it from the air and making it available to crops through nitrogen-fixing legumes, encouraging mineral release and recycling from soil reserves, making water available to crops by applying water harvesting and other enhanced soil moisture retention strategies, selecting crop varieties on the basis of their resistance or tolerance of insects and diseases, construction of bunds and terraces to control soil erosion, modifying planting dates and other cultural practice, control of management and labour by the farm family. Lefroy *et al.,* (1999) focused on issues of sustainable land management, especially in slope lands in South-East Asia, and begin with the premise that land management involves issues that go beyond the subject of soil quality. Sustainable land management encompasses the need for long term preservation of the resource base to allow adequate future food production in a manner that is socially acceptable economically viable and environmentally sound. In this definition included aspects of the three components of sustainability are environment, economy, and society.

Meerman *et al.,* (1996) have described that land reclamation, soil and water management, cropping practices, pest management and use of plant genetic resources are the practices to achieve high productivity with sustainable agriculture. Sustainable agriculture aims at presenting biodiversity, maintaining soil fertility and water purity, conservation and improvement of the chemical, physical and biological, quantities of the soil recycles natural resources and conserves energy and produces diverse forms of high quality foods and fibre (Oxfam, 1999).

The above studies help for selecting the variables for conducting further research on sustainable agricultural development from soil and water management. The study area covered the Jhansi division, which is very backward division of Uttar Pradesh and the agriculture is the main source of income for majority of people. The present study helps to get the information regarding awareness and knowledge of farmers about soil and water management and agricultural productivity. This helps to agricultural scientist, policy makers and researchers to make a sustainable action plan. Therefore, the study focuses on the following objectives: (1) to know the opinion of farmers on reasons of increasing agricultural productivity; (2) to know the framer's knowledge about soil management; (3) to know the awareness of farmers about water management; and (4) to check the sustainable impact of different selected variables on total per acre output.

The present study is divided into four sections. Section I contains introduction with objectives of the study while sampling and used models are presented in Section II. Section III presents results and discussion and at last conclusion and policy implications are present in Section IV.

Methodology

The present study is based on primary information collected from Jhansi division of Uttar Pradesh. Thus, the universe of the study is Jhansi division. Jhansi division consists three districts namely Jhansi, Lalitpur and Jalaun.

Sampling

Soil type was the main criteria for differentiating the areas for sampling. Therefore, from Jhansi district red soil type containing block, i.e., Babina, from Lalitpur district *rakar* soil type containing block, i.e., Jakhora and from Jalaun district *kabar* soil type containing block, i.e., Madhavganj were selected. From each selected block two villages were undertaken. From each village 25 respondents were surveyed from each farm size categories, i.e., marginal (up to 2.5 acre land), small (> 2.5 acre land to 5 acre land), and large (> 5 acre land). The data were collected on the basis of 150 sample sizes from each district by multistage stratified random sampling method. Therefore, 450 respondents were obtained for the fulfilment of the objectives of the study. The reference period was 2008-09.

Model

To analyze the facts and figure on the basis of collected information for first three objectives simple percentage method has been used. In Tables 13.1, 13.2, 13.3, and 13.4 total numbers of sampled farmers with their respective answers have been presented. To check the sustainable impact on total per acre output of different selected variables multiple regression analysis has been used. The model is:

$$Q_t = \beta_t + \beta_{1t} + \beta_{2t} + \beta_3 X_{3t} + \beta_4 D_1 + B_5 D_2 + \beta_6 D_3 + \beta_7 D_4 + \beta_8 D_5 + \beta_9 D_6 + U_t$$

Where,

Q_t = Total per Acre Output in Quintals

X_{1t} = Investment on Farm Yard Manure (FYM) in Rupees per Acre

X_{2t} = Investment on Insecticides and Pesticides in Rupees per Acre

X_{3t} = Investment on Fertilizers in Rupees per Acre

D_1 = Farmer's knowledge about yield increment by use of FYM (Yes = 1, Otherwise = 0)

D_2 = Farmer's knowledge about yield increment by use of Fertilizers (Yes = 1, Otherwise = 0)

D_3 = Farmer's knowledge about yield increment by interchange and mixed crop pattern (Yes = 1, Otherwise = 0)

D_4 = Farmer's knowledge about yield increment by protection of soil erosion (Yes = 1, Otherwise = 0)

D_5 = Farmer's knowledge about yield increment by use of Insecticides and Pesticides (Yes = 1, Otherwise = 0)

D_6 = Farmer's knowledge about yield increment by decrement in soil moisture (Yes = 1, Otherwise = 0)

Results and Discussion

Opinion of Farmers about Reasons of Increasing Agricultural Productivity

Table 13.1 shows farmer's opinions on reasons of increasing agricultural productivity. The reasons are explained as below:

Use of Farm Yard Manure, Fertilizers and Insecticides and Pesticides

Farm Yard Manure (FYM), fertilizers and insecticides and pesticides are critical inputs of agriculture. These help in providing the nutrients to crop and protect from the insects and pests, which enhance the plant growth.

Now-a-days continuous use of land for agriculture seriously deteriorates the fertility of soil. Therefore, the inputs like FYM, fertilizers, insecticides and pesticides with other inputs play an important role for increasing agricultural productivity.

In Jhansi division, majority of marginal, small and large farmers answered that with the use of farm yard manure (FYM), fertilizers and insecticides and pesticides the agricultural productivity has increased. Table 13.1 shows in Jhansi division, the 6.67 per cent marginal farmers, 5.33 per cent small farmers and 7.33 per cent large farmers answered that they 'don't know' about the FYM is helpful for increasing the agricultural productivity. The 8.67 per cent marginal, 9.33 per cent small and 8 per cent large farmers are unaware about use of fertilizers. Twelve per cent marginal, 14.67 per cent small and large farmers are unaware about use of insecticides and 13.33 percent marginal, 14.67 per cent small and large farmers are unaware about use of pesticides increased the agricultural productivity.

This implies that farmer's opinion about the use of compost and chemicals is better for agricultural growth. The awareness is helpful to use proper quantity of inputs which protect water and soil pollution.

Crop Inter-changed and Mixed Crop

Crop inter-changed and mixed cropping pattern are helpful to control the nitrogen component in the soil. These maintain the sustainable agricultural development.

Table 13.1 shows in Jhansi division, 10 per cent large farmers answered that they 'don't know' the impact of crop interchange. The percentage of marginal and small farmers answered 'no' is 1.3 per cent and 8 per cent respectively. It means these farmers have seen negative performance of crop interchanged. The percentage of marginal and small farmers answered 'don't know' is 11.33 per cent and 8 per cent respectively. It means these farmers are not aware regarding impact of crop interchange.

The farmer's opinion about impact of mixed crop is distributed between 'yes', 'no' and 'don't know'. The percentage of farmers answered 'yes' is 53.33 per cent marginal, 50 per cent small and 70 per cent large farm size holding. The percentage of farmers answered 'don't know' is 38 per cent marginal, 30.67 per cent small and 29.33 per cent large farm size holding. The 19.33 per cent small farmers answered 'no' followed by marginal (8.67%) and large (0.67%) farmers.

This implies that answer of the farmers give information regarding their knowledge about increment of agricultural productivity by using crop interchanged and mixed cropping pattern.

Table 13.1 : Total Numbers of Sampled Farmer's Opinion on Reasons of Increasing Agricultural Productivity

Districts	Villages	Farm Size Categories	Sample Size	Surveyed Farmers Opinion on Reasons of Increasing Soil Productivity																							
				Use of FYM			Use of Fertilizers			Crop Interchanged			Mixed Crop			Water Conservation			Protecting Soil Erosion			Use of Insecticides			Use of Pesticides		
				Yes	No	Don't Know	Yes	No	Don't Know	Yes	No	Don't Know	Yes	No	Don't Know	Yes	No	Don't Know	Yes	No	Don't Know	Yes	No	Don't Know	Yes	No	Don't Know
1	2	3	4	5	6	7	8	9	10	11	12	13	14	15	16	17	18	19	20	21	22	23	24	25	26	27	28
Jhansi	1. Dikouly	Marginal	25	23	0	2	23	1	1	21	0	4	14	1	10	22	0	3	24	0	1	19	2	4	19	2	4
		Small	25	24	0	1	22	0	3	23	0	2	17	0	8	25	0	0	23	0	2	20	0	5	20	0	5
		Large	25	23	0	2	23	0	2	24	0	1	18	0	7	25	0	0	23	0	2	22	0	3	22	0	3
	2. Nayakheda	Marginal	25	24	0	1	20	0	5	23	0	2	15	0	10	25	0	0	21	0	4	22	0	3	22	0	3
		Small	25	22	0	3	21	0	4	24	0	1	17	0	8	25	0	0	22	0	3	23	0	2	23	0	2
		Large	25	24	0	1	23	0	2	24	0	1	16	0	9	25	0	0	20	0	5	21	0	4	21	0	4
	Total	Marginal	50	47	0	3	43	1	6	44	0	6	29	1	20	47	0	3	45	0	5	41	2	7	41	2	7
		Small	50	46	0	4	43	0	7	47	0	3	34	0	16	50	0	0	45	0	5	43	0	7	43	0	7
		Large	50	47	0	3	46	0	4	48	0	2	34	0	16	50	0	0	43	0	7	43	0	7	43	0	7
Lalitpur	1. Kalyanpura	Marginal	25	23	1	1	23	2	0	23	1	1	8	8	9	22	0	3	20	0	5	24	1	0	23	0	2
		Small	25	23	2	0	21	0	4	20	1	4	9	7	9	24	0	1	23	1	1	18	2	5	18	2	5
		Large	25	24	0	1	23	0	2	18	0	7	13	1	11	24	0	1	20	0	5	22	0	3	22	0	3
	2. Jamoramaphi	Marginal	25	22	0	3	22	0	3	19	0	6	8	1	16	20	0	5	24	0	1	23	0	2	23	0	2
		Small	25	24	0	1	23	0	2	22	0	3	16	0	9	24	0	1	24	0	1	18	3	4	18	3	4
		Large	25	24	0	1	22	1	2	22	0	3	21	0	4	23	0	2	24	0	1	22	0	3	22	0	3
	Total	Marginal	50	45	1	4	45	2	3	42	1	7	16	9	25	42	0	8	44	0	6	47	1	2	46	0	4
		Small	50	47	2	1	44	0	6	42	1	7	25	7	18	48	0	2	47	1	2	36	5	9	36	5	9
		Large	50	48	0	2	45	1	4	40	0	10	34	1	15	47	0	3	44	0	6	44	0	6	44	0	6

1	2	3	4	5	6	7	8	9	10	11	12	13	14	15	16	17	18	19	20	21	22	23	24	25	26	27	28
Jalaun	1. Kursenda	Marginal	25	24	0	1	23	0	2	24	0	1	20	0	5	25	0	0	23	0	2	22	0	3	22	0	3
		Small	25	23	0	2	21	4	0	18	5	2	7	10	8	25	0	0	24	0	1	23	0	2	23	0	2
		Large	25	22	0	3	23	0	2	24	0	1	19	0	6	25	0	0	23	0	2	21	0	4	21	0	4
	2. Rupapur	Marginal	25	22	1	2	22	1	2	21	1	3	15	3	7	25	0	0	22	0	3	19	0	6	19	0	6
		Small	25	24	0	1	17	7	1	19	6	0	9	12	4	25	0	0	20	0	5	21	0	4	21	0	4
		Large	25	22	0	3	23	0	2	23	0	2	18	0	7	25	0	0	21	0	4	20	0	5	20	0	5
	Total	Marginal	50	46	1	3	45	1	4	45	1	4	35	3	12	50	0	0	45	0	5	41	0	9	41	0	9
		Small	50	47	0	3	38	11	1	37	11	2	16	22	12	50	0	0	44	0	6	44	0	6	44	0	6
		Large	50	44	0	6	46	0	4	47	0	3	37	0	13	50	0	0	44	0	6	41	0	9	41	0	9
Jhansi Division		Marginal	150	138	2	10	133	4	13	131	2	17	80	13	57	139	0	11	134	0	16	129	3	18	128	2	20
		Small	150	140	2	8	125	11	14	126	12	12	75	29	46	148	0	2	136	1	13	123	5	22	123	5	22
		Large	150	139	0	11	137	1	12	135	0	15	105	1	44	147	0	3	131	0	19	128	0	22	128	0	22

Source: Primary Survey.

Water Conservation

Now-a-days water crisis is the main problem. Droughtness and floods fluctuate agricultural production. This problem can be short out by adopting proper water conservation methods. Therefore, farmer's awareness and their knowledge play an important role in water conservation. In Jhansi division, majority of farmers answered 'yes' except 7.33 per cent marginal, 1.33 per cent small and 2 per cent large farmers answered 'don't know' (Table 13.1).

This implies that the opinion of farmers about water conservation is helpful to know the awareness of farmers. This is positive sign for increasing agricultural productivity.

Protecting Soil Erosion

Soil erosion is major problem which affect agricultural productivity adversity. Therefore, its protection is very essential. Though it is positive sign for agriculture that majority of all farm size categories answered 'yes' that they are very much conscious about soil erosion except 10.67 percent marginal, 8.67 percent small and 12.67 percent large farmers answered 'don't know', means they don't know about soil erosion.

This implies that knowledge of protecting soil erosion is economically as well as environmentally viable. Therefore, its knowledge is helpful for increasing agricultural productivity.

Farmer's Knowledge about Soil Management

Soil is the main medium of agriculture and its proper management increases the agricultural productivity. Thus to protect soil erosion its knowledge is very essential. So that, one can takes remedial action for protection of soil erosion at right time.

Table 13.2 shows different methods of soil erosion viz., from excess use of fertilizers, from bullocks (at the time of ploughing), from tractor (at the time of ploughing), from excess of irrigation, from low water level, from decreasing soil moisture, from air and from heavy rainfall. It also intimates the total numbers of sampled farmers having information regarding soil erosion.

In Jhansi division, majority of all farm size categories have the information regarding soil erosion. The information of farmers regarding soil erosion from excess use of fertilizer is varied in 'yes', 'no' and 'don't know'. The majority of all farm size categories are answered 'yes'. The 36 percent marginal, 44 per cent small and 34 per cent large farmers answered 'no'. The 24 per cent marginal, 7.33 per cent small and 12.67 per cent large farmers answered 'don't know'.

Table 13.2 : Total Numbers of Sampled Farmers Having Information Regarding Soil Erosion

Districts	Villages	Farm Size Categories	Sample Size	Do you know about Soil erosion?		Reasons of Soil Erosion																							
						From Fertilizers			Bullocks (At the time of Ploughing)			Tractor (At the time of Ploughing)			From Excess of Irrigation			Low Water Level			Decreasing Soil Moisture			Air			Heavy Rainfall		
				Yes	No	Yes	No	Don't Know	Yes	No	Don't Know	Yes	No	Don't Know	Yes	No	Don't Know	Yes	No	Don't Know	Yes	No	Don't Know	Yes	No	Don't Know	Yes	No	Don't Know
1	2	3	4	5	6	7	8	9	10	11	12	13	14	15	16	17	18	19	20	21	22	23	24	25	26	27	28	29	30
Jhansi	1. Dikouly	Marginal	25	24	1	5	13	7	0	21	4	1	14	10	25	0	0	24	0	1	10	0	15	25	0	0	25	0	0
		Small	25	21	4	24	0	1	3	20	2	7	10	8	24	0	1	25	0	0	17	0	8	25	0	0	25	0	0
		Large	25	25	0	20	0	5	3	17	5	11	2	12	25	0	0	25	0	0	15	0	10	25	0	0	25	0	0
	2. Nayakheda	Marginal	25	25	0	12	10	3	0	25	0	6	12	7	25	0	0	25	0	0	15	0	10	25	0	0	25	0	0
		Small	25	24	1	22	3	0	4	17	4	10	5	10	22	0	3	24	0	1	24	0	1	25	0	0	25	0	0
		Large	25	25	0	21	0	4	4	21	0	5	12	8	25	0	0	25	0	0	14	0	11	25	0	0	25	0	0
	Total	Marginal	50	49	1	17	23	10	0	46	4	7	26	17	50	0	0	49	0	1	25	0	25	50	0	0	50	0	0
		Small	50	45	5	46	3	1	7	37	6	17	15	18	46	0	4	49	0	1	41	0	9	50	0	0	50	0	0
		Large	50	50	0	41	0	9	7	38	5	16	14	20	50	0	0	50	0	0	29	0	21	50	0	0	50	0	0
Lalitpur	1. Kalyanpura	Marginal	25	19	6	12	7	6	3	22	0	11	5	9	24	0	1	22	0	3	19	1	5	25	0	0	25	0	0
		Small	25	21	4	11	11	3	0	25	0	14	7	4	22	0	3	21	0	4	24	0	1	25	0	0	25	0	0
		Large	25	24	1	6	15	4	0	18	7	2	16	7	25	0	0	24	0	1	24	0	1	25	0	0	25	0	0
	2. Jamoramaphi	Marginal	25	24	1	2	9	14	1	24	0	1	9	15	22	0	3	25	0	0	18	2	5	25	0	0	25	0	0
		Small	25	25	0	6	12	7	3	22	0	5	10	10	23	0	2	20	0	5	20	0	5	25	0	0	25	0	0
		Large	25	25	0	2	20	3	2	23	0	2	15	8	25	0	0	19	0	6	19	0	6	25	0	0	25	0	0

1	2	3	4	5	6	7	8	9	10	11	12	13	14	15	16	17	18	19	20	21	22	23	24	25	26	27	28	29	30
	Total	Marginal	50	43	7	14	16	20	4	46	0	12	14	24	46	0	4	47	0	3	37	3	10	50	0	0	50	0	0
		Small	50	46	4	17	23	10	3	47	0	19	17	14	45	0	5	41	0	9	44	0	6	50	0	0	50	0	0
		Large	50	49	1	8	35	7	2	41	7	4	31	15	50	0	0	43	0	7	43	0	7	50	0	0	50	0	0
Jalaun	1. Kursenda	Marginal	25	25	0	18	6	1	12	13	0	12	0	13	25	0	0	25	0	0	20	0	5	25	0	0	25	0	0
		Small	25	25	0	5	20	0	1	24	0	1	22	2	19	6	0	16	9	0	15	8	2	25	0	0	25	0	0
		Large	25	25	0	15	7	3	12	13	0	13	1	11	25	0	0	25	0	0	19	0	6	25	0	0	25	0	0
	2. Rupapur	Marginal	25	25	0	11	9	5	6	18	1	7	6	12	25	0	0	25	0	0	17	0	8	25	0	0	25	0	0
		Small	25	25	0	5	20	0	0	25	0	1	24	0	16	9	0	11	11	3	12	9	4	24	1	0	24	1	0
		Large	25	25	0	16	9	0	9	16	0	10	8	7	25	0	0	25	0	0	21	2	2	25	0	0	25	0	0
	Total	Marginal	50	50	0	29	15	6	18	31	1	19	6	25	50	0	0	50	0	0	37	0	13	50	0	0	50	0	0
		Small	50	50	0	10	40	0	1	49	0	2	46	2	35	15	0	27	20	3	27	17	6	49	1	0	49	1	0
		Large	50	50	0	31	16	3	21	29	0	23	9	18	50	0	0	50	0	0	40	2	8	50	0	0	50	0	0
	Jhansi Division	Marginal	150	142	8	60	54	36	22	123	5	38	46	66	146	0	4	146	0	4	99	3	48	150	0	0	150	0	0
		Small	150	141	9	73	66	11	11	133	6	38	78	34	126	15	9	117	20	13	112	17	21	149	1	0	149	1	0
		Large	150	149	1	80	51	19	30	108	12	43	54	53	150	0	0	143	0	7	112	2	36	150	0	0	150	0	0

Source: Primary Survey.

Ploughing with bullocks is very old method and without ploughing agricultural production is not possible. Thus the majority of all farm size farmers answered 'no'. It means that the soil erosion is not very high through bullocks (at the time of ploughing) because 14 per cent marginal, 7.33 per cent small and 20 per cent large farmers answered 'yes'. The soil erosion from tractor (at the time of ploughing) is distributed between 'yes', 'no', and 'don't know' by all farm size farmers in Jhansi division. The percentage of farmers answered 'yes' are 25.33 per cent marginal and small and 28.67 percent large farmers. The percentage of farmers answered 'no' is 30.67 percent marginal, 57 per cent small and 36 per cent large. The percentage of farmers answered ' don't know' is 44 per cent marginal, 22.67 per cent small and 35.33 per cent large. This implies that at the time of ploughing from tractor causes soil erosion. It can also be analyzed that majority of small and large farmers are able to use tractor power but majority of marginal farmers are not able because of their weak economic condition and their land holding is very small in size.

Water is essential for plant growth. It is one of the major inputs of agriculture. It maintains the moisture in soil so that the plant can grow easily. Its proper quantity maintains the soil alkalinity, which helps to maintain agricultural productivity. Thus each and every crop requires proper quantity of water. It can be possible through proper numbers of irrigation. The excess quantity of water reduces the agricultural productivity. In Jhansi division, the majority of all farm size farmers answered 'yes' for soil erosion from excess of irrigation water. The percentage of farmers having information of soil erosion from low water level is 97.33 percent marginal, 78 percent small and 95.33 percent large. The farmers having information of soil erosion from decreasing soil moisture are 66 percent marginal, 74.67 percent small and large farmers. In this context the farmers answered 'don't know are 32 percent marginal, 14 percent small and 24 percent large farmers. The cent percent farmers answered 'yes' for soil erosion from air and heavy rainfall it means all the farmers are aware about these cause which affect the soil.

Protection of Soil Erosion

Table 11.3 shows protection of soil erosion methods adopted by total numbers of sampled farmers in selected regions of Jhansi division. The adopted methods are: (*a*) small mud wall around the field, (*b*) after harvesting left with deep ploughing, (*c*) planting around field, (*d*) arrangement of water flow on one side of the field, (*e*) leveled the soil, (*f*) partition of field by the soil and (*g*) burn the left part of the crop after harvesting in the field.

About 11.33 per cent marginal, 51.33 per cent small and 29.33 per cent large farmers made small mud wall around the field for protecting soil erosion.

Table 13.3 : Methods Adopted by Total numbers of Sampled Farmers for Protecting Soil Erosion

Districts	Villages	Farm Size Categories	Methods of Protecting Soil Erosion											
			a	b	c	d	e	f	g	ab	ad	ag	N A	Sample Size
1	2	3	4	5	6	7	8	9	10	11	12	13	14	15
Jhansi	1. Dikouly	Marginal	3	1	0	0	0	0	0	0	0	0	21	25
		Small	8	0	0	0	0	0	0	0	0	0	17	25
		Large	11	0	0	0	0	0	0	1	0	0	13	25
	2. Nayakheda	Marginal	7	1	0	0	0	0	0	0	0	0	17	25
		Small	12	0	0	0	0	0	0	2	0	0	11	25
		Large	9	0	0	0	0	0	0	3	0	0	13	25
	Total	Marginal	10	2	0	0	0	0	0	0	0	0	38	50
		Small	20	0	0	0	0	0	0	2	0	0	28	50
		Large	20	0	0	0	0	0	0	4	0	0	26	50
Lalitpur	1. Kalyanpura	Marginal	6	0	1	0	0	0	0	1	0	0	17	25
		Small	13	0	0	0	1	0	0	0	1	0	10	25
		Large	11	1	0	0	0	1	0	0	0	0	12	25
	2. Jamoramaphi	Marginal	1	0	0	0	0	0	0	0	0	0	24	25
		Small	16	0	0	0	0	0	0	0	0	0	9	25
		Large	11	0	0	0	0	0	0	0	0	0	14	25

1	2	3	4	5	6	7	8	9	10	11	12	13	14	15
	Total	Marginal	7	0	1	0	0	0	0	1	0	0	41	50
		Small	29	0	0	0	1	0	0	0	1	0	19	50
		Large	22	1	0	0	0	1	0	0	0	0	26	50
Jalaun	1. Kursenda	Marginal	0	0	0	0	0	0	0	0	0	0	25	25
		Small	16	0	0	0	0	0	0	0	0	0	9	25
		Large	0	0	0	0	0	0	1	0	0	2	22	25
	2. Rupapur	Marginal	0	0	0	0	0	0	0	0	0	2	23	25
		Small	12	0	2	0	0	0	0	0	0	0	11	25
		Large	2	0	0	0	0	0	1	0	0	7	15	25
	Total	Marginal	0	0	0	0	0	0	0	0	0	2	48	50
		Small	28	0	2	0	0	0	0	0	0	0	20	50
		Large	2	0	0	0	0	0	2	0	0	9	37	50
Jhansi Division		Marginal	17	2	1	0	0	0	0	1	0	2	127	150
		Small	77	0	2	0	1	0	0	2	1	0	67	150
		Large	44	1	0	0	0	1	2	4	0	9	89	150

Source: Primary Survey.

Notes: NA = Not Answered

Methods of Protecting Soil Erosion used by Farmers are: (a) made small mud wall around the field, (b) After harvesting left with deep ploughing, (c) Planting around field, (d) Arrangement of water flow on one side of the field, (e) Level the soil, (f) Partition of field by the soil, and (g) Burn the left part of the crop in the field.

The 0.67 percent marginal, 1.33 percent small and 2.67 percent large farmers adopted both 'a' and 'b' methods. The 1.33 percent marginal and 6 percent large farmers adopted both 'a' and 'g' methods. The 84.67 percent marginal, 44.67 percent small and 59.33 percent large farmers are not answered.

This implies that the most popular methods for protecting soil erosion are: made small mud wall around the field, after harvesting left the field with deep ploughing and burn the left part of the crop in the field.

Farmers Awareness about Water Management

Table 13.4 shows total numbers of sampled farmers aware about water conservation and adopted methods for it. In Jhansi division, 17.33 percent marginal, 54 percent small and 36 percent large farmers are answered that they knew about fall of water level in the last years. The majority of all farm size farmers answered that they 'don't know' about fall of water level. According to the sampled farmers the reasons behind fall of water level are: (a) due to low rainfall, (b) excess use of water, (c) lack of conservation of rain water, and (d) due to pollution. About 9.33 percent marginal, 47.33 percent small and 24.67 percent large farmers are suggested that 'a' is the main reason behind fall of water level. The 2.67 percent marginal, 2 percent small and 0.67 percent large farmers suggested that 'a' is the main reason behind fall of water level. The majority of all farm size farmers are not answered.

In the Jhansi division, the adopted methods for conserving water by farmers are: (a) from well deepening, (b) making small pond in the field, (c) field banding and (d) new well digging. About 5.33 per cent marginal, 18.67 percent small and 15.33 per cent large farmers are adopted 'a' method and the 5.33 per cent large farmers are adopted 'b' method and followed by small (4.67%) and marginal (3.33%) farmers for conserving water. The majority of all farm size farmers are not answered.

Sustainable Impact of Different Selected Variables on Total per Acre Output

Sustainable agriculture development mainly depends on knowledge of proper utilization of resources and distribution of capital among these inputs. The chemical inputs raised the productivity but their excess use also hazardous for environment (soil and water) and human health. The sustainability of agriculture is checked through investment on FYM, pesticides and fertilizers and also through the knowledge of farmers about the use of the variables and also about cropping pattern and environment. The results obtained through multiple regression are shown in Table 13.4. The coefficient of investment on FYM is positive and significant in Lalitpur district for marginal

Table 13.4 : Total Numbers of Sampled Farmers Having Awareness about Water Conservation

Districts	Villages	Farm Size Categories	Total Numbers of Farmers	Do you know about fall of water level in the previous years?		Surveyed Farmers Opinions															
						What are the reasons behind fall of water level?										Which methods you have adopted for conserving water?					
				yes	No	a	b	c	d	ab	ac	ad	bc	abc	NA	a	b	c	d	ab	NA
1	2	3	4	5	6	7	8	9	10	11	12	13	14	15	16	17	18	19	20	21	22
Jhansi	1. Dikouly	Marginal	25	8	17	4	0	0	0	1	0	0	0	0	20	4	1	0	0	0	20
		Small	25	10	15	7	1	0	0	2	0	0	0	0	15	5	1	1	0	1	17
		Large	25	11	14	9	0	1	0	0	0	0	0	1	14	5	1	0	0	3	16
	2. Nayakheda	Marginal	25	7	18	1	1	1	0	3	0	0	0	0	19	4	2	0	0	2	17
		Small	25	10	15	8	0	0	0	1	0	0	0	1	15	6	5	0	0	0	14
		Large	25	12	13	8	0	1	0	0	1	0	0	0	15	9	2	0	0	0	14
	Total	Marginal	50	15	35	5	1	1	0	4	0	0	0	0	39	8	3	0	0	2	37
		Small	50	20	30	15	1	0	0	3	0	0	0	1	30	11	6	1	0	1	31
		Large	50	23	27	17	0	2	0	0	1	0	0	1	29	14	3	0	0	3	30
Lalitpur	1. Kalyanpura	Marginal	25	6	19	5	1	0	0	0	0	0	0	0	19	0	1	0	0	0	24
		Small	25	15	10	13	0	0	0	0	0	0	0	0	12	9	0	0	2	0	14
		Large	25	13	12	10	2	1	0	0	0	0	0	0	12	6	4	3	0	0	12

1	2	3	4	5	6	7	8	9	10	11	12	13	14	15	16	17	18	19	20	21	22
	2. Jamoramaphi	Marginal	25	3	22	3	0	0	0	0	0	0	0	0	22	0	0	0	0	0	25
		Small	25	13	12	12	0	0	0	0	0	0	0	0	13	7	0	0	0	0	18
		Large	25	8	17	3	0	1	0	0	2	1	1	0	17	3	1	0	0	0	21
	Total	Marginal	50	9	41	8	1	0	0	0	0	0	0	0	41	0	1	0	0	0	49
		Small	50	28	22	25	0	0	0	0	0	0	0	0	25	16	0	0	2	0	32
		Large	50	21	29	13	2	2	0	0	2	1	1	0	29	9	5	3	0	0	33
Jalaun	1. Kursenda	Marginal	25	0	25	0	0	0	0	0	0	0	0	0	25	0	0	0	0	0	25
		Small	25	18	7	18	0	0	0	0	0	0	0	0	7	1	1	0	0	0	23
		Large	25	3	22	3	0	0	0	0	0	0	0	0	22	0	0	0	0	0	25
	2. Rupapur	Marginal	25	2	23	1	0	0	0	0	0	0	0	0	24	0	1	0	0	0	24
		Small	25	15	10	13	0	0	2	0	0	0	0	0	10	0	0	0	0	0	25
		Large	25	7	18	4	1	0	0	1	0	1	0	0	18	0	0	0	0	0	25
	Total	Marginal	50	2	48	1	0	0	0	0	0	0	0	0	49	0	1	0	0	0	49
		Small	50	33	17	31	0	0	2	0	0	0	0	0	17	1	1	0	0	0	48
		Large	50	10	40	7	1	0	0	1	0	1	0	0	40	0	0	0	0	0	50
Overall	Jhansi Division	Marginal	150	26	124	14	2	1	0	4	0	0	0	0	129	8	5	0	0	2	135
		Small	150	81	69	71	1	0	2	3	0	0	0	1	72	28	7	1	2	1	111
		Large	150	54	96	37	3	4	0	1	3	2	1	1	98	23	8	3	0	3	113

Source: Primary Survey.
Notes: NA = Not Answered
What are the reasons behind fall of water level?
(a) Due to low rain fall; (b) Excess use of water; (c) Lack of conservation of rain water; (d) Due to pollution.
Which method u have adopted for conserving water?
(a) From well deepening; (b) Making small pond in the field; (c) Field banding; (d) New well digging.

and small farmers. The coefficient of investment on insecticides and pesticides is negative and significant for marginal (-0.004) and large (-0.003) farmers in Lalitpur district and for large farmers in Jalaun district (-0.04) and Jhansi division (-0.006). The coefficient of investment on fertilizers is positive and significant for small (0.005) and large (0.005) farmers in Jhansi division. This shows that the large farmers are applying excess amount of pesticides and insecticides. This is having an adverse impact on soil quality.

The variables from x_4 to x_9 are related to farmers' knowledge about yield increment. The coefficient of the farmer's knowledge about yield increment by the use of FYM is positive and significant for marginal farmers in Jhansi district (1.46) and Jalaun district (8.66), for small farmers (2.08) in and for large farmers (2.17) in Lalitpur district and for large farmers (3.37) in Jhansi division. The coefficient of farmer's knowledge about yield increment by use of fertilizers is positive and significant for large farmers (1.12) in Lalitpur district and for marginal farmers (3.03) in Jalaun district. The coefficient of farmer's knowledge about yield increment by interchange and mixed cropping pattern is positive and significant for large farmers (1.46) in Jhansi division. The coefficient of the farmer's knowledge about yield increment by protection from soil erosion is negative and significant for large farmers (-2.06) in Jhansi division and for rest of the farm sizes it is insignificant. The coefficient of the farmers knowledge about yield increment by use of insecticides and pesticides is negative and significant for marginal farmers in Jalaun district (-6.90) and Jhansi division (-1.56). The coefficient for farmer's knowledge about yield increment by decrement in soil moisture is negative and significant for large farmers in Jhansi district (-3.04) and Jhansi division (-1.24) and for small farmers (-3.005) in Jhansi division. It is positive and significant for marginal farmers (0.73) in Jhansi district. As in depth analysis of the table show that most of the variables in the selected region are found to be having a poor significance level. This indicates that the knowledge of farmers regarding environment issues is too low to show a significant sign of agricultural sustainability.

Conclusion and Policy Implications

From above discussion it can be concluded that in all the selected regions, majority of marginal, small and large farmers answered that with the use of farm yard manure (FYM), fertilizers and insecticides and pesticides the agricultural productivity has increased.

The farmer's opinion about the use of compost and chemicals is better for agricultural growth. This awareness is helpful to use proper quantity of these inputs which protect water and soil pollution. The answer of the

Table 13.5 : Sustainable Impact on Productivity by Different Variables in Selected Regions: Multiple Regression Analysis

Sl.No.	Districts	Farm Size Categories	Variables											R^2	F-value
			Intercept	Investment on FYM	Investment on Pesticides	Investmenton Fertilizers	D_1	D_2	D_3	D_4	D_5	D_6			
				X_1	X_2	X_3	X_4	X_5	X_6	X_7	X_8	X_9			
1	2	3	4	5	6	7	8	9	10	11	12	13		14	15
1.	JhansiDistrict	Marginal	10.969	-0.004 (1.177)	-0.001 (0.395)	-0.001 (0.652)	1.458** (2.255)	-2.738*** (1.776)	-0.005 (0.016)	1.048 (1.150)	-0.413 (0.762)	0.729*** (1.783)		0.2296	1.325
		Small	8.883	0.0001 (0.030)	-0.002 (1.107)	0.00006 (0.030)	0.017 (0.039)	-0.122 (0.207)	0.094 (0.275)	1.055**** (1.476)	0.513 (1.008)	-0.331 (0.297)		0.1583	0.836
		Large	9.436	0.0001 (0.042)	-0.004 (1.097)	0.0006 (0.390)	-1.316 (1.046)	0.554 (0.691)	-0.085 (0.360)	0.430 (0.870)	0.061 (0.220)	0.184 (0.722)		0.0715	0.342
2.	LalitpurDistrict	Marginal	10.137	0.002*** (1.696)	-0.004* (2.861)	0.0007 (0.714)	0.709 (0.614)	-1.596*** (1.738)	0.237 (0.767)	-0.741 (0.754)	0.460 (0.612)	0.107 (0.170)		0.2976	1.883
		Small	7.219	0.003** (2.245)	0.001 (0.762)	-0.0005 (0.539)	2.080* (3.361)	-0.779 (1.096)	0.160 (0.712)	-0.852**** (1.444)	0.346 (0.683)	0.076 (0.122)		0.360	2.500
		Large	5.493	-0.0009 (0.685)	-0.003* (2.800)	0.00009 (0.128)	2.172* (2.966)	1.121** (2.175)	0.129 (0.402)	-0.136 (0.141)	0.043 (0.101)	0.575 (1.200)		0.366	2.571
3.	JalaunDistrict	Marginal	4.130	0.003 (0.705)	-0.005 (0.375)	0.002 (0.388)	8.662** (2.143)	3.032*** (1.812)	0.515 (0.485)	0.135 (0.090)	-6.902* (2.965)	-0.009 (0.007)		0.2336	1.354
		Small	14.760	0.019 (0.315)	0.004 (0.226)	-0.0008 (0.056)	-2.416 (0.558)	-2.970**** (1.370)	-2.111 (0.897)	4.176**** (1.482)	-0.491 (0.162)	-0.883 (0.544)		0.1223	0.619
		Large	44.996	0.008 (0.509)	-0.042** (2.336)	-0.024** (2.168)	1.282 (0.285)	-2.262**** (1.280)	2.418**** (1.675)	-1.660 (0.886)	2.920**** (1.292)	-3.037** (2.066)		0.3167	2.060

1	2	3	4	5	6	7	8	9	10	11	12	13	14	15
4.	Overall	Marginal	9.134	0.002**** (1.301)	-0.001 (0.580)	0.0007 (0.621)	1.274**** (1.442)	0.584 (0.774)	0.248 (0.728)	0.002 (0.004)	-1.555** (2.239)	-0.322 (0.651)	0.0661	1.101
		Small	10.429	0.0006 (0.113)	0.003 (0.763)	0.005**** (1.607)	0.164 (0.149)	-3.10* (3.048)	-1.203*** (1.765)	2.464 (1.921)	0.259 (0.222)	-3.005* (3.354)	0.2657	5.630
		Large	7.661	-0.0002 (0.047)	-0.006**** (1.581)	0.005** (2.373)	3.366*** (1.797)	-1.273 (1.258)	1.461** (2.253)	-2.061*** (1.779)	0.863 (1.030)	-1.243*** (1.686)	0.1461	2.661

Source: Computed

Notes: 1. *, **, *** significant at 1%, 5%, 10% level of significance respectively. 2. Figures in parenthesis () shows t-values.

Q = Total per Acre Output; x_1 = Investment on FYM (In Rs / Acre); x_2 = Investment on Insecticides and Pesticides (In Rs / Acre); x_3 = Investment on Fertilizer (In Rs / Acre)

x_4 = Farmers knowledge about yield increment by use of FYM (Yes = 1, Otherwise = 0)

x_5 = Farmers knowledge about yield increment by use of Fertilizers (Yes = 1, Otherwise = 0)

x_6 = Farmers knowledge about yield increment by interchange and mixed crop pattern (Yes = 1, Otherwise = 0)

x_7 = Farmers knowledge about yield increment by protection of soil erosion (Yes = 1, Otherwise = 0)

x_8 = Farmers knowledge about yield increment by use of Insecticides and Pesticides (Yes = 1, Otherwise = 0)

x_9 = Farmers knowledge about yield increment by decrement in soil moisture (Yes = 1, Otherwise = 0) farmers give information regarding their knowledge about increment of agricultural productivity by using crop interchanged and mixed cropping pattern. This shows that the opinion of farmers about water conservation is helpful to know the awareness of farmers. This is positive sign for increasing agricultural productivity.

The knowledge of protection of soil erosion is economically as well as environmentally viable. Therefore, its knowledge is helpful for increasing agricultural productivity. In Jhansi division, majority of all farm size categories have the information regarding soil erosion. The information of farmers regarding soil erosion from excess use of fertilizer is varied in 'yes', 'no' and 'don't know'. The majority of all farm size categories are answered 'yes'. The 36 percent marginal, 44 percent small and 34 percent large farmers answered 'no'. The 24 percent marginal, 7.33 percent small and 12.67 percent large farmers answered 'don't know'.

Water is essential for plant growth. It is one of the major inputs of agriculture. It maintains the moisture in soil so that the plant can grow easily. Its proper quantity maintains the soil alkalinity, which helps to maintain agricultural productivity. Thus each and every crop requires proper quantity of water. It can be possible through proper numbers of irrigation. The excess quantity of water reduces the agricultural productivity. In Jhansi division, the majority of all farm size farmers answered 'yes' for soil erosion from excess of irrigation water. The percentage of farmers having information of soil erosion from low water level is 97.33 percent marginal, 78 percent small and 95.33 percent large. The farmers having information of soil erosion from decreasing soil moisture are 66 percent marginal, 74.67 percent small and large farmers. In this context the farmers answered 'don't know are 32 percent marginal, 14 percent small and 24 percent large farmers. The cent percent farmers answered 'yes' for soil erosion from air and heavy rainfall it means all the farmers are aware about these cause which affect the soil erosion. The most popular methods for protecting soil erosion are: made small mud wall around the field, after harvesting left the field with deep ploughing and burn the left part of the crop in the field.

Sustainable agriculture development mainly depends on knowledge of proper utilization of resources and distribution of capital among the inputs. The chemical inputs raised the productivity but their excess use also hazardous for environment (soil and water).

On the basis of above conclusion it may be recommended that the reallocation of resources in proper manner is required to check the wastage of resources. Therefore, agricultural extension education should be launched to educate farmers for proper quantity allocation of inputs. Their follow-up is essential in order to maintain sustainable agricultural development.

REFERENCES

Cmpbell, B. M., P. Bradley and S. E. Carter (1997), "Sustainability and Peasant Farming System: Observation from Zimbabwe", *Agriculture and Human Values: 14,* pp. 159-68.

Lefroy, R. D. B., H. D. Beehstedt and M. Rais (1999), *"Indicators for Sustainable Land Management based on Farmer Surveys in Vietnam, Indonesia and Thailand"*, Agriculture, Ecosystems and the Environment.

Meerman, F., G. W. J. Van de Ven, H. Van Keulen and H. Breman (1996), "Integrated Crop Management: An Approach to Sustainable Agricultural Development", *International Journal of Pest Management: 42,* pp. 13-24.

Misra, V. N. and M. Govinda Rao (2003), "Trade Policy, Agricultural Growth and Rural Poor, Indian Experience 1978-79 to 1999-2000", *Economic and Political Weekly*, October 25, pp. 4588-4603.

Oxfam (1999), 'Genetically Modified Crops World Trade and Food Security', November (http://www.oxfam.org.uk)

Taylor, D. C., Z. A. Mohamed, M. N. Shamsudin, M. G. Mohayidin and E. F. C. Chiew (1999), "Greeting a Farmer Sustainability Index: A Malaysian Case Study", *American Journal of Alternative Agriculture: 8,* pp. 175-84.

Institutional Credit and Rural Development in India

—Dr. G. Parimalarani

Introduction

Rural development is must for country like India where more than 72.2 per cent of the populations are leading their life in 5,93,732 villages. The importance of the rural development has been emphasized by Mahatma Gandhi that "The true India is to be found not in its few cities, but in its seven hundred thousand villages, if the villages perish, India will perish too". So the main thrust of the country is the development of the rural sector. In this regard The Government of India has taken adequate steps in improving the standard of living of the rural segments by initiating more programmes, some of them are Bharat Nirman for rural infrastructure (US$34.84 billion), National Rural Health Mission (US$ 3 million), Credit and Debit-Wavier for farmers (US$13.86 billion), Sarva Shiksha Abhiyan, Mid-day meals in schools etc., and schemes such as Pradhan Mantri Gram Sadak Yojana, Swarnjayanti Gram Swarozgar Yojana, Sampoorna Gramin Rozgar Yojana, Indira Awaas Yojana etc. During the Third Plan period (1961-66) the Government has allocated Rs. 1088.9 crore for agriculture and allied sectors and subsequently in the annual plan (2006-07) the amount allocated has been increased to Rs. 16,573 crore. For rural development in the Annual Plan (2006-07) the allocated amount stands to Rs 30,154 crore.

Apart from the Government of India the Non-governmental Organizations (NGOs), Local or regional authorities take effective steps for improving the standard of living of the rural masses. Other than these agencies the institutional credit also plays a vital role in the development process of the rural segment.

Institutional credit and rural development are always inter-linked. In India we have a well-developed banking network which plays a vital role in the development process of the economy by accepting the surplus amount of the society in the form of deposits and lending loans and advances for the development of the society. Srimathi Indira Gandhi has nationalized the commercial banks on two phases, *i.e.* on 1969 and1980 with the intention of routing the credit from banks to the needed rural sectors. The nationalization of the bank as well as setting up of Regional Rural Banks (1975) has further strengthened the rural credit together with co-operative banks. The present study highlight the role played by the commercial bank in developing the rural segment by comparing with Regional Rural Banks (RRBs) and Co-Operative Banks(COBs).

Objectives: The study has the following objectives:-

1. To elaborate the role played by the commercial Banks in rural development
2. To compare the performance of commercial banks in the area of rural credit with Regional Rural Banks and Co-operative Banks.

Hypotheses:

1. Commercial Banks have more number of branches than the RRBs.
2. The role played by the commercial Banks is more than the RRBs and COBs in terms of rural advances.

Methodology

Sources of Data: The study fully deals with secondary data

Tools for analysis: Used simple tools like percentage analysis, growth rate and Average.

Role of Commercial Banks in Economic Development

Among the banking institutions in the organized sector commercial banks are the oldest institution, which function at the gross root level. The role played by the commercial bank particularly the public sector bank since nationalization is quiet notable. We know that if the banking system in a country is effective, efficient and disciplined it brings about a rapid growth in the various sectors of the economy. It helps in –

- Capital formation
- Development of agriculture

- Investment in new enterprises
- Balanced development of different region
- Export promotion cell
- Promotion of trade & Industry etc.,

Commercial Banks and Rural Development

In India we have multiagency rural credit delivery structure comprising rural credit delivery structure comprising Commercial Banks, RRBs and COBs with large network of branches. The main purpose behind nationalizing the Commercial Banks on Two Phases are:-

To provide banking services in previously unbanked or under-banked rural areas

To provide substantial credit to agriculture and cottage industries and

To provide credit to certain groups like dalit household.

In fact the role played by the Commercial Banks since its nationalization are quiet notable. The Government of India and the Reserve Bank of India give specific direction to commercial banks regarding social and development banking like:-

- Setting targets for the expansion of rural branches
- Setting guidelines for the sectoral allocation of credit
- Lead Bank scheme was evolved
- Minimum target lending to priority sectors, such as agriculture, small scale business, retail trade etc.,
- Lending under poverty alleviative and employment generation schemes

Apart from funding the above programmes the commercial banks also play a lead role for various schemes specially meant for rural development. Some of the programs are Self-help Groups (SHGs), Training of Rural Youth for Self-employment Scheme (TRYSEM) for Land Development, 20 point programme, Differential Rate of Interest schemes etc., During 1980s the commercial banks played a lead role in Integrated Rural Development Programme (IRDP). The scheme is meant for the creation of productive income bearing assets among the poor through the allocation of subsidized credit.

The effective role played by the commercial bank for rural development can be analyzed through various parameters like branches, loans and advances to agriculture, credit to micro and small enterprises, credit to weaker section and Self-help Group and provision of Kisan Credit Cards.

Table 14.1: Bank Branches of Commercial Banks and Regional Rural Banks in Rural Areas for the period June 2009

Banks	Rural Branches (as on 30-06-2009)	Percentage of Rural Branches to Total Number of Branches (as on 30-06-2009)
State Bank & Associates	5619	34.49
Nationalized Banks	13425	33.81
Regional Rural Banks	11644	76.61
Other Scheduled Commercial Banks	1126	12.54
Foreign Banks	4	1.36
Non-scheduled Commercial Banks	11	25

Source: *Economic Survey 2010.*

The branch expansion in the rural area was the major intention of nationalization. Table 14.1 enumerates the branches opened by the commercial banks and regional rural banks during the period June, 2009. The nationalized banks are having more number of branches (13,425) followed by the Regional Rural Banks (11,644). When we analyze the share of rural branches to total number of branches the figure states that The RRBs are having 76.61 per cent of their banks in rural area followed by State Bank and Associates to the tune of 34.49 per cent. The share of rural branches of Nationalized Banks is 33.81 per cent only. From the Report on Trend and Progress of Banking 2009-10, it is clear that the Reserve Bank of India (RBI) has taken effective steps in reaching the banking services i.e., During November 2009, the RBI has advised banks to draw up a roadmap to provide banking services through a banking outlets in every village having a population of over 2000 by march 2010. At the end of June 2010, about 73,000 villages have been allocated to various banks for the provision of banking facilities in villages having population of more than 2000.

The hypothesis "commercial banks have more number of branches than the RRBs" accepted. Through percentage analysis it has been analyzed that the commercial banks are having 80.84 per cent of their bank branches in rural area followed by the RRBs.

The credit flow from commercial banks, RRBs and COBs to agriculture and allied activities are of in increasing trend from 2002-03 to 2008-09. The credit disbursement by all these banks during the year 2009-10 was very less comparing to the previous year (Table 14.2).

Table 14.2 : Flow of Institutional Credit to Agriculture and Allied Activities

(Rs. in crore)

Banks	02-03	03-04	04-05	05-06	06-07	07-08	08-09	09-10
Commercial Banks	39774 (5)	52441 (60)	81481 (65)	125477 (70)	166486 (73)	181088 (71)	228951 (78)	112449 (-51)
Growth rate	—	31.85	55.38	60	32.68	8.77	26.43	-50.89
Regional Rural Banks	6070 (9)	7581 (9)	12404 (10)	15223 (8)	20435 (9)	25312 (10)	26724 (9)	20065 (12)
Growth rate	—	24.89	63.61	22.73	34.24	23.87	5.58	-24.92
Co-operative Banks	23716 (34)	26959 (31)	31424 (25)	39786 (22)	42480 (18)	48258 (19)	36762 (13)	32925 (20)
Growth rate	—	13.67	16.56	26.61	6.77	13.60	-23.82	-10.44
Total	69560	86981	125309	180486	229401	254658	292437	165439
Growth Rate	**—**	**25.04**	**44.04**	**44.03**	**27.10**	**11.01**	**14.84**	**-43.43**

Source: Report on Trend and Progress of Banking 2005-06 , 2009-10

Overall the credit disbursement made by all these bank for agriculture and allied activities have increased by 2.4 times from 2002-03 to 2009-10.

Quantum-wise the disbursement made by the commercial bank is higher than that of the RRBs and COBs. But when we compare that with that of the times of increase RRBs registered the highest level of 3.31 per cent followed by commercial bank at 2.83 per cent and co-operative bank at 1.39 per cent.

The growth rate of advances of all the banks to the agriculture and allied activities are in increasing trend for all the year except 2009-10.

The hypothesis "The role played by the commercial banks are more than the RRBs and COBs in terms of advances" is accepted. By considering the quantum-wise disbursement made by these banks as well by comparing with that of the growth rate it is clear that the performance of commercial bank in disbursing agricultural credit is more commanding.

Special Agricultural Credit Plans (SACP)

The Reserve Bank of India had advised public sector banks to prepare SACP on an annual basis since 1994-95 with a view to achieving distinct and marked improvement in the flow of credit to agriculture. Under SACP, the banks are required to fix self-set targets for achievement during the year (April-March). The target are generally fixed by the banks showing an increase of about 20-25 per cent over the disbursement made in the previous year. Under SACP during 2008-09 the banks provided credit to the extent of Rs. 2,28,951 crore.

Self-help Group and Bank linkage

Self-help group are formed with the objectives of improving their livelihood through the collective savings and investments in income generation activities. The bank provides credit to the SHGs after observing their operations and their ability to absorb credit.

Table 14.3 : Agency-wise SHGs-Bank linking position

Agency	SHGs- credit linked (In 000)			Bank loan disbursed (In crore)		
	2006-07	2007-08	2008-09	2006-07	2007-08	2008-09
Commercial Banks	572 (52)	312 (42)	1005 (62.42)	3919 (60)	2043 (48)	8061 (65.78)
Regional Rural Banks	381 (34)	241 (33)	406 (25.22)	2053 (31)	1599 (38)	3193 (20.06)
Co-operative banks	153 (14)	187 (25)	199 (12.36)	599 (09)	586 (14)	999 (8.16)
Total	**1106**	**740**	**1610**	**6570**	**4228**	**12254**

Source: NABARD, Figures in the parentheses are percentage to the total.

The credit linkage to SHGs through the commercial Bank, RRBs and COB are in increasing trend. The amount disbursed by the commercial bank very high to the level of Rs. 8061 followed by RRBs (Rs 3193) and COBs (Rs. 999) (Table 14.3).

The shares of the commercial bank in disbursing the loans to SHGs are very high to the tune of 65.78 per cent followed by RRBs (20.06%) and COBs (8.16%).The total amount disbursed by these agencies is Rs 12254 crore.

Kisan Credit Cards

This is the widely accepted mechanism for delivering of credit to farmers. Currently the schemes now also cover borrowers of the long-term co-operatative credit structure flow of institutional credit to agriculture and allied activities. As per the Report on Trend and Progress of Banking 2009-10, it known that the total amount sanctioned by the commercial banks, COB and RRBs together stands at Rs. 4,27,748 crore. In that the share of Commercial Bank is high to the extent of Rs. 2,33,190 crore followed by

COBs to the tune of Rs1,40,594 and RRBs have sanctioned Rs53,964 crore. The role played by the Commercial Bank in this regard is highly commendable.

Apart from above facilities provided by the Banking institution for the rural development the reserve Bank of India has given an instruction to the all domestic scheduled commercial banks both in the public and private sector are required to meet a target of 40 per cent of their Adjusted Net Bank Credit (ANBC) or credit equivalent amount of off balance- sheet exposures, whichever is higher for lending to the priority sectors. Of this 18 per cent and 10 per cent of ANBC or credit equivalent amount of off balance sheet exposures whichever is higher have been stipulated for lending to agriculture and weaker sections respectively.

Conclusion

Indian economy has emerged as one of the fastest growing economies in the world. The contribution of the banking and financial sector to the current economic growth of the Indian economy is very significant. The statistical report states that the rural economy is estimated to increase from $220 billion in 2004-05 to about $ 425 billion in 2010-11 at a compounded annual growth rate of 12%. For developing the rural area the role played by the commercial bank are quiet commendable, and it is evident from the analysis.

REFERENCES

Agrawal, B.P. (1983): *Commercial Banking in India*, The Capital Publishing House, delhi.

Basu, S.K. (1979) : *Commercial Banks and Agricultural Credit* (Bombay, Allied Publishers Private Limited.

Channa, Chanjut: *Agricultural Finance in India-Role* of Commercial Banks, Marketing and Economic Research Bureau, New Delhi.

Choubey, B.N. (1977): *Institutional Finance for Agricultural Development* : Pune, Shubdada Saraswat.

Jha, N.K. (1985) : Bank Finance and Green Revolution in India, Amar Prakshan, Delhi.

Joshi, P.L. (1985): Institutional Financing in India, Delhi, Deep and Deep Publications.

Naidu, L.K. (1986): Bank Finance for Rural Development, Ashish Publishing House, New Delhi.

Pandey Kishore: *Commercial Banks and Rural Development,* Asian Publications Services, New Delhi.

Rangarajan, C. (1996) : Rural India: The Role of credit", First Ravi Matthai Memorial Lecture, IIM, Ahmedabad, Published in *Reserve Bank of India Bulletin*, May.

Report on Trend and Progress of Banking in India, Reserve Bank of India (Various issues from 1994 to 2010).

Common Property Resources and Their Linkages with Livelihood in South Asia

A Review

—Sudarshan Prasad Regmi
—Dr. Ravinder Sharma

ABSTRACT

About fifty literatures published during 1980 to date were reviewed for the common property resources, (CPRs), especially pasture lands. They were categorized in three aspects viz. linkages, livelihood and share of income, and effect on CPRs and role of CPRs. It was analyzed for their linkages, the strong and the weak linkages were identified. A framework of the linkages was developed. It is revealed that management of CPRs plays a vital role for the sustainable productivity of common pastureland and to private farm land. It was observed that the socio-economic aspects of range land/pasture land in the context of Nepal, as well as in the regional level (ICIMOD), that accounts for 40 per cent of high hills, has been neglected and a strong policy implication should be implemented based on research findings.

Introduction

Common properly resources (CPRs) are those natural resources in which a group of people has equal rights to use. These resources are characterized by free access for all individuals of the locality and lies outside the market framework. They play vital role in substance of hill farming system in particular. Because of meager size of operational holding, poor infrastructure facilities in hill agriculture CPRs directly or indirectly play an important role in enhancing and stabilizing the income, employment and substance of village community by providing multiple products to various activity of their farming system.

Interpreting natural resource in a broad way, those arrests that provide the many and varied ecosystem services upon which life is based (Dasgupta and Maler, 2004). A number have a global reach, but many are local. Nature's services are not only of direct value of use they offer indirect benefits too: a multitude support and promote the natural resource base on which our economic activities are founded [e.g. mangrove frost, Pasture land].

The numerous roles nature plays in the lines of rural people into world poorest continues. Some 60-70 per cent of people in the world's poorest countries live in rural area basically Asian and African continents.

Common properly resources are the local resource base, which comprise such assets such as ponds, stream, woodland and forests, grazing land (rangeland and pastureland), village tanks and fisheries and wetland. They are for the most part common property and one frequently managed by communitarian institutions.

Dasgupta, (1982, 1993, 2003a), Dasgupta and Maler (1991, 1995) have attempted to uncover the pathways by which poverty and reproductive behavior among rural people is linked to the state of their local resource based.

Though it has been neglected (Stern, 1989; Brown, 2000) we would not obtain a clean picture of rural life in the world's poorest region, if we neglect the direct role, the local resource base play there. And if we do so they may manage to create in order to cope with those needs. For them - and they are among the poorest in society - there are no frequently alternative source of livelihood, nor is migration usually an option. The poor suffered from lack of substitution possibilities in always the rich don't (Agrawal, 1986; Jodha, 2001, and Campbell *et al.*, 2001). The CPRs are asset with differ in characteristics, but are facing different economic circumstance. When a resource in not individually or state owned it requires a collective of people to organize and protect the resources in order to avert open-access plunder.

South Asia CPRs

South Asia is experiencing rapid changes with increasing integration into the world economy, a rapid growing population increasing per capita income, but with large numbers still living in absolute poverty. Given that a large number of people still depend on CPRs, the concern for their sustainable use is obvious. There have also been experiments at expanding community control over their resources.

Large scale changes in property right have been witnessed across South Asia – in India and Nepal, such as handing over of forests to communities is a great success in Nepal.

The extent of livelihood dependence on natural resource management in South Asia by various estimates ranges from 15 to 29 per cent whereas in part of Africa it has been found to be higher as 35-51 per cent (Cavandish 2000; Chopra, Kadekodi, and Murty 1990; Jodha 1986, 2001; Kerapeletswe and Lovett 2001). Earlier studies suggested that both the rich and the poor (relatively more) depend on natural resources for their livelihood, especially on CPRs. The CPRs have been found to act not only as buffer during period of crisis when normal source of income fail, but also act a source of income during normal time.

The literature points out the use of two definitions of sustainability: one is the efficient measure of maximizing the net benefit value of intertemporal consumption and the other seeks to ensure that the future level of consumption do not fall below present one. Consequently, except in some isolated tribal communities, CPR in South Asia remain community resource mainly in a *de facto* sense, subject to any change as state decides.

A number of CPRs have been degraded or privatized, as Jodha (2008) recorded there have been a 40-50 per cent decline in CPRs area in his study area and 25-85 per cent reported degradation.

In South Asia more over the research and study of CPRs has been centered on and around following only:

1. Forestry : Nepal, Bangladesh, India Sri Lanka
2. Water and Fisheries : India, Bangladesh, Sri Lanka
3. Land management : India, Pakistan
4. Irrigation : India, Sri Lanka, Nepal
5. Pastureland; and rangeland : Some works in India Model has been Developed by Dasgupta (2008) but waiting for the empirical study.

The review of some studies has been done in this chapter.

Problems in Mountain

At the production level, the smallholder in mountain faces problems of acute fodder shortage and is still largely isolated from appropriate and beneficial technology option (Tulachan and Neupaue, 1999). Dhar (1997) reported that Uttarakhand the shortage of feed and fodder is estimated to be 65 per cent. In Nepal especially during the winter and the dry period livestock are generally underfed by one-third of the amount required. The situation is much worse in the mountains because of small land holdings and the limited support land for grazing. This has resulted in late maturity, high mortality, poor lifetime performance and infertility (Sherchand and Pradhan 1997). This affinity affected the livelihood of the people.

The primary reason for shortage of fodder and the shrinking per capita land moldings and loss of forest and degraded pasture land; which has reduced the resources base per head of livestock. Animal number per household have decreased while the total livestock unties (LU) have gradually increased. Many common property resource, where farmers used to graze their livestock unimpeded, are also becoming protected area.

Even in well managed community forests, fodders species and grasses area still scarce. There are restrictions imposed to collected fodder and graze livestock in the community forest area.

Livestock contributes to the maintained of soil fertility. There is scope for contributing to the sustainable management of soil through better management of livestock. In a semi-stall fed system, about 46% of manure produced during the day time is lost while animals are grazing in the forest or on communal fallow land (Bajracharya, 1998).

The amount to support land in terms of pasture and grassland has declined over time. One hectare of agriculture land has 0.45 hectares of support land, which is much less than desired.

Livestock contributes 20 per cent of household cash income in the hills and mountain without taking home consumption of livestock product in to account (Nepal Rastra Bank, 1988).

Percentage charge in number of buffalo and goat are a positive indication of their importance, while the charge in cattle and sheep is negative and shows their decreasing importance in total hard composition and in the economy. To noticeable change is in sheep population in Nepal (Table 15.1).

An analysis of temporal changes in livestock population and composition from 1978-1988 in U P (now Uttarakhand) and H.P. from 1982-1992, (Table 15.2), show that whereas the cattle population has declined the buffalo population has greatly increases. Among small ruminants the sheep population has declined. It is interesting to observe that there has been a significant increase in goat population. The percentage share of both buffalo and goat has increase, while percentage share of sheep and cattle has decreased or gone down.

Table 15.1 : Livestock Population and Composition in Mountain and Hills of Nepal

Livestock class	Mountain		Hills	
	Change in population 88/89 to 96/97	Change in Share 88/89 -96/97	Change in population 88-/89 to 96-97	Change in Share 88/89 to 96-97
Cattle	+ 3.17	+ 0.89	+ 5.77	-0.51
Buffalo	+ 0.58	0	+ 8.30	+ 0.21
Sheep	-9.59	-1.70	-2.53	-9.59
Goat	+ 2.87	+ 0.80	+9.37	+ 2.87

Source: Agricultural statistic of Nepal (1990) and Statistical information on Nepalese Agriculture (1996-97) HMG/MOAC/ Agricultural statistical division, Nepal.

Table 15.2 : Livestock Population and Composition in Indian Himalayas

Livestock Species	Central Himalaya Uttarakhand (1978-1988)		Western Himalayas (H.P.) (1982-92)	
Cattle	-5.2	-3.0	-1.06	-0.71
Buffalo	+15.1	+2.5	+13.64	+1.62
Sheep	-9.1	-1.0	-8.15	-1.91
Goat	+7.1	+1.4	+5.25	+1.00

Source: (1) Directorate of land resource (1992) Livestock Census, Government of H.P., Shimla, India.

(2) Revenue Department, Livestock Census, Government of U.P., Lucknow, India.

Pasture Land Scenario

Animal husbandry has bean the integral component of traditional family system in hills of South Asian countries. Pasture land provides grazing resources, are now susceptible to degradation due to heavy grazing pressure through repeated seasonal grazing. The system of nomadic grazing for economic and ecological sustenance is also losing ground day after day because of shrinking forest area and degrading pastures and rangelands.

The rained pasture resource degradation is a challenging problem. Although pasture land and rangeland constitute about nearly equivalent to cropped area yet very title research has been make on silvi-pastoral, pastoral farming and improvement of fodder resources.

The linkages of pastoral farming, socio-economic factors consideration along with research and development effects are the prominent aspects to analyses for efficient resource utilization in CPRs. That is, conservation and effective harnessing of most precious grasslands. Nepal's total rangelands are estimated to cover about 1.75 million hectares, or nearly 12 per cent of Nepal's total land area. The key sources of pastureland/ rangeland in Nepal come primarily from high mountains and high Himalaya's areas which make up nearly 79.83% of Nepal's total pastureland.

Table 15.3: Distribution of Pastureland in Nepal (km^2)

Physiographic Region	Total Land Area		Pastureland		
	hectare (x000,000)	%	hectare (x000)	% of Total Land	% of Rangeland
Tarai (plain)	2.1	14.4	49.7	0.3	2.9
Siwaliks	1.9	12.7	20.6	0.1	1.2
Middle Mountains	4.4	29.5	292.8	2.0	17.2
High Mountains	2.9	19.7	507.1	3.4	29.8
High Himalaya	3.5	23.7	831.5	5.6	48.9
Total	14.8	100.0	1701.7	11.4	100

Source: Land Resource Mapping Project (1986).

Objective

The main objective of this chapter is to review the different research works performed in South Asian region on common property resources especially on pastures and linkages with livelihood. This also aims to find out the gaps in the research areas for the linkages with livelihood opportunity.

Review of Literature

How commons are important has been studied by Jodha (1986) in 21 dry districts in India. The study reveals that among poor families the proportion of income based directly on their local commons in the range 15-25 per cent. Similarly, Cavendish (2000) study supported even larger estimates the proportion of income based directly on the local commons is 35 per cent with the figure for the poorest quintile reaching 40 percent. Both the research discovered and concluded on samples those richer households draw a smaller proportion of their total income from the common than poor households.

Pathania *et al.*, (2008) revealed that the consumption of different products from CPR lands has been found to increase with decrease in the size of landholdings, which underlines the need to increase the productivity of CPR lands. The analysis of linkages between different farm sectors has revealed strong forward linkages of CPRs with livestock and agriculture and weak backward linkages with other sectors.

The CPRs management through viewed as complex of interpersonal networks and Das Gupta (1993) Pretty and Ward (2001) hints at the basis upon which co-operation had traditionally built. Seabright (1997) in a study on South Indian village found that cooperation in one sphere of life (managing the commons) makes cooperation in other spheres (marketing milk) that much easier : cooperation begets cooperation. They organically cope with resource allocation problem.

Beteille (1983) the management of local commons is entitlement to products the commons is frequently based on private holding: Richer household enjoy a greater proportion of benefit from the common.

Agrawal (2001) recorded in his study on communal forestry that women are sometimes excluded as in participation and decision making.

A recent empirical study on South Africa has tested the theory that rapid population growth in the world poorest region has been accompanied by increase deforestation, reduced fallows biomass declined, environmental destruction and poverty (Agrawal et al., 2001; Das Gupta 1993 and 2003a) deterioration of pastureland.

A study in NE Kenya on privatization of common grazing lands established that the transformation took place with the consent of elder of the tribe. The elders were from the stronger families which lead to privatization accentuated in equality with in tribe (Ensminger's, 1990 and North and Thomas, 1973).

Sheep enterprise was a continuous source of income (three shearing in a year) and contributed about 50 percent household income on medium farms in Bharmaur tehsil of HP, India (Oberoi and Moorti, 1986).

In order to increase the total biomass production of foage from unproductive lands was emphasis by Krishnamurthy et al, (1987) in their article and stated on importance of silvi-pastoral and rangeland management. Similarly Pathak and Roy (1987) pointed out that national forage needs can be achieved by half by managing pastoral land and rangeland land use capability and land use system.

In Ethiopia, Tothill (1988) found strong linkages between livestock and crop production on small farm in hills. The relation was leguminous forage with soil fertility status.

Using input out put model Parasnis (1976) and Batini (1977) stressed the need to view the integration between forestry and agriculture in general land use scheme.

Sharma *et al.,* (1991) observed linkages of farming system with common property resources. He emphasizes key issues on increased pressure on common property resource and inequality in income generation in different agro climatic zones of H.P. India.

Comparing dynamics to linkages between two periods 1959-60 and 1990-91, Singh et al (1995) observed that latter year market oriented input were increased due to introduction of improved livestock and degradation of forest and grazing lands.

The livelihood security to the resource poor and landless has been identified as one of the biggest challenges confronting development agencies (Hedge, 2004). Although all natural resources providing gainful self employment, are not properly managed rather under utilized.

Hedge (2004) suggested that integrated livestock and development of community pastures can play very important role in achieving sustainable livelihood.

Paul, D. K. (2004) suggested the participating approach to natural resource management which led to address natural resource degradation problem and provide economically viable measures for sustainable food and livelihood security.

Hedge (2004) mutinied that community pastures management in Rajsthan had increased the output in the form of fodder and fuel food (about Rs.6000 to 7000 one yr) and directly increment in production of livestock.

There is need of strong analytical method to capture and preserve interactions between crop and livestock production, considering the importance of common property resources in natural resource degradation (Dixon *et al.,* 1990).

A common property resources are neither exclusive nor discriminative is permitted in respect of their access by all members that differentiate with private property. Exclusivity is the major factor and is not found in common property resource (Harwick and Olewiler, 1986; Fischer and Krutila 1974).

Jodha (1986b) defined common properly resources are the resources accessible to whole community of village and to which no individual has exclusive property rights. In Indian and Nepalese context the CPRs are village common lands, community pastures, thrusting floor, rivers, and rivers banks.

Garen (1993) and Singh (1994) classified resources as common property resource, open access resource on the basis of property rights characteristics. They pointed out principal differences between CPRs and open access in that in the CPR case the property right holder has well defined property right but is absent or exist in the latter.

Gibbs et al (1989) defined institution right as the rules and conventions which establish the people relationship to resources, translating interest into claims and into property origins. The CP Rights are special types of rights which assume individuals access so resource over which they have collective claim.

Levine *et al.,* (1986) reported that rural poor in India are dependent for their livelihood upon a mix of private land and C P resources when the role of CPR is critical for very poor people and stress that planning should be done refereeing these factors.

Damodaran (1988) examined for grazing crisis faced by sedentary village communities of Indian which own the animals. Deteriorating common pastures and other grass land severe under nourishment of livestock were identified as major facet of crises.

Sexena (1988) mentioned that grazing lands play major role in the well being of desert people where each village has at least one common grazing land

Wade (1988) argued that some villages develop and finance joint institutions for cooperative management of C.P. resource in grazing and irrigation, but other do not.

Mukaiyama and Kawanada (1989) studied the contribution of pasture land to the farming economy and found that multipurpose cows and milk production contributed most to the farm income but pasture production and feed self-supply contributed slightly. He recommended for efficient technique for production and utilization of pasture.

Trampling during grazing pasture near home stead allowed eroded and degraded scenario in Australians arid grazing lands (Pick up, 1989), which has changed botanical composition of pastures and reduced productivity of pasture land overtime.

Singh (1989) observed that small farmer were more dependent on CPRs in meeting their day to day needs for fuel and fodder and timber.

Their relationship between the productivity of natural grazing lands and atmospheric precipitation was conducted in sub-mountaineer zone of Turkmenia and Artykov (1990) found that annual precipitation in the region is low (90-431) and directly related with the productivity of grass lands.

Chopra et al (1990) found that peoples participation in common property resource management would increase the productivity of privately own assets in lower Shiwalik rage of Himalayas.

Jodha (1990) realized that CPR play vital role in sustaining the income and employment in the rural mass by contributing about 30 percent of input to the farm activities. The CPRs shared substantial proportion 48-55% of arable land for crop husbandry.

Moorti et al (1990) found that about 60 per cent of farm income was contributed by sheep and goats.

Jodha (1991, and 1992) documented micro level evidence of the contribution of CPRs toward the standard of living of low income farmers. There has been direct effect of management and degradation of common property resources. He emphasized the need for inclusion of CPRs as one of the components of sustainable rural develops for arid and hilly states of India.

Pasha (1991) studied in Karnataka on role of common property resources and ruminant on the small and marginal farmers and found that due to declining productivity of grazing lands the composition of ruminant changed toward sheep and goats. They can withstand on poor pasture and stabilized income and asset accumulation.

Gupta et al (1992) analyses the composition of different fodders and their source wise availability and found that in J&K, Kashmir share of grasses to total available fodder was maximum (53 per cent) and similarly firewood was 30-40 per cent from public land there were similar response by Chauhan (1995) and Pathania and Vashist (1995)

Garen (1993) reported that most of CPRs in Indian have been degraded due to their conversion into open access resource, increasing presume, technological advancement and commercialization and rural sector.

Using game theory Sahu (1995) found that rich responded by withdrawing regular use of CPRs because of high opportunity cost. However, the poor responded by maximizing the use of CPRs products even by accepting inferior options. It was concluded that CPR loss is both individual and communal loss.

Sharma and Bhati (1995) found role of CPR and forests and decided that in low mid and high hills zone public land play a significant role in meeting day-to-day household needs. Annual value of these inputs was estimated at Rs. 5562, Rs. 8964 and RS. 42604 in the low, mid and high hill zone respectively.

Singh and Bati (1995) stated that the depended on common pool resource was found highest among marginal farm (69 per cent) in rural household of Himachal Pradesh, India.

Singh and Dhillon (1995) in his finding revealed that where there are no project activities the proportion of household grazing decreased by two per cent (60 to 58 per cent) while the share of green fodder increased from 58.4 to 60.7 per cent to the total requirement in the project activities area.

Gupta (1986) forwarded the view that technological solution to low productivity of grazing land of arid and semi arid region are limited closure of pasture land affected the landless livestock farmer more adversely.

Frederick and Sedijo (1991) examined the USA, water forest, rangeland, soil and cropland and wild life resources. The paper, stress on height in the importance of establishing institutions that would lead to a socially optimal resource development. It is argued the sustainability is not possible without management and management is not possible without a set of institution that establishes the economic incentives for producing or conserving resources.

A comparison by the two time photographs 1992 and 1989 for tree coverage in Jhiku Khola, Nepal showed that there was increase in the common land categories significantly from 1972 to 1989 (Gilmow and Nurse 1991). They revealed it as a strong indication of afforestation by farms to maintain the tree based farming system.

Methodology

As this paper is a review of papers, so following method is used.

The research papers and literatures regarding the common property resources were reviewed. Different results were presented as the sub-heading of the common property resources findings. It was basically whether the pastureland and its role, contribution to livelihood are reflected or not. The related findings were reviewed and presented as tabular form. The gaps regarding linkages to livelihood were indicated as the findings.

Result and Discussion

Increased population of human and livestock in developing countries has increased significantly, indicating tremendous pressure on limited land and other natural resources. To attain the self sufficiency in food grain production new technologies, infrastructure incentive, and research has been put on to farmers through government, but no attention has been paid toward the CPRs, especially the pastureland. The area and productivity has declined due to over exploitation, encroachment and poor management. These researches are treated as free goods by society and kept outside the policy issues by planners and policy maker.

Motivation and training of weaker section of society awareness generation about natural resource introduction of multidisciplinary programs and appropriate technologies and establishment of people's organization have been suggested as key to success for ensuring sustainable livelihood to the rural poor. Lack of infrastructure, inadequate financial resource and poor managerial capabilities, come in the way of tackling poverty and ensuring livelihood opportunities.

Table 15.4: Review of literature based on the specified Area as Mentioned Below

Area of study and country			
Definitions CPRs and Open Access	**Linkages**	**Livelihood and Share of Income**	**Effect on CPRs and Roles**
Garen (1993) - India	Artykov (1990): weather and environment - India	Jodha (1986) - India	Agrawal et al (2001) - India
Gibbsetal (1989) - India	Bitini (1977): foresry and agriculture - India	Cavendesh (2000) - Zimbabwe	Pasha (1991) - India
Jodha (1986) - India	Dixon *et al* (1990): livestock - India	Oberoi and Moorti (1986) - India	Dasgupta (1993) - India
Singh (1994) - India	Gupta (1989): technology and production - India	Hedge (2004) - India	Jodha (1990) - India
	Hedge (2000): livestock and pasture - India	Paul (2004) - India	Garen (1993) - India
	Parasnis (1976): Forestry & agriculture;	Mukaiyama and Kawanada (1989) - Japan	Levine et al (1986) - India
	Sharma *et al.,* (1991): livestock & forestry-India	Moorti *et al.*, (1990) - India	Sharma & Bhati (1995) - India
	Tothill(1988): Crop & livestock - Ethopia	Beteille (1983) - India	Damodaran (1988) India
		Jodha (1990) - India	Saxena (1989) - India
		Jodha (1991, 1992) - India	Pickup (1989) - Australia
		Gupta (1992) - India	
		Sahu (1995) - India	
		Singh & Bati (1995) - India	
		Singh & Dhillon (1995) - India	

New, CPRs has become the focus of research scholars, environmental economics and NR specialist during 1980s on ward.

Summary and Conclusion

On the basis of the observed and reviewed literature followings can be reflected.

- Common property resources are basically the primary assets for the livelihood of about 75 per cent rural people of India, Nepal and other South Asian countries.
- The income difference has increased the dependencies in to the common property resources in the rural context.
- The output from pastureland to the marketable framework is still the managerial concept for an efficient use of resources available and utilization.
- Increment in population and migration from remote to sub urban and urban region has an effect on utilization of available traditional occupation mainly sheep husbandry, which were the basic livelihood of the area.
- The net benefit from farm land and pastureland at zero transaction cost , would be maximized at higher if some incentives and motivation with new technologies would be provided to the rural poor. It needs a strong policy for devolution or property rights to community level.
- The proper and strong property rights mechanism would drive strong motivation to sustain the farming / enterprise for their livelihood.
- It has been noted that rangeland or pastureland management has been neglected due to different reasons (maybe remoteness, lack of proper government policy, state ownership, property rights and so on). There has been insufficient research work strongly recommending the policy implications of findings. The in-depth knowledge of linkages with various socioeconomic factors has still been interrelated with biological factors of grazing land management.
- The technical linkage of pastureland with socioeconomic factors to livelihood security has to be established for its maximizing net benefit and rather strong political commitments.
- A frame-work of functional linkages - relation among different components can be drawn with strong in the bold arrows (Fig. 15.1).

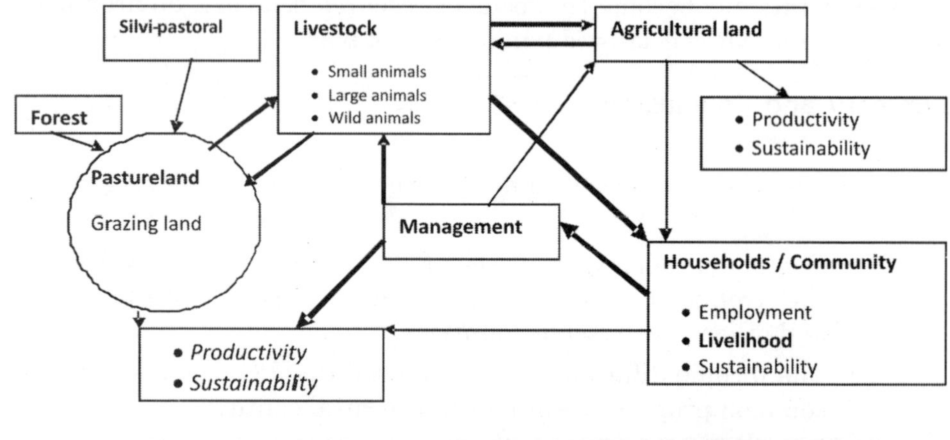

Functional Linkage among Key elements of Pastoral- Livelihood Framework

Pastureland Productivity α Livestock Productivity α Household Productivity α Livelihood

Fig. 15.1 : Functional Linkage among Key Elements of Pastoral – Livelihood Framework

Note: Thinner linings indicate weaker linkages and thicker linings indicate strong linkages. α indicates direct proportionate to.

REFERENCES

Agarwal, A. K. 1988. Forestry development in north east: an approach. *Advances in Forestry Research in India* 2: 105-116.

Agarwal, B.1986. *Cold Hearths and Barren Slopes: The Wood-fuel Crisis in the Third World*. New Delhi: Allied Publishers.

Aggrwal, R. S. Netanyahu, K. and Romano C. 2001. Access to natural resources and the fertility decision of women: The case of South Africa. *Environment and Development Economics* 6(2): 209-236.

Artykov, K. 1990. The cycle of precipitation and forecasting the productivity of pastures. *Problemy Osvoeniya Pustyn*. 3: 28-32.

Beteille, A., (ed.) 1983. *Equality and inequality: Theory and Practice* (Delhi Oxford University Press).

Cavendish, W. 2000. Empirical regularities sin the poverty environment relationships of rural households: Evidence from Zimbabwe, *World Development* 28(11): 1979-2003.

Chauhan, K. K. S., Verma, R,. C. and Shukla, G,. C. 1974. Impact of commercial crops on farm incomes and resources use in Jaipur district of Rajsthan. *Indian Journal of Agricultural Economics* 29(3): 106-114.

Chauhan, S. K. 1995. Extent of wastelands and strategy for their rehabilitation in western Himalayas. Paper presented in *International Seminar on Natural Resource Management and Therio linkages with farming systems*. June 8-9, 1995, UHF, Nauni Solan (HP).

Chopra, K,., Kadekodi, G. K. and Murty, M. N. 1990. *Participatory development people and common property resources*. Sage Publications, New Delhi 163 pp.

Compbel, B., Manando, A., Nemarundwe, N., Sithole, B., Dejong, W., Luckert, M. and Maltose, F. 2001. Challenges to proponents of common property resource system: Despairing virces from society forest of Zimbabwe, *World Developmetn* 29(4): 589-600.

Damodaran, A. 1988. Morphology of grazing and its crisis in sedentary communities. *Economic and Political Weekly*. 23: A29-A34.

Dasgupta, P and Maler, K. G. 1995. Poverty institutions and the environmental resource base in J. Behrman and T. N. Srinivasan eds., *Handbook of Development Economics* Vol. III(A) (Amsterdam: North Holland)

Dasgupta, P. 1982. *The control of resources* (Cambridge, MA: Harvard University Press).

Dasgupta, P. 2003a. Population, poverty, and the natural environment in K-G Maler and J. Vicent, ed., *Handbook of environmental Economics* Vol. 1: *Environmental Degradation and Institutional Responses* (Amsterdam: Elsevier Science).

Dasgupta, P. and Maler, K. G. 1991. *The environment and emerging development issues*. Proceeding of the World Bank Annual Conference on Developmet Economics 1990, 101-132.

Dasgupta, P. and Maler, K. G. 2002. *Environmental and resource economics: Some recent development special issue*, working paper No 7-04 South Asian Network for Development and Environmental Economics (SANDEE) Kathmandu July 2004 57p.

Dasgupta, P.1993. *An inquiry into well being and destitution* (Oxford: Clarendon Press).

Dixon, J,. A., Reyes, B. N. L. and Reyes, D. L. 1990. Issues of sustainability and agricultural development in Asian Uplands. Farm *Management Notes for Asia and the far east* 13: 1-10.

Ensminger, J. 1990. Co-opting the Elders: the Political Economy of State Incorporation in Africa. *American Anthropologist* 92.

Fischer, A. C. and Krutilla, J. 1974. *Managing the public lands: assessment of property rights and valuation of resources*. Haefele 35-59.

Garen, J. 1993. Aspects of common property resource use in India. *TRI News,* Spring 18-19.

Gibbs, C. J. N., Bromley, D. W. and Berkes, F. 1989. Institutional arrangements for management for rural resources common property regimes. In: *Ecology and Community Based Sustainable Development* (ed. Berkes, F.) 22-32.

Gupta, R., Rana, U., Pathania, M. S., Joorel, J. P. S., Negi, Y. S. and Kaushal, P. K. 1992. *Status of fuel wood and fodder balance and its impact on farm woman in Himachal Pradesh and Jammu and Kashmir*. Regional Centre, AAEB, UHF, Nauni-Solan, 80pp.

Hartiwick J W and Olewiler N C. 1986. *The economics of natural resource use*. Harper Collins Publishers 527pp

Hedge, N. G. 2004. Management of Natural Resource for Sustainable Livelihood: BAIF's Approach. In: *Natural Resource Management and Livelihood Security: Survival Strategies and Sustainable Policies*. Edited by Sundaram, K. V., Moni, M. and Jha, M. M. New Dehli: Bhoovigyan Vikas Foundation. 3-33p.

Jodha, N. S. 1986. Common property resources and the rural poor. *Economic and Political Weekly* 21, 1169-1181.

Jodha, N. S. 1986b. Common property resources and rural poor in dry region of India. *Economic and Political Weekly* 30(27): 1169-1181.

Jodha, N. S. 1990. Rural common property resources contribution and crisis. *Economic and Political Weekly 25*(260: A65-A78.

Jodha, N. S. 1991. Rural common property resources: a growing crisis. Gatekeeper Series Sustainable Agriculture Programme, *International Institute for Environment and Development No. 24*: 16pp.

Jodha, N. S. 1992. Common property resources: a missing dimension of development strategies. *World Bank Technical Paper 169*: 87pp.

Jodha, N. S. 2001. *Life on the edge, sustaining agriculture and community resources in fragile Environments* (Delhi: Oxford University Press).

Jodha, N. S. 2008. Some places again: a 'restricted' revisit to dry regions of india. In *Promise, Trust, and Evolution: Managing the Commons of South Asia.* Ed. Ghate, Rucha, Jodha, N. S. and Mukhopadhyay. New York, Oxford University Press, 1651-69pp

Levine, G. Bentley, W. R., Brockbank B. and Ghildyal, B. P. 1986. *Problems and solutions lesions from experience with rural resource development project*. Discussion paper series, Ford Foundation, India 20: 14.

Moorti, T. V, Oberoi R. C. and Thakur D. R. 1990. Impact of sheep and goats on the economy and environment of high altitude areas of Himachal Pradesh. *Final Technical Report, Department* of Agriculture Economics, HPKV, Palampur 213pp.

Mukaiyama, S. A Kawanabe, S. 1989. Dairy farming on the west slope of Mt. Fuji with reference to pasture utilization. *Proceedings of XIV International Grassland Congress* 4-11 October, Nice, France 1301-1302.

Negi, Y. S. 1999. Sustainable livestock management in mixed crop livestock family system of Himachal Pradesh, India. Paper presented at the joint ICIMOX_FAO workshop on mixed crop livestock family system in high pressure area of the Himalayas. ICIMOD, Kathmandu, Nepal

North, D. and Thomas, R. P. 1973. *The Rise of the Western World: A New Economic History* (Cambridge: Cambridge University Press).

Oberoi, R. and MoortyT. V. 1986. Economic Analysis of Sheep Farming in Tribal Farm of Bharmaur Tehsil. *Himanchal Journal of Agricultural Research*. **12** (1): 35-46.

Pasha, S. A. 1991. Sustainabilityad viability of small and marginal farmer's animal husbandry and common property resources. *Economic and Political Weekly* 26(13): A27-A30.

Paul, D. K. 2004. Natural Resource Management for food Security and Sustaining Agricultural. In: *Natural Resource Management and Livelihood Security: Survival Strategies and Sustainable Policies*. Edited by Sundaram, K. V., Moni, M. and Jha, M. M. New Dehli: Bhoovigyan Vikas Foundation. 34-55p.

Pathania, M.S.; Sharma, K. D. and Harbans, Lal. 2008. System Synergy of Farming System and Common Property Resources in Mountain Regions: A Case Study of Himachal Pradesh. *Agricultural Economics Research Review* Vol.: 21, No.: 1, June 2008.

Pickup, G. 1989. New land degradation survey techniques for arid Australia problem and prospects. *Austrailian Rangeland Journal* 11(2): 74-82.

Pretty, J. and Ward, H. 2001. Social Capital and the Environment, *World Development* 29(2): 209-227.

Sahu, A. 1995. Games theory and the tragedy of commons. *Yojna,* June 1995: 35-36.

Seabright, P. 1997. Is cooperation habit forming in P. Dasgupta and K-G Male reds., *The Environment and Emerging Development Issues* Vol.-II (Oxford: Clarendon Press).

Sexena, S. K. 1988. Present status of common village grazing lands of Indian desert and there possible management rangeland resource management. *Proceedings of the National Rangeland Management Symposium*, IGFRI, Jhansi, Nov. 9-12 (Eds, Singh, P. and P.s. Pathak). 84-92.

Sharma, L. R. and Bhati, J. P. 1995. Role of Forest in Mountain Farming System of Himachal Pradesh. Preper presented in *Internation Seminar on Natural Resource management and their Linkages with Farming System*. June 8-9, 1995. UHF, nauni-Solan (HP).

Sherchand, L. and Pradhan, S. L. 1997. *Domestic animal genetic resource management and utilization in Nepal. Kathmadu*: Dept. of Livestock Services.

Singh, D. V. and Bati, J. P. 1995. Role of Common Pool Resourcesin Household Energy need in Himachal Pradesh. Paper Presented in *International Seminar on Natural Resource management and their Linkages with Farming Systems*. June 8-9, 1995, UHF, Nauni-Solan (HP).

Singh, K. 1994. Managing common pool resources principles and case studies, Oxford University Press, New Delhi, p. 357.

Singh, K. and Ballabh, V. 1989. Afforestation of village common lands: A case study of Aslali village woodlot in Gujrat. *Institute of Rural Management*, Anand 28 pp.

Smith, M. F. 1986. The impact of changing agricultural systems on the nutritional status of farm households in developing countries. *Food and Nutrition Bulletin* 8(3): 25-29.

Thakur, D. R, Sharma, K. D. and Thakur, D. C. 1995. Impact of sheep and goats farming on natural resources of Himachal Pradesh. Paper presented in international Seminar on Natural Resource Management and Their Linkages with Farming Systems, June 8-9, 1995, UHF, Nauni - Solan, HP

Tulachan, P. M. and Neupane, T. 1999. *Livestock in mixed farming system of the Hindu-Kush-Himalayas: Trends and sustainability*. FAO. ICIMOD, Kathmandu, p. 116.

Wade, R. 1988. *Village Republics: Economic Conditions for Collective Action in South India. Cambridge South Asian Studies*, Cambridge University Press, p. 238.

Sustainable Development and Phom Tribes of Nagaland

—Dr. Mithilesh Kumar Jha
—Kumari Anupma Jha

Concept of Sustainable Development

The word 'sustainable' meaning able to be sustained has been derived from the old French word *'soustenir'* or from Latin word *'sustinere'* which is the combination of two words sub-means from below and tenure means hold (Pearsall, 2000). When the inonogram development placed right after the term 'sustainable' a new word order forms as sustainable development. The concept of sustainable development got momentum very recently. The etymon 'sustainable' development was first introduced by world conservation strategy presented by the International Union for the Conservation of Nature and Natural Resources in 1980 (Jhingan *et al.,* 2008). But the need of sustainable development was felt at the outset of development process commenced. Scientists developed the sundry machines and mechanical devices to assist and upliftment of the peoples' unfavourable condition of life. But development economist mooted the plan to use these scientific developments to give the boost in developmental process. They considered development as $D = G + \Delta G$, where, D = Development, G = Growth and Δ = additional change. For the robust amalgamation of ΔG rampant destruction of environment was ignored and environmental condition had begun to deteriorate.

By the 1970s, globally it was realized that development strategies in which only economic considerations were implied, had begun to suffer from erious environmental problems due to air and water pollution, waste nanagement, deforestation and variety of other ill effects that seriously ffected peoples' well-being and health. There were also serious equity issues etween the 'haves' and 'have-nots' in society, everywhere. The disparity in he lifestyles between the affluent and indigent was made worse by these nsustainable development strategies (Bharucha, 2006). The maneuvers f rampant exploitations and inefficient use of environmental resources orced the policy makers to forge the sound plan in which development hould be less harmful and based on sustainable development. Therefore, urrent development strategies have come to be considered unsustainable or the world's long-term development. The newer concept of development as come to be known as 'sustainable development'. Thus, for the first time ustainable development was the concept of popularized by the world onservation strategy (WCN, 1980) (Nayak, 2008), and was commonly used nd very strongly defined by the influential Brundtland report, entitled *ur common future*, of the World Commission on Environment and Development in 1987. It defined sustainable development as "meeting the eeds of the present generation without compromising the needs of future enerations." (Jhingan, *et al.*, 2008).This definition of sustainable evelopment is similar to the Neo-classical definition of income "A person's ncome is what he can consume during the week and still be as well of the nd of the week as was at the beginning."

The term 'sustainability' has been derived from ecology, which provides he means to sustain ecological processes, functions, biodiversity and roductivity in the long term. This requires that natural resources should e used at a rate at which it can be replaced naturally. In the real sense the oncept of sustainability has long been in use with varied connotations and neanings. When any activity is defined as sustainable, it is always in ontemporary terms on the basis of what is known at the given time.

The easiest definition of sustainable development is what we, the present eneration, have inherited a certain amount of ecology and environmental urrounding in terms of land, water and air; when we leave it to the next eneration, we should leave it at least in the same condition, if not in a etter condition that development, putting in the elementary terms (Nayak, 008). Achieving sustainable development involved achieving equity both vithin generation (intra-generational equity) and across generations intergenerational equity) (Hanley, *et al.*, 2008). As Ashcim puts it, sustainable development is a requirement to our generation to manage he resource base such that average quality to our generation to manage he resource base such that the average quality of life we ensure ourselves an potentially be shared by future generations"(Hanley, *et al.*, 2008). It lso considers the equity between countries and continents, races and classes, gender and ages. It includes social development and economic opportunity on the one hand, and the requirements of the environment on the other. It is based on improving the quality of life for all. It is a process which leads to a better quality of life while reducing the impact on the environment (Bharucha, 2006). As pointed out by Pearce and Warford, "Sustainable development describes a process in which natural resource base is not allowed to deteriorate. It emphasizes the neither to unappreciated role of environmental quality and environmental inputs in the process of raising real income and quality of life."

The concept of sustainable development is not a new concept in Indian context. It is lucidly explained in Vedic literature as

"आप: शान्ति: औषधाय: शान्ति:, वनस्पतय: शान्ति:।
पृथ्वी शान्ति: अन्तरिक्ष शान्ति:शान्तिरेव च।।"

(Aapah Shantih, Aaushadhyah Shantih, Vanaspatyah Shantih,
Prithvi Shantih, Antriksh Shantih, Shanti Reb Chh)

It meant that human being, herbs, flora and fauna of the earth should grow in healthy atmosphere. Not only Earth but the whole universe should develop without any hindrance. It signifies the importance of the whole universe, and its robust development not confined only on the Earth. While preparing the developmental policy, policy maker should keep it in their mind that whole universe should be protected. Pondering about the development one can say that Vedic cognizance had touched the perfection. It is beyond the present sustainable development which confines only onto Earth.

Many decades ago, Mahatma Gandhi envisioned a reformed village community based on robust environmental management. He emphasized on the need for sanitation based on recycling human and animal manure and well-ventilated cottages built of recyclable material. He envisioned roads as being tidy and free of dirt and dust. His main aim was to promote and use village made goods instead of industrial products. All these tenets are now considered part of robust long term development. Being a visionary Gandhiji had designed a sustainable lifestyle for himself when these concepts were not a part of general thinking (Bharucha, 2006).

At present, Gandhian thought of developmental strategy is proclaimed by the experts on development across the world. It is based on his concept that the God has provided sufficient things on earth to satisfy people's needs but not their lavish greed. It has obvious that the quality of human life has worsened as economic grew. Due to the detriment of environment the world now appears to be at a crossroads. It has chosen the path of short-term economic growth and now bounded to face the consequences of environmental detriment and degradation at the cost of loss of 'quality of human life.' The Earth cannot fulfil the amount of resources utilized and wasted by the economically affluent sectors of society as well the day to day needs of the ever-growing population in developing countries. That is why; the present developmental process is de trop by expert. Thus society has to transform its unsustainable development strategy to a new form where development will not destroy and harm the sound environment. This form of sustainable development can only be possible when an individual take a strong decision to practice a sustainable lifestyle based on caring for the Earth (Nayak, 2008).

The world conservation strategy, while indicating the requirement for sustainable development, emphasizes on three important objectives of living resource conservation viz. (1) To maintain essential ecological processes and life support system on which human survival and development depend; (2) To preserve genetic diversity on which depend the functioning of ecological process and life support system; and (3) To ensure the sustainable utilization of resources and ecosystem which support millions of rural communities as well as major industries. Therefore, if the degradation of the planet Earth is to halted, then a major shift has to take in social, economic and political aspects. A kind of revolution is necessary to involve a change in lifestyles, a major shift in human reproductive behavior and a restructuring of the global economy (Nayak, 2008).

Under the umbrella of UN, the First Conference on Human Environment held at Stockholm in1972. The difference in the environmental problems of the developed and developing countries become the issues of discussion between the North and South. The concerns of developing countries were well highlighted at the plenary session of the Stockholm Conference by the then Prime Minister of India Ms Indira Gandhi. She competently enunciated the conditions of poverty and its rapport with environmental problems in the following words:

> "Are not poverty and need the greatest pollutants" For instance, unless we are in position to provide employment and purchasing power for the daily necessities of the tribal people and those who live in or around our forests, we cannot prevent them from combing the forest for food and livelihood, from poaching and from despoiling the vegetation. When they themselves feel deprived, how can we urge the preservation of animals? How can we speak to those who live in villages and in slum about keeping the oceans, the rivers and the air clean when their own lives are contaminated at the sources."[13]

This meant that while the affluent nations had serious environmental problems, the developing countries in Asia, Africa and South America had a different set of environmental problems linked to poverty. Developing countries were suffering the consequences of rapidly expanding human population with all its effects on the over utilization of natural resources.

The main achievement of the conference was that the western countries commenced to observe the fault of its developmental path. It was realized that technology gain could not be the solution of environmental problems in the developing countries as many of them arise basically from the conditions of poverty, socio-economic inequality, and underdevelopment and from the unintended negative effects of the very process of development. These issues brought into focus the need for developing a congenial social environment for sustainable development (Nayak, 2008). It has become obvious that development must begin to change from aiming at short term-economic gains to a long-term sustainable growth that would not only support the well-being and quality of life of all people living in the world today but that of future generations as well (Bharucha, 2006).

Sustainable development is closely linked to economic development. To ensure sustainable development, any activity that is expected to bring about economic growth must also consider its environmental impacts so that it is more consistent with long-term growth and development. Many 'development projects' such as dams, mines, roads, industries and tourism development have severe environmental consequences and these must be evaluated before they are even commence. Thus, for every project, there must be a scientifically and honestly 'Environmental Impact Assessment' (EIA) and conduct of 'Public Hearing'.

Phom Tribes and Their Norms towards Sustainable Development

The Phoms, the major tribes of Nagaland are living in the northern part of Nagaland under Longleng, the smallest district of Nagaland. Longleng became district on January, 24, 2004. The total population of the district is according to the Census of India 2011, 50593, males 26,528 females 24,005. It was 121,581 in 2001 census. Its percentage decadal growth during 2001 -2011 is -58.39 and change in percentage decadal growth is highest in India that is -137.97. The whole Phome domains are abundantly blessed and adorned by natural beauty. The Phoms are having various norms, lore to up-keep the environment (By environment we meant the whole complex of climatic, soil, water and biotic factors on which we all subsist, and on which our entire agricultural and industrial development depends). Not a single norms and practices are familiar to outside the community (As Khejri movement of Bisnoi community of Rajasthan), which are up-keeping the environment from the days of Yore. Due to negligence of intellectual, lack of script, common dialect and unawareness of the people. The study is based on primary sources of data which was collected through questionnaire and interview from 50 persons (25 through questionnaire and rest from interview) during the year 2003-04.

All the facts are as follows:-

1. **Regarding Forest Pollution**:- Like other parts of Nagaland the flora and fauna of the Phom's forest is very prosperous. It stretches over its deep picturesque gorge and vale which spells-bound the visitors and force them to rapt and buoyant in its natural beauty. They forget to haunt of brooding dust and obtain the natural bliss, tranquillity, stilled with ecstasies. There is a symbiotic relationship between Phom and forest. The large chunks of forest belong to two types. First, forest belongs to individual and second, belongs to Clan. Morung plays dominant role to frame the thumb of rules and its implementation in *toto*. Generally trees are planted and nurtured by individual in this area since yore days (In the beginning period the genesis of plants were taking naturally). But planting and nurturing is also in existence since long ago. Generally all the trees of the road side, outside the village and in some particular areas forest is reserved for the villages but to preserve it Morung is the sole responsible. People are bound to plant and nurture the tree on the land preserve by the Morung. If anybody is found damaging, making pilferage, or stealing, cutting the tree or trees of preserved area then that accusation (He/ She or They) is responsible to pay fine (hang or lad) whatever Morung imposes that is fixity. Culprit presents the pig otherwise whole the property is confiscated by the villagers.

   If forest belongs to an individual and if anybody is found damaging, making pilferage and cutting or stealing then culprit is bounded to pay 250 gram *hum* (salt), if not then higher quality of Dao, if not then precious pot and incase if the culprit is unable to pay then *langha* (Brass Plate) is taken in lieu. At the present time instead of these items money is also imposed as a fine according to the capacity of culprit. Above discussed both the rules and regulations are up till practisising in this region.

   The pompous life of affluent lured the innocent Phom to sell their "Green Gold" (Forest). This attraction made the hill denuded of trees. At the present time only that Jungle is virgin Jungle which is not accessible to man. That is why people are thinking to prepare one strong rule to save the forest. If it will happen then the dream of late Rajiv Gandhi will fulfil, "We shall develop a people's movement for afforestation".

2. **Regarding Water Pollution**: Water, the ambrosia of human being is available here in three ways:- First, rain water second, spring water and third, tap water. The supply of the tap water is in the worst condition in this area. Phom vicinity is one of the wettest regions in Nagaland. So, people are mainly depends on rest two sources (rain water and spring water). In winter season, when the flow of spring becomes narrow then people are totally dependent on well water. Wells are shallow. Well, well-head and drainage are prepared by the villagers since ancient times. The area of well-spring and drainage are prepared by the villagers since ancient times. The area of community well and drainage is strictly prohibited for washing clothes, using soaps and taking bath, because such actions are making drinking water polluted. Rearing of domestic cattle nears the well and well-spring is also prohibited. *Yungkok* Daupu and *Pheyungsho Shupu* (all are Phom words) is the process by which Phom are keeping and maintaining the well and drainage. Here the word *"yungkok"* indicates well and *daupu* indicates cleaning. Thus *"Yungkok Daupu"* means cleaning of the village well. This function is organized by *morung* in the month of October and November, after the rainy season.

   The word *"Pheyungsho"* indicates drainage and *"Shupu"* indicates digging. Thus *"Pheyungsho Shupu"* means digging the drainage. This function is also organized by Morung during the month of May and June. Fencing work is done by Morung people during October and November every year. By above discussed process, Morung people maintaining the well and drainage. The students Union has been taken initiative in this regard since from the decade of 1960. They impose fine Rs. 150 on those person who did not participate in the social work.

Long long ago, there was a dearth of written thumb of rule, only verbal rules and regulations based on lore were influencing the community. Following norms are practiced here to protect the water pollution:-

(*a*) If anybody makes the drinking water dirty then culprit is apprehended by the Morung authority and punished as imprisoned for one day or night without a food and a single drop of water, in special custody of Morung.

(*b*) The culprit may be punished by restricting him, her or them from fetching water from the common well, restricted cultivation with the fellow villagers. In brief, he she or they are completely debarred from the social circle, till the solution debarment leads the isolated life.

In spite of the various precaution taken by the villagers to up-keep their living condition, yet some villages are disease prone, specially malaria and epidemic. Yachem village which is the second biggest village in Phom area was known as diseases prone some decade back. After the persistently efforts of Student Union, the villages are changing its all the defective scene. Nowadays village folks are not allowed to rear cows, pigs, buffaloes, mithun and goat openly as before, in Yachem village. If any of the above mentioned animals is found loitering freely, then the animal will be gunned down and the cost of the bullets will be charged from the owner of that killed animal in the form of fine Rs. 50.

Some years before when people come to know about the fish killing medicine, they adopted to use this chemical for killing the fish. After observing its adverse effect these days it is prohibited and traditional poisonous fruits are common in killing fish which are not so harmful for human being and water also. *Kai* (Fruits), *Nguhnyu* (Leaves/Fruits/bark), *Chauch Vu* (root), *Nguh Lak* (Leaves) etc. are toxic flora. Its botanical nature could not collect.

3. **Regarding Air Pollution**:- Air pollution is primarily a byproduct of energy consumption. Discovery of fire, started the air pollution. Being a backward region in the sphere of industrial development the Phoms are not having much air pollution, but it has already commenced. During the beginning of rainy season, people are getting "black water". This is the indication of air pollution. Due to shifting cultivation known as slash-and-burn agriculture, hoe and burn, migratory primitive agriculture, nomadic agriculture and in north east "jhumming" (originated in the Neolithic period, 10,000 years before) this problem has started. This is the symbol of undevelopment as Benjamin Higgins believes.

   Indoor Air Pollution:- A large section of the district's population (Around 99%) - Ignancy sacks calls them "Eco-system people" depends on Forest firewood which is basic for human survival. Smokes and fumes from indoor use of firewood pose much greater health risk than any outdoor pollution. Women and children suffer most from this form of pollution, and its effects on health are often equivalent to those of smoking several packs of cigarettes a day (Meier and Rauch, 2006). People are bounded to suffer this pollution before 2010 because there was no authorized dealer of Liquefied Petroleum Gas (LPG). After the commencement of LPG agency also people are still apply the traditional fuels, *i.e.* fire wood. Earlier there was a lack of air pollution. So, not a single rule is in practice.

4. **Regarding Soil Erosion**:- Soil erosion can be defined as the movement of surface litter and topsoil from one place to another Soil erosion takes place when the surface soil is washed away through excessive rains, it occurs because of indiscriminate falling of trees and conversion of forest into cultivated land through Jhumming. To protect the Soil erosion people are practicing two types of norms. First, people plant the cactus and bamboo in particular area where soil erosion or landslide started. In the field during sowing time people accustomed to the piece of bamboo, small log and make step covered the whole field in order to protect the soil erosion. This process is known as *"Mang-Phang"* (bamboo line) here, since the days of Yore.

   Second, a religious faith, when soil erosions occurs the people buried the parrots head in particular location to make the "God of Earth" in cheerful to stop the soil erosions. But after the influence of Christianity, this process is not so popular.

   Due to lack of scientific knowledge to protect the "Soil Erosion" the annual soil loss from erosion is tremendous and the consequences are disastrous.

   Now come to the ecological sustainability of Phom. The word "Ecology" is a combination of two Greek words *"Oikos"* house or home and *"Logia"* means study. So, the literally meaning of Ecology is the study of the homes. In other words, it is the study of the habitude of all livings. Ecology also called Bioecology, Binomics or Environmental Bilogy study the relationship between organisms and their environment.

   At the present time, ecological balance in Phom area is in reverse conditions. The species of flora and fauna are in danger. Peacock, the national bird of India is totally vanished and Lion the King of forest is fully extinct from this area.

   The vanishing of the birds and animals which is rapidly occurring in this area is mainly due to two major reasons. The most dreaded reason is because of the rampant killing by the native people as the flesh of the wild animals formed one of the staple foods of the people. The second reason is due to the universal change in the climate and environment, due to depletion of forest land, deforestation, soil and various pollutions.

   At the present time the following birds and animals from this vicinity have been extinguished and are the edge of extinction:-

(A) Birds:- Peacock, Hornbill, Vulture, Sea gulf, Kingfisher, Skylark, Swan and Crow etc.

(B) Animals:- Lion, Tiger, Elephant, Rabbit, Rhinoceros, Hippopotamus, Monkey, Chimpanzee, and Mongoose etc.

The extinction effects of animals and birds have been felt by the people where the beautiful sky is without birds and dense forest with deteriorating number of animals. But not a single norm is taking birth here to protect the wild life. The above discussed norms and practices still influence the bucolic life of Phom. Morung is playing a significant role in maintaining the law and order situation in this area. Like Indian Panel Code (IPC) Morung is also having special tribal rule known as "Pangkhum". By the help of *"Pangkhum"* Morung plays the dominant role to control everything. If intellectuals can take interest to improve all the norms and practices then undoubtedly Phom will become developed community. It is obvious that no citizen of the earth can afford to be ignorant of environmental issues. Environmental management has become a part of health care sector. Managing environmental hazards and preventing possible disasters has become an urgent need. The aforesaid discussion proves that the Phoms maintain the thumb of rules to protect the environment which leads to sustainable development.

REFERENCES

Bharucha, Erach, (2006) *Textbook of Environmental Studies for Undergraduate Courses*, University Press (India) Pvt. Ltd., Hydrabad – 29.

Chengppa, Raj, (2008), *Burning Earth, India today* (Hindi) July'16 New Delhi.

Datt, Ruddar and Sundharam, K.P.M. (2007), *Indian Economy*, S. Chand & Company Ltd. New Delhi.

Dhingra, Ishwar C., (2006), *The Indian Economy Environment and Policy*, Sultan Chand & Sons, New Delhi.

Government of India, (2011) *Census of India 2011 Provisional Population Totals Paper 1 of 2011 Nagaland Series* 14, Directorate of Census Operations, Kohima , Nagaland.

Hanley, Nick and et al (2008) *Environmental Economics*, Macmillan India Limited, Chennai.

Higgins, Benjamin, (1959), *Economic Development*, Norton, New York.

Jha, Mithilest Kumar, (1998) *The tribal norms and practices for environmental up-keep special context to Phom Community* (Seminar Paper).

Jhingan, M.L. and *et al.*, (2008) *Environmental Economics, Theory, Management & Policy*, Vrinda Publications (P) Ltd., Delhi – 91.

Kolstad, Charles D., (2006) *Environmental Economics*, Oxford University Press Inc, New York

Macropaedia, *The New Encyclopaedia Britannica, Encyclopaedia Britannica*, Inc London, Vol. 4

Meier, Gerald M. and Rauch, James E., (2006), *Leading Issues in Economic Development*, Oxford University Press, Inc, New York Edition-8th

Nayak, Krupasindhu, (2008) *Sustainable Development for Vulnerable Poor*, Kurukshetra, March, Vol. 56, No. 5.

Pearsall, Judy, (Ed),(2000), *Concise Oxford Dictionary*, London, Oxford University Press p. 1444.

Sirohi, Seema., (2008), *Hot Currents, Economic Might is Right in Climate Debate*, Outlook, July 14.

Population Growth and Its Impact on Land-use and Forest in North-Eastern Region of India

—Dulal Ch. Karmakar

Introduction

North-Eastern Region (NER) has its own identification for its geographical isolation, economic and socio-cultural features. The region is rich in natural resources, but they have not been fully explored. Since long time, it has been suffering from diverse problems. It has vast potentiality of economic development. North-Eastern Region refers to a region of India situated in extremely north east direction is composed of seven States - Assam, Arunachal Pradesh, Meghalaya, Monipur, Mizoram, Nagaland and Tripura and a sister State of Sikkim and part of West Bengal with the district of Cooch Behar, Jalpaiguri and Darjeeling. The region shares 98% (4,600 km with international borders with Bangladesh 1,500 km, Myanmar 1,450, China 1,000 km and Bhutan 650 km) while India shares only 2% (23 km) with international border. It is linked with rest of the parts of the country through a chicken neck of 21 km to the northern part of W.B.

The region is situated between 21-28 degree North latitude and 89-97 East longitude. It is surrounded by foreign countries. Bhutan and China are to the northern part, Myanmar is in the eastern part, Bangladesh is to the south-western part of NER.

Total geographical area of the region is 2,55,083 square km which accounts for 7.76% of the total land mass of India. According to 2001 Census, total population of the region is 3.84 crore. In 2011 Census, the population becomes 4.56 crore. The decadal growth rate of population is almost around the national average of 17.64 per cent. Interestingly, Nagaland recorded at negative 0.40 per cent. Eighty eight per cent of the total population lives in rural areas and the remaining 12 per cent live in urban areas. Seventy three per cent of the total geographical area is surrounded by forest area.

North-Eastern Region is a land of tribal people living in plain as well as hilly areas. The people are very simple and depending on agriculture and its allied activities for their livelihood. The region is backward in all respects - socially, economically and politically. It is suffering from high illiteracy, capital deficiency, problem of immigration, unemployment problem, weak infra-structural base and a leading unpeace of the region. These are greatly responsible to the backwardness of the region. For the socio-cultural growth of the different ethnic groups and proper utilization of economic resources in the tribal areas, a number of agencies have been formed. They are NEC, Tribal Development Agency Projects, Hill Area Development Projects, etc.

The gap between NE region and the rest of India has been widening since independence and particularly after inception of economic reform in 1991.

Population and environment are related to each other. Increasing size of population brings more area of land for cultivation as well as inhabitation. To meet the growing needs of the people, new industries are established. This leaves hazardous wastes in the environment. Accordingly, water and air are polluted. Present growing urbanization is also the result of high growth of population. Area of land under forests is declining. Soil erosion due to *jhum* cultivation in hilly areas makes the river bed shallow causing devastating flood in plain areas that take thousands lives and properties.

Population is required for the development of the nation. But over size population is not desired and if so, it distorts the environment. Growth of population is very high in our country. According to 2001 Census, urban population increases to 27.8 per cent of total population. It has two reasons, one is natural increase and the other is migration of people from rural areas to urban areas. Side by side industrialization is also growing. Both urbanization and industrialization are associated with the process of development. But this development is unsustainable because it degrades the environment. Industrial wastes are polluting air and water. Thus, the development is for the present only leaving poisonous and harmful environment for the future generations. Massive deforestation is the root cause of environmental degradation. Poverty as a result of high growth of population causes deforestation. The poor people make the forest land into cultivable land for their livelihood. They also live on forest produce. 33 percent coverage of forest was fixed by 1952 forest policy. But it was not achieved. Deforestation continues at an alarming rate of 1.3 to 1.5 million hectares per year. Deforestation results in flood, soil erosion. It increases suffering of landless labourers, marginal and small farmers who have lost their grazing field for their cattle, fuel wood and in turn, they use cow dung as a substitute of fuel wood that in turn, vanishes a huge quantity of organic manure.

Objectives of the Study

The chapter aims at showing how population growth causes changing land use pattern and forest degradation. Some important objectives of the study are:

- to study the trend, population growth and density of population for last five decades,
- to study the growth of urbanization,
- to examine the land use pattern,
- to examine the extent to which forests are degrading and
- to make suggestions for improvement relating to the objectives of 3rd and 4th points.

Methodology

Data are collected from secondary sources. Data include population data, land-use, urbanization and forest. Data on population are collected from different reports. Land-use classification data are compiled. Data on land-use pattern-use follows Economic Survey and government report. Density of population is measured as a ratio of persons living to per square km and measured as man-land ratio. Urbanization is measured as: (*i*) Number of persons living is 5000; and (*ii*) male persons working constitute 75% engaged in non-agricultural pursuit and density of population is 400 per sq km. Indicators of development are: (*i*) literacy; (*ii*) per capita income; and (*iii*) below poverty line.

Land-use Pattern in NER

There are three geographical divisions of the NER. They are: the Surama Valley, North Eastern Hill Basin and The Brahmaputra Valley. A significant difference found in between the hills and plain regions in terms of population, water, soil quality, forestry and bio-diversity. The Brahmaputra Valley and Surama Valley having large water channels are suitable for agricultural works whereas the people of hilly region having river to neither irrigate nor water storage facility largely depend on shifting cultivation. Pattern of land use is diversified in North-Eastern Region. Total area of land is classified under the following categories:

- forest land
- land not available for cultivation
- other uncultivated land excluding fallow land
- current fallow
- net area sown
- Area sown more than once
- Other grazing land
- Land under miscellaneous trees and groves not included in net sown area

Table 17.1 shows the comparative resource (land-use) of NER, 2000-01 (per cent)

Table 17.1

States	Forest/ land	Net area sown/ land	Area sown more than once/ net area sown	Net area sown/ total cropped area	Area sown more than once / total cropped area	& other grazing lands/ land	Land under misc. trees & groves not included in net	Culti-vable waste land/ and	Fallow lands other current fallows/ land	Current fallows/ land
Arunachal Pradesh	94.0	3.0	60.0	62.0	38.0	0.1	0.8	0.8	0.9	0.5
Assam	25.0	35.0	49.0	68.0	33.0	2.1	3.0	1.0	0.8	1.4
Manipur	28.0	6.0	49.0	68.0	33.0	-	1.1	-	-	-
Meghalaya	43.0	10.0	20.0	83.0	18.0	-	8.0	19.8	8.3	2.9
Mizoram	88.0	4.0	-	100.0	-	1.1	1.5	6.0	8.4	1.8
Nagaland	54.0	19.0	5.0	96.0	4.0	-	8.9	4.1	5.0	5.8
Sikkim	36.0	13.0	33.0	85.0	25.0	9.8	0.8	0.1	1.3	0.6
Tripura	58.0	28.0	53.0	65.0	35.0	-	2.6	0.1	0.1	0.1
North-East	52.0	18.0	43.0	80.0	30.0	1.1	2.8	3.2	2.2	1.4
India	23.0	46.0	33.0	85.0	25.0	3.6	1.1	4.5	3.3	4.8

Source: Statistical Abstract of India 2003-04.

North-Eastern Region Vision 2020, Vol-II: Ministry of Development of North-Eastern Region & North Eastern Council.

(**Note:** Figures are fractions of total available land unless otherwise specified).

Growth of Population in NE India since 1951

North-Eastern Region (NER) is a region consisting of seven states like Assam, Arunachal Pradesh, Mizoram, Monipur, Meghalaya, Nagaland and Tripura. The region has vast diversities and complexities of topographies, societies, culture, histories, politics, languages, and society traditions. It is a place of fertile valley, dense forest, blue hills and a number of rivers where one can find natural peace. It is engulfed in acute problems in the sectors of economic, social, political and infra-structures. Total geographical area of the region is 2, 55,083 sq. km accounting for 7.76% of the country's total geographical area.

Growth of population is very high. The region absorbs 3.81 per cent of the total population of the country. In Assam, growth rate of population is very high resulting in a huge size of population. According to 2001 census, total population of entire North-Eastern States stands at 3.84 crore. Of all the States, Assam has the highest population. As per 2001 census, total population of Assam stands at 2,66,55,528 of which 1,37,77,037 and 1,28,78,491 are males and females respectively. Total numbers of urban and rural population are 34,39,240 and 2,32,16,288 respectively, that is, number of people living in urban areas constitutes only 12.7 per cent. In other words, people live in rural areas constitute 89 percent. But percentage of urban population is the highest in the state of Mizoram, it is 43.5 per cent followed by Manipur (23.9%). It is 19.6 percent in Meghalaya, 17.7 per cent in Nagaland, 17.0 per cent in Tripura and 5.4 per cent in Arunachal

Table 17.2 : Population Trend in NE states (in thousand)

Census Year	Arunachal Pradesh	Assam	Manipur	Meghalaya	Mizoram	Nagaland	Tripura	All India
1951	-	8024	578	606	196	213	646	360940
1961	337	10837	780	769	266	369	1142	439073
1971	467	14625	1073	1012	332	516	1556	547950
1981	632	19897#	1421	1336	494	775	2053	683810
1991	864	22414	1837	1774	689	1209	2757	846302
2001	1091	26638	2388	2306	891	1988	3191	1027015
2011	1382*	31169*	2721*	2964*	1091*	1980*	3671*	1210193*

Population figure in 1981 is an interpolated figure since 1981 census was not held.

* Provisional population figure of 2011 census

Source: Census of India, 1981

Population of India-A Bose

The *Economy of Assam including economy of NE India*, Dr P.K. Dhar

Pradesh while annual growth rate of population is 27.8 percent during the same period in all India. Annual growth rate of population in the State of Nagaland is 4.97 percent during (1991-2001) as per 2001 census. It is 1.73 percent during the same period in Assam. While during the same period all India annual growth rate of population was 1.93 percent. Density of population of Assam is the highest. It is 340 while it is the lowest being 13 in 2001 census in the state of Arunachal Pradesh. Trend of population in the states of NE since 1951 is shown in Table 17.2.

Table 17.2 reveals that size of population of Assam has increased from 80.24 lakh in 1951 to 311.69 lakh in 2011. In Manipur, size of population has increased from 5.78 lakh in 1951 to 27.21 lakh in 2011. In Meghalaya, population size increases sharply from 6.06 in 1951 to 29.64 lakh in 2011. We see an increasing trend of the size of population in Nagaland also during the period of 1951-2001. It has increased to 19.88 lakh in 2001 from 2.13 lakh in 1951. But its size has decreased to 19.80 lakh in 2011 from 19.88 lakh in 2001.

Urbanization in NER

Urbanization is an important property of economic development. Rural surplus population is migrated to urban areas. The degree of urbanization depends on the growth of industries and other ancillary activities that offer continuous job opportunities. Urbanization also depends on development of infra-structural facilities and expansion of market. Thus, urbanization is associated with economic development.

Trend of Urban Population in North-East India

North-East India is under-urbanized region. As for distribution of population between rural and urban areas, the region has always remained rural in character. Slow urbanization has resulted due to slow industrialization, poor infra-structural facilities and mean market size. Though the trend of urban population is positive but it is very slow. According to 2001 Census, 43.5 per cent of the total population constitutes the urban population in Mizoram, the highest percentage of urban population in NER followed by Manipur's 23.9 per cent as against 27.80 per cent of the total population of all India. Degree of urbanization is not same over the years. The trend of urbanization in Assam from 1901 to 2001 is shown in the following table:

Table 17.3 shows that urban population of the state increases from 77074 in 1901 to 34,59,240 in 2001. Over the period percentage of urban population to total population increases from 2.34 to 12.90 as against 10.84 per cent of the total population of India in 1901 increases to 27.80 percent in 2001. However, decadal growth rate of uran population in Assam is much more than that of India. It is 20.5% in 1901 in Assam increases to 36.22% in 2001 while it is 0.35% in 1901 for India and it increases to 31.34% in 2001. Thus, pace of urbanization in Assam increases and with it land use pattern of the state is changing.

Table 17.3 : Trend of Urbanization in NER states in 2001

Census year	Urban population of Assam	Percentage of urban population to total population		Growth rate (Decadal) of urban population (%)	
		India	Assam	India	Assam
1901	77074	10.84	2.34	-	-
1911	92,916	10.29	2.41	0.35	20.5
1921	1,27,107	11.18	2.74	8.27	36.80
1931	1,62,166	11.99	2.92	19.12	27.58
1941	2,08,067	13.86	3.11	31.97	28.30
1951	3,44,831	17.29	4.29	41.42	65.73
1961	7,81,288	17.97	7.21	26.41	126.57
1971	12,89,222	19.91	8.82	38.23	65.01
1981	-	23.34	-	46.14	-
1991	24,87,795	26.73	11.10	36.47	*92.97
2001	34,59,240	27.80	12.90	31.34	36.22

*Growth rate during 1971-91 as census was not held in 1981 n Assam.

Source: *Census of India, The economy of Assam* by Dr P K Dhar, p-48

Forest Base in Assam

The State of Assam is known for its extensive forest areas. The area under forest is more than 35 percent of the total geographical area of the state. In 2004-05, total forest area of the state is 20,881 sq. km of which reserved forest covered 13,869 sq. km, proposed area under reserved forest covered 3,102.7 sq. km and area of 3,909 sq. km covered by forests under District Council.

Forest area in Assam has been degrading since past 20 years due to various biotic factors and resultantly, rich bio-diversity has been losing continuously. To meet the needs of the increasing population, lands for cultivation are extended at the cost of forest and grass lands. This results in deforestation.

Deforestation

The term 'deforestation' is defined as declining of forest vegetation. Deforestation in Assam consequent upon urbanization and its resulting factors is estimated at 2352.77 sq. km in 1991-92 and is classified as forest waste land.

Degradation of forest occurring in the State is acute due to mis-management. The other factors responsible for deforestation is growing demand for raw materials for forest-based industries and increasing demand for State revenue from forest resources, *i.e.,* depletion of forest resources. Forest land of 41,000 hectares in the State was destroyed of which 20,000 hectares destroyed in Sonitpur district during 1996-99. A total of 611 forest-based mills and factories like paper, match and plywood factories depending on forest raw materials are now running. Requirement of bamboos in Nagaon Paper Mill at Jagiroad is supplied from Karbi Anglong forest and this results in large scale deforestation in the district. Other forest-based industries those have grown in different parts of Assam such as Saw Mills, Plywood factories, Vaneer Mills are depleting forest resources. Data of National Remote Sensing Agency shows that during 1975-82, about 64 million hectares of forest areas were depleted in N.E. Regions. Present trend of small tea gardens also degrade forest area. Forest areas are destroyed due to construction of roads, setting up new towns, communication towns and electric lines. Requirement of lime stones in cement industry at Bokajan depletes forest areas. A huge amount of revenue earned by the State government from the forest is shown in table 17.4 :

Table 17.4 : Revenue Receipt

Year	Timber	Others	Total
2000-2001	286.40	1,190.10	1,476.50
2001-2002	117.67	1,090.10	1,207.77
2002-2003	67.37	1,786.63	1,854.00
2003-2004	158.07	1,758.75	1,916.82
2004-2005	201.60	2,176.24	2,377.84

Source: Economic Survey, Assam-2005-2006.

Cutting the trees in the forest the rural poor set firewood for their livelihood. This way pace of deforestation is intensified.

Both area and density of forest are changing. Forest area is decreasing due to encroachment, shifting cultivation, erosion of river banks, etc. and density of forest is contracting due to biotic pressure like *jhum* cultivation, grazing and smuggling, etc. Shifting cultivation is a process of agricultural practice done in hilly areas and after some years (normally 8 to 10 years) the patch of cultivated area is shifted to other else due to losing of soil quality and soil erosion of that place. It causes soil erosion, triggering landslide, siltation in the plains and flash floods. This leads to degradation of forest and pastures for the animals. Per capita forest land stood at 0.13 hectare. Karbi Anglong and N.C. Hills are two hilly districts of Assam where shifting cultivation is practised exclusively. Out of 4,23,885 hectares of land under *jhum* cultivation in Karbi Anglong district, 6844 hectares of forest land have become degraded forest land. Similarly, out of 2,92,309 hectares in N.C. Hills, 7938 hectares of the land have been degraded.

Large scale deforestation in the state made the government ban (by law) on logging and movement of timber by trucks. The National Forest Policy of 1988 lays down those forest-based industries will meet their needs of raw materials from private plantations. The government of the State has formulated some programmes of forestry development such as forestation and social forestry, wild life management, etc.

Summary and Conclusions

Total geographical area of the North-Eastern Region is 2,55,083 square km which accounts for 7.76% of the total land mass of India. In 2011 census, the population becomes 4.56 crore. Population size in all the States of the region has been increasing alarmingly since 1951. We see an increasing trend of the size of population in Nagaland during the period of 1951-2001. It has increased to 19.88 lakh in 2001 from 2.13 lakh in 1951. But its size has decreased to 19.80 lakh in 2011 from 19.88 lakh in 2001. The changes in land-use and forest so made are irreparable immediately. Explosive growth of population has made a pressure on land, encroaching forest areas, felling trees illegally to meet the incresing needs of food for growing people and raw materials for the forest-based industries. Present increasing of urbanization is the result of high growth of population. The trend of urban population is positive but it is very slow. According to 2001 census, in Assam, only 12.90 per cent of the total population constitute the urban population as against it is 27.80 per cent of the total population of India. Degree of urbanization is not same over the years. Growing fallow lands are the creations of high population. Total area of diversified land in Assam is classified as forest land, land not available for cultivation, other uncultivated land excluding fallow land, current fallow, net area sown and area sown more than once. Forest area has been degrading over the years. The factors responsible for degrading are various biotic factors. Degradation of forest occurring in the region is acute due to mismanagement. The other factors responsible for deforestation is growing demand for raw materials for forest-based industries and increasing demand for state revenue from forest resources, i.e., depletion of forest resources. To recover the situation, explosive growth of population should be checked with strong hand. A provision should be made to support the poor economically so that they do not depend upon forest resources for their livelihood. Aforestation and social forestry should be implemented with sound financial support. Private plantation should be encouraged. The revenue deptt. Of the state should be strict in giving settlement right (Patta) in forest areas. Information of remote sensing should be used in monitoring and managing the forest area. Farmers of *jhum* cultivation should be provided alternative economic activities to arrest *jhum* cultivation.

REFERENCES

Bhattacharya, Rabindra N (2003): *Environmental Economics*, Oxford University Press.

Dhar, P.K. (2007): *The Economy of Assam*, Kalyani Publishers, New Delhi.

Dutt, Rudder and Sunderam, K.P.M. (2007): *Indian Economy*, S Chand & Company Ltd., New Delhi.

Gossami, P.C. (1988); *The Economic Development of Assam*, Kalyani Publishers, New Delhi.

Nagdeve, Dr.D.A. : *Population, Poverty and Environment in India.*

Purkayastha, Gautam (2009): *A Concise Book of Indian Economy and North-East Economy,* Bani Mandir, Guwahati

Sengupta, Ramprasad (2003): *Ecology and Economics - An Approach to Sustainable Development*, Oxford University Press.

Sharma, H.S. and Chattopadhyay (1998): *Sustainable Development - Issues and Case Studies,* Concept Publishing Company, New Delhi.

Sharma, U.C. (2003): *Impact of Population Growth and Climate Change on the Quantity and Quality of water Resources in the north east of India.*

Srivastava, Shalini; Sing, T.P.; Sing, Harnam; Kushwaha, S.P.S. and Roy, P.S. (2002): *Assessment of Large scale Deforestation in Sonitpur District of Assam.*

Survey of the Environment, 2005

Statistical Hand Book, Assam, 2005

Economic Survey, Assam- 2005-06

National Information Centre, Guwahati

Sustainable Growth through Watershed Development

A Case Study of Mizoram

—Dr. Rahul Verma

ABSTRACT

The State of Mizoram occupies the north eastern corner of India. It is bordered by Myanmar in the east and by Bangladesh in the west. Mizoram is typically rugged and hilly terrain being a part of Indo-Myanmar ranges. The aerial view of Mizoram is very green and picturesque. The entire State is densely forested. Urbanization what so ever is concentrated around the few townships spread in the vicinity of eight District Headquarters, namely Aizawl, Kolasib, Lunglei, Saiha, Lawngtlai, Champai, Thenzawl and Saituwal.

It is noteworthy to mention about Mizoram that out of its total geographical area (21081 sq.km), Mizoram has only 21.20% of wasteland. While other hilly States like Himachal Pradesh, Jammu & Kashmir, and Manipur, have more than 50% of wasteland.

The relatively lower percentage of wasteland is attributed to the State's initiative and local efforts for the protection of biotic resources and application of primitive techniques of water conservation.

Groundwater sustainability is a matter of great concern for the provision of potable water to State's population.

Since, the monsoon is unpredictable and uncontrollable as well; water conservation is the only option within the watershed, through all possible sources. This task can be achieved through four major aims:

- *Prevention and reduction of damages by soil erosion.*
- *Reduction of pollution in the water and soil.*
- *Improvement of water quality*
- *Protection of wildlife and bio-diversity*

The sustainable growth of the Watershed Managements aims at

(1) *Protection and enrichment of Groundwater Table*

(2) *Improvement of Productivity of Degraded Land*

(3) *Prevention of Land through reduction of Land Degradation*

(4) *Conservation of Eco-Fragile Lands*

(5) *Increment of Fuel, Food and Fodder*

(6) *Improvement of cattle and milk production*

(7) *Improvement of Rural Economy through entrepreneurship.*

In Mizoram, sincere efforts are being made for the adaptation of these measures by local people. Almost every house hold has a self-designed "rain water harvesting system" on the roof top. The people use traditional method of collecting ground water through rock fractures, seepages, joints and run-off channels.

Practice of plantation on the slopes, constriction of retaining walls, contour and graded bunds, diversion channels, check dams, are very common measures to check soil erosion, In all, the people do use a good combination of vegetative and engineering structures.

Vegetable forms for production of Passion Fruit, Bird's Eye chilly etc., nursery (especially for "anthurium"), pig-farms, cottage industries (handloom and handicrafts) are getting ample support and funding from the government and other NGOs. Khadi and Village Industries (KVI), Micro-Small and Medium Enterprises (MSME) and National Bank of Agricultural and Rural Development (NABARD) are apex government agencies in this sector. Exclusive handicrafts made of bamboo and traditional Mizo Powerloom and Handloom industries are flourishing in the State.

The major share through self-entrepreneurship income comes through the export of handicrafts, "passion fruit", "anthurium flower" and "bamboo-shoots". "Thenzawl" nearly 100 kilometres away from the Capital Aizawl, is famous as the "weaving township".

All the above mentioned products are related to the sustainable use and management of watersheds. The agro-farm products are well linked with the cottage industry products. The success story is very well reflected in the overall above-average socio-economic status of people, highest literacy rate (up to secondary level) and more or less semi-urbanized life style.

The State has done commendable progress against many odds like-most adverse geography and topography, very poor transportation network and connectivity with the main land. The State is slowly but steadily growing through the effective management of watershed development. The socio-economic growth of the state is very well reflected by the two factors: (a) Reduction in Poverty (b) Reduction in Migration.

The case of Mizoram is quite inspiring for other States as trend setter, for achieving a happy, peaceful and respectful life.

Introduction

Mizoram is the southernmost State among Seven Sister States in North Eastern India. It shares State boundary with Tripura, Assam and, Manipur, It also shares international borders with Bangladesh to its east and Myanmar to its west. Mizoram got statehood of India on 20th February 1987. Its population at the 2011 census has crossed ten lakhs. Mizoram ranks second in India with a literacy rate of 88.49%.

Geography

Climate

Mizoram, by virtue of its tropical location combined with the high altitude, has a mild climate throughout the year. It is neither very warm in summer nor very cold in winter. During winter, the temperature varies from 11°C to 21°C and in summer it varies between 20°C to 29°C. The entire area is under the regular influence of monsoons from May to September and the average rainfall is 254 cm, per annum. The average annual rainfall in Aizawl and Lunglei are 208 centimeters and 350 centimeters, respectively. Winters in Mizoram are normally rain-free.

Topography

Mizoram is a land of rolling hills, valleys, rivers and lakes. There are 21 major hills ranges or peaks of different heights within the State, with plains scattered here and there. The average height of the hills to the west of the State is about 1,000 metres. These gradually rise up to 1300 metres to the east. Some areas, however, have higher ranges which go up to a height of over 2000 metres. "Phawngpui Tlang" popularly known as the Blue

Mountain, situated in the south-eastern part of the State, is the highest peak in Mizoram.

Rivers

The major strike of Mizoram Hills being North-South, most of the rivers flow either to the north or south creating deep gorges between the hill ranges. Most of the rivers in Mizoram originate in the Central part and flow either towards south or north.

The northerly flowing rivers mostly drain into the Barak River and constitute a part of "Barak Basin". The main northerly flowing rivers of Mizoram are, Tlawng, Tut, Tian, Tuichawng, Tuirial, Tuipui, Tuivawl, Teirei, Tuirini and Serlui. Tlawng (Dhaleshwari) with a length of 185.15 km, is the largest of them. Tlwang and Tut rivers drain into the Barak River directly. All other rivers meet the Barak River through indirect and subsidiary channels either via Tripura-Bangladesh or via Manipur.

Although many more rivers and streams drain the hill ranges, the most important and useful rivers are the Tlawng (also known as Dhaleswari or Katakhal), Tut (Gutur), Tuirial (Sonai) and Tuivawl which flow through the northern territory and eventually join the Barak River in Cachar District.

The biggest river in Mizoram is "Kolodoyne" also known as Chhimtuipui Lui in local Mizo language. It originates from Chin State in Myanmar and flows southwards till it enters India. It takes a northward turn through Saiha and Lawngtlai districts in Southern Mizoram. It reaches the extreme north at 22° 562 213 N 92° 582 553 E, and then flows southward till it goes back to Myanmar's Rakhine State, finally it enters Bay of Bengal at Akyab, a very popular port in Sittwe, Myanmar. Indian government has invested millions of rupees to set up inland water ways along this river to trade with Myanmar. The project name is known as "Kolodoyne Multipurpose project".

Lakes (Dil)

There are many lakes within the state, but the most important among these are Palak Dil (Pala Tipo), Tam Dil, Rung Dil, and Reng Dil. The Palak Dil, the biggest lake in Mizoram is situated in Mara Autonomous District Council (MADC) within Saiha District which is part of southern Mizoram and covers an area of 30 hectares. It is believed that the lake was created as a result of an earthquake or a flood. The local people believe that a village which was submerged still remains intact deep under the waters. The Tam Dil is a natural lake situated 110 km from Aizawl. Legend has it that a huge mustard plant once stood in this place.

However, the most significant lake in Mizo history "Rih Dil" is ironically located in Myanmar, a few kilometers from the India-Myanmar border. It was believed that the departed souls pass through this lake before making their way to "Pialral" or heaven.

Economy

In terms of economic development, Mizoram lags behind in comparison to the rest of the country. The State does not have any large scale industry due to the lack of raw materials, communication problems and infrastructure. However, cottage industry and other small-scale industries play an important role in its current economy. There is a much wider scope for the development of forest product based industries. The 10th Five-year Plan has given more emphasis to the "agro-based industry" as nearly 70% of the population is engaged in agriculture.

Land-use Systems

Land-use systems are focused on the cropping system and agro-forestry. Suitable location specific crop production technologies have been developed and implemented for tillage, seeding, weed control, water and fertilizer application and crop management for enhanced productivity. Land use systems have been developed for desert areas involving suitable trees, grasses and legumes.

The biggest challenge to the growth of the watershed is "Land degradation". It is badly affecting healthy environment and reducing the basic live support systems. Agro-forestry is being viewed as a restoration agent, rehabilitation process, bio remediation, and mechanism to high input agriculture on fragile lands.

Agri-horti System

In the region, the commonly preferred horticulture based agro-forestry systems are agri-silvi-horticulture and silvi-horticulture. Agri-horticulture system in the region envisages growing of trees and woody perennial on terrace risers, terrace edges, field bunds in the field as intercrops, as alley cropping in the shape of the hedge row type of plantation, etc.

The tree species grown in association with hilly crops in this region are: *Grevillea robusta*, *Albizia lebbek*, *Malia azadarach*, *Alianthus excelsa*, *Moringa pterygosperma*, *Morus alba*, *Bauhinia purpurea*, *Grewia optiva*, *Populus xeriramericana*, *Eucalyptus globules*, etc. Agriculture crops such as peas, potato, cauliflower, mustard, etc., during winter season maize, tomato, pepper, beans, etc., are grown in first few years during summer with following tree species in north eastern region. Toky *et al.* (1989) reported that the total above ground biomass in agrohorti-silvicultural or agrihorticultural system was around 48 t/ha and it was about two fold higher than agrisilviculturtal systems. In fodder tress, significant percentage of annual production up to 48% was allocated in current twigs, while in horticultural trees, a major portion, up to 63% was partitioned in fruits.

Bamboo as a Backbone of Agro-Economy

Mizoram, with an area of 21,090 sq. km has an abundant reserve of bamboo forest covering 12,54,400 ha, contributing to 14% of All India Bamboo Distribution. Bamboo is distributed thoroughly between 400-1520 m altitude. Thirty per cent of Mizoram is covered with wild bamboo forests, and most of them are still unexploited. Mizoram harvests 40% of India's 80 million-ton annual bamboo crop. The current State administration aims to increase revenue streams from bamboo and aside from uses as a substitute for timber, there is research underway to utilize bamboo more widely such as using bamboo chippings for paper mills, bamboo charcoal for fuel, and a type of "bamboo vinegar" which was introduced by Japanese Scientist Mr. Hitoshi Yokota, and used as a fertilizer.

Melocanna baccifera (Mautak) is the major component of bamboo in Mizoram. The total bamboo yield works out to be 32, 37,689 mt/year. 20 species of bamboo have been recorded in the forests of Mizoram. Out of these species, *Melocanna baccifera* is the predominant and occupies 95% of the bamboo-afforested land in the state. It is a very versatile species; the culms grow to 20 metres tall and are strong and durable with slender fibres and inconspicuous nodes. These qualities, renders them ideal for house building, weaving, pulping and for the production of small softwood products such as incense sticks, chopsticks and toothpicks. The shoots can also be eaten, and are of high quality.

Multiple Use of Bamboo for Sustainable Development

Bamboo in Agriculture: Bamboo pipes are used to irrigate vast tracts of agricultural land in different agro-ecological settings and applications. More than a million bamboo pumps are in current use. Bamboo is also used in making dams, dikes, sluice gates, farm implements, props, stakes; floats fish trap, silk cocoon trays, chicken coops, windbreak barriers and several other articles.

Bamboo in Construction: Bamboo houses are traditional in many countries. It is used for pillars, post, stilts, rafters, roofing, flooring, walling, scaffolding and a host of other purposes. Bamboo's mechanical properties also make it an ideal material for earthquake resistant and emergency housing.

Bamboo in Handicrafts: Bamboo's natural elegance and easy workability make it a choice material for handicrafts. It is possible to manufacture more than 8000 bamboo and rattan items. From buttons to baskets, lamps to lacquer ware, mats to musical instruments and from toys to walking sticks, bamboo can make it all.

Bamboo in Transportation: Bamboo culms float in water as they are lightweight and the inteodes are filled with air. This property has been put to use for thousands of years in making rafts, junks and boats. Bamboo is also used in making wagon floor, carts and their hoods, and suspension bridges.

Bamboo in Micro Entrepreneurship: Micro enterprises make extensive use of bamboo in furniture, handmade paper, handlooms, curtains and blinds, toothpicks, chopsticks, incense sticks and various other products. The incense stick industry in India has over 3800 production units that generate nearly US $ 400 million from domestic and export markets.

Agro-horticulture

Organic Varieties: Use of fertilizer and pesticides in agriculture and horticulture fields in Mizoram is minimal. As such, all agri-horticulture output of Mizoram are organic products of very high-value in national and international market.

The crops mentioned below have tremendous potentials for marketing outside the state:

Fruit Crops: Fruits like Mandarin Orange, Passion Fruit, Pineapple, Hatkora, Banana and Papaya

Vegetables Crops: Tomato, Brinjal, Bean, Pea and Iskut (Chow Chow).

Spices Crops: Bird's eye chillies, Garlic, Ginger, turmeric, Black Pepper, Cardamom and Betel vine.

Root & Tuber Crops: Potato, Sweet Potato and Colocasia.

Plantation Crops: Tung, Coffee, Coconut and Areca nut.

Potential Agro-horti Products

Sesame: Sesamum (*Chhawhchhi*) is one of the most important edible oil seeds cultivated in Mizoram. It is grown as mixed crops in Jhum land.

Sesamum is rich in oil (50%) and protein (18-20%). A 100 g of seed provide 592 calories. Sesamum produced in Mizoram are mainly marketed to Assam. Traders collect the produce from farmers and carry to nearby market i.e. at Karimganj or Silchar.

Cotton: Cotton is the most important crop cultivated in Mizoram. It is sown as mixed crop in *jhum* land. It is grown mainly in the western part of Mizoram. There is vast potential for cultivation of cotton in Mizoram. At present the utilization of cotton in the State is concentrated only for making of quilts, pillows, cushions etc as there is no cottage industry for other purposes like making threads etc. The approximate cost of cotton in Mizoram is Rs. 50 per kg.

Tung: Tung (*Aleurites montana*) is found all over Mizoram. It is generally grown in homestead and garden lands in a scattered manner. Sometimes, it is grown in *jhum* lands in compact blocks having 275 plants per ha. The tung oil is used largely in paint industry and is considered ampng the best of the available oils in India.

Orchids: Mizoram has a wide range of orchids growing from the lower elevations to the high hills. The Orchids grown in the high hills fetch a good price in the market at Delhi and Calcutta. More than 200 varieties of Orchids have been identified in Mizoram till date. In view of the right agro-climatic conditions prevailing in Mizoram, there is an immense potential of Orchids production for large-scale commercial purposes.

Coffee: The climatic conditions of the mid-hill ranges of Mizoram are congenial with successful cultivation of coffee. A high rainfall and sufficient warmth almost throughout the year aided with fertile, well drained, mildly acidic soil, is suitable for the growth of coffee. Considering higher economic return for the farmers on a permanent basis, the government of Mizoram is planning to establish coffee plantations in an area of 10,000 hectares over a period of 10 years.

Tea: The tea produced in Mizoram has a distinct touch of quality and flavour similar to tea grown in high altitudes like that of Nilgiris and Darjeeling. Biate has the largest area under tea, followed by Ngopa, Khawdungsei, NE Bualpui, Pawlrang, and Thungvei.

Bird-eye chilly: Mizoram is famous for bird-eye chilly. It is a high prized-item in spices' market abroad. This is a short-gestation crops and the yield can be increased within a matter of a year or two.

Food Processing

The climate of Mizoram is conducive to agricultural and horticultural crops. Moreover, a strong and effective food-processing sector plays a significant supportive role. The total production of fruits, vegetables and spices is likely to increase in few years as more number of farmers are weaning away from "*jhum* cultivation" and are taking up diversification towards cash-crops.

Food processing industry would help in diversification and commercialization of agriculture and horticulture and lead to value addition. This will surely result in employment generation in rural areas thereby providing income revenue and potential export prospects. Above all it would help in better utilization of local resources.

Importance of Food Processing Unit in Mizoram

Mizoram accounts for about 12 per cent of the total output of fruits in the Northeast.

- There is significant production of Orange (28,000 TPA), Banana (15,000 TPA), Pineapple (7,000 TPA), Passion fruit (4000 TPA). Besides Lemon, Papaya, Hatkora and a host of other fruits are grown in the State.
- As a matter of fact, the per hectare yields of fruit crops in Mizoram are significantly lower. However, better input of improved agro horticulture practices, the per capita yield may grow by 50 percent.

Existing Food Processing Units

The existing Food Processing units in the State of Mizoram are as follows:

- Food Processing Plant, Sairang, Aizawl: This plant was commissioned in August 1994 the current actual installed capacity is reported to be 460 TPA. Mostly Pineapple is processed here.
- Fruit Juice Concentrate Plant, Chhingchhip, Aizawl: This plant was commissioned in May 1998.The present production is 600 TPA concentrate & 800 TPA single strength juice (both in terms of output).

Pig Production in Aizawl District, Mizoram, India

Pig is the most important livestock in the state and plays a major role in the livelihood of the small farmers.

All the farmers follow stall feeding and supply kitchen waste with certain weeds, after boiling, to their pigs while 50% of them offer concentrate feeds (maximum 1 kg per pig). Pigs are marketed at the age of one year or above when they attained body weight of 90 kg or more and the market price of pork was INR 180. Thus the pig farming is economically a very productive occupation. On an average, sale of one pig is worth profit of Rs. 5,000.

Problems and Challenges

Shifting Cultivation

"*Jhum* Cultivation" (shifting cultivation) is the transition from "food gathering or hunting" to "food production". This traditional practice is still predominant in this region. With the increasing load of population in the state, demand for food and fuel has also risen. As a result, the jhum cycle of 10-15 years has been reduced to 3 years.

Indiscriminate felling of trees on the hill slopes has brought an undesirable eco-imbalance. Further, the hill tops are the main source of water; deforestation of this hill top led to the elimination of water source. This in fact, ended in the losses of top soil. Coupled with this, deforestation drastically reduced the retentive capacity of the soil. Erosion of soil in the catchment area resulted in silting of the reservoirs and streams leading to unprecedented floods. Sincere efforts are needed on top priority, to keep the ecological balance intact. This can be forced by discouraging the Jhoom cultivation.

Unscientific Land-use on Hill Slopes

Horticultural crops grown on the hill slopes without proper soil and water conservation accelerate the rate of soil erosion. The soil erosion is induced with the extent of disturbances caused to the soil surface. Colocasia, tapioca, sweet potato, turmeric and ginger are the crops, which resulted in movement of soil to the foot hills during the process of harvesting (Table 18.1). Vegetable crops grown on the slope without proper soil and water conservation measures also resulted in this type of soil loss.

Table 18.1: Soil Erosion on Hill Slopes

Land use/practice	Soil loss (t/ha/yr.)	Reference
"Bun" system for raising tuber crops	40-50	
Pineapple along the slope	24-62.6	Ghosh (1976)

Over Exploitation of Forest

Exploitation of forest indiscriminately, again increases the soil erosion on hills and flood in downstream areas, thereby damaging the forests wealth decreases. In long run, the loss of forest wealth leads to acute fuel shortage.

Even excessive grazing by cattle may also damage forest. The overall impact results in more denudation, environmental degradation and loss of biological components of soil and vegetation.

Groundwater Conservation

Sound steps are needed conserve the water. In the absence of proper water conservation policy, even the most ranier areas may face acute shortage of water. The best example is Cherrapunji in Meghalaya, which has been famous till recently for recoding the highest rainfall in world. The place is suffering from acute scarcity of drinking water. With an average rainfall of over 1150 cm or more one would expect Cherrapunji to be clothed in lush green forest. But what one sees now is a desertified barren bed along the slope. Heavy deforestation for augmenting fuel/fire need and building and furniture's, has engraved this problem. Cutting down the hill slopes result in the loosening of the soil thereby rendering the high possibilities of surface runoff, solifluction and mud flows.

Land Degradation

The extent of land degradation of forest areas for agriculture is largely dependent on the level of management. Apart from soil loss that accompanies land clearing and early stages of plantations, there is also severe nutrient loss. The practice of *jhuming* cultivation in North-East region has increased the problem of land degradation. The involvement of such a large area in shifting cultivation has caused large scale deforestation, soil erosion, loss of productivity, ecological imbalance and land degradation. Rapid population pressure has resulted in misuse of land resource and rational options for high value plantation crops have severely affected the tropical forests.

Planing Water Shed Management

The master plan for watershed management in Mizoram needs emphasis on several target areas. These are discussed under the following heads:

Watershed Parameters

The following are the main parameters for the watershed managements:

(1) Watershed Area

(2) Channel Length

(3) Length of Stream in the watershed

(4) Channel Slope

(5) Channel Slope Length

Key Locations

The key locations for watershed development are:

(1) Water, wetlands, transition areas.

(2) Flood hazard areas.

(3) Areas with high capacity for groundwater recharge, well-head protection areas.

(4) Forests.

(5) Steep slopes

(6) Wildlife corridors.

(7) Habitat for threatened and endangered species.

(8) Farmland.

(9) Significant soils.

Effective Watershed Management

The effective watershed management is possible only through the implementation several strong preventive measures which are as the following:

- Preventive the soil erosion through effective plantation.
- Reduction and control of Pollution.
- Improvement of Water quality.
- Protection of Wildlife.

Objectives of Watershed Development Projects

The targets mentioned under the effective watershed management can be achieved through the following major activities as prime objectives:

(a) Raising groundwater table through ground water conservation.

(b) Improving productivity of degraded / wastelands through suitable crop combination.

(c) Preventing land degradation through aggressive forestation and slope protection.

(d) Conserving eco-fragile lands through some suitable combination of plantation /cropping.

(e) Increasing fuel, food and fodder in the watershed. Improving rural economy through the promotion of "cottage industries, agro-horticulture and cattle production. Land Development including in-situ soil and moisture conservation.

(f) Contour and graded bunds fortified by vegetation, bench terracing in hilly terrain.

(g) Drainage line treatment with a combination of vegetative and engineering structures.

(h) Development of small water harvesting structures such as low-cost farm ponds, check-dams and percolation tanks.

(i) Nursery raising for fodder, timber, fuel wood and horticultural species

(j) Afforestation including block plantations, shelter belts, sand dune stabilization, etc.

(k) Agro-forestry and horticultural development.

(l) Pasture development either by itself or in conjunction with plantations.

(m) Setting up revolving fund not exceeding Rs.1 lakh to be given as seed money to SHGs at a rate not exceeding Rs. 10,000 per SHG for undertaking income generating activities.

Benefits from Watershed Development

The proper implementation of watershed development may result in the fulfilling of the following major goals

(a) Improvement in ground water level.

(b) Improvement in cultivated area.

(c) Improvement in productivity of Land.

(d) Decrease in soil erosion.

(e) Runoff loss and silting of ponds, tanks and dams.

(f) Increase in availability of fuel-wood.

(g) Increase in availability of fodder.

(h) Increase in availability of milk production.

(i) Increase in availability of employment.

(j) Growth of agro based cottage industries.

(k) Improvement in overall socio-economic status of people.

Initiatives in Watershed Developement

Agriculture

(1) Agriculture is the main occupation with more than 80% of the population involved in agriculture and allied sector. In order to

do away with wasteful and soil detrimental practice of *Jhum*, "Contour Farming System" has been introduced in the hill areas.

(2) Mechanization of farming and introduction of improved varieties of seeds coupled with massive irrigation projects are likely to transform the agriculture scenario in Mizoram.

(3) The main food grain crops are rice and maize. Cash crops such as ginger, coffee, areca nut, pepper and tea are being undertaken on a large-scale. The local markets are now flooded with home-grown vegetables throughout the year.

(4) Watershed Development Projects in Shifting Cultivation Areas (WDPSCA) has been implemented in Mizoram during XIth Plan period with a total target of 30,000 ha area. During 2007-08, a total area of 5,500 ha has been targeted with the main objectives of Control of Shifting Cultivation.

(5) Under National Watershed Development Programme in Rain-fed Areas (NWDPRA), a total area of 17,500 ha has been targeted. In order to reduce the area under *jhum* cultivation, major thrust is given on Oil Palm cultivation under ISOPOM where the net revenue returns per hectares tends to be higher.

(6) A high level working Group constituted by Govt. of India under the chairmanship of Dr. K. L. Chadha, has identified 61,000 ha potential area for Oil Palm cultivation in Mizoram. At present, the seven districts are selected for cultivation of Oil Palm.

(7) Under National Projection Organic Farming, sanction proposal amounting to Rs.388.68 lakh have been submitted to the Government of India for implementation of various components of Organic Farming Programmes in Mizoram.

Horticulture

The main horticultural produces are Orange, Banana, Pineapple, and Passion Fruit. Assam Lemon, Hatkora, which grow abundantly in all parts of the state. Oranges, Pineapples and Bananas are supplied to neighboring states. Other fruits such as pear, plum, guavas, are also grown.

Fruit preservation and processing units have been set up at Chhingchhip, Sairang and Vairengte. The State Government is giving high priority to upgrade the horticulture sector to increase the products of horticulture crops. Besides, steps have been taken for extensive cultivation of passion fruits, anthurium and grapes for supply to the neighboring States.

Handloom and Handicrafts

Handloom and handicrafts are the most important cottage industrial activities in Mizoram. Mizoram Handloom and Handicraft Development Corporation Limited was established in 1988 to promote and operate scheme for the development of handloom and handicrafts industries in the State.

The beautiful "shawls" and "Puan" of different designs reflect the weaving skill of the Mizo women. Crafts Development Centers have been opened at Aizawl and Lunglei in the year 1991 and 2001 respectively. The Tribal Handloom Development Project was started in 1992. Under this Project, four emporia have been opened inside the state. Besides, one emporium and a showroom at Kolkata, and a permanent sales outlet in New Delhi, is set up. About 180 persons had been trained in various institutions.

Rain Water Harvesting

In Mizoram, most of the villages situated in the hilltops, have a great shortage of drinking water. To combat this problem, rooftop rainwater harvesting has been a traditional practice of the Mizo community for a long time.

Having an average annual rainfall of 250 cm, much of the valuable and chemical-free rainwater gets drained off and wasted annually in the State. The PHE Department faces huge crisis to meet the growing demands of the rapidly increasing population, particularly in the urban areas. In order to harvest the rainfall received, the PHE Department of Mizoram had taken up construction of rainwater harvesting works since 1986 and has drawn up plans for large scale water collection like Impounding Dam and also Rainwater Treatment for drinking purposes. The Department had completed construction of 24,185 nos. of Rain Water Harvesting Tanks, 32 nos. of impounding Reservoirs in the State up to 2006-07.

Sanitation

A comprehensive Sewerage and Drainage Scheme for Aizawl has been prepared and undertaken by the newly formed SIPMIU, funded by Asian Development Bank. Other towns throughout Mizoram are also proposed to be undertaken through UIDSSMT for which surveying and preparation of project reports is in good progress.

The total sanitation campaign was started during 2003-07 and is currently being implemented in all districts of Mizoram. The up to date achievement under the project is 45,356 nos. of individual household latrines

(BPL), 10,000 nos. of individual Household Latrines (APL) and 236 nos. of community sanitary complex.

Power and Electricity

Small Hydel Projects completed during 10th Plan are Teirei SHP (3MW), Kau-Tlabung SHP (3MW) and Tuipanglui SHP (3MW). Some small Hydel Projects are also under construction such as Serlui 'B' (12MW) Hydel Project with an estimated cost of Rs. 135.20 crore out of which Rs. 22.50 crore will be funded by MNES. Proposed Tuiwal Hydel Project HEP (3×70MW) at the estimated cost of Rs. 1500 Crore envisages construction of a 115m high rock-filled dam over Tuivawl River near Ngopa Village of Champhai District in Mizoram and the water impounded is to be utilized for generating two 10MW of Hydro Power. It is intended that the Project be taken up on priority in the form of Public Private Partnership (PPP) and the proposal has been submitted to the Department of Economic Affairs. MOF. Government of India for obtaining Viability Gap Funding (VGF).

Concluding Remarks

For a successful implementation of the watershed development, the diverse issues, mandates and opportunities need due consideration to all possible aspects affecting people's life such as geology, geography, economics, sociology, commerce, management etc. The combined efforts in these diverse areas can be summarized under the following heads:

(a) Public Education.
(b) Nonpoint Source Pollutant Loadings.
(c) Storm water Management.
(d) Flood Damage Reductions.
(e) Surface Water Control Plans.
(f) Water Quality Assessment.
(g) Open Space for Watershed Protection.
(h) Water Supply Management.
(i) Wastewater Management.
(j) Land Development Management.
(k) Aquatic Habitat Restoration.

A proper implementation of Watershed development methods may finally yield good results. The major benefits will be reflected in - increase in the productivity, growth of agriculture allied sectors, growth in Micro-enterprises, enrichment of groundwater level and conservation of groundwater. The biggest socio-economic impact will be the reduction in migration, self-sufficiency and overall reduction of poverty.

REFERENCES

Anonymous (1987). *Annual Progress Report of AICRIP on Agroforestry. Technical Bulletin,* ICAR Research Complex for NEH Region, Shillong.

Anonymous (1988). *Annual Progress Report of AICRIP on Agroforestry. Technical Bulletin,* ICAR Research Complex for NEH Region, Shillong.

Anonymous (1990). Studies on the production potential of some silvi-horti-pastoral systems. *Biennial Report of the AICRPA*, ICAR, New Delhi.

Ghosh, S.P. (1976). *Development of suitable planting technique of pineapple in hill slope. Annual Report of ICAR Research Complex for NEH Region*, Shillong.

Toky, O.P., Kumar, P. and Khosla, P.K. (1989). *Structure and function of traditional agroforestry systems in the Western Himalayas-I.* Biomass and Productivity. Agroforestry Systems 9: 47-70.

Verma R (2009) *Role of Watershed Development in the Sustainable Growth: A Case Study of Mizoram*, pp. 276-284, Proc.Volume.National Seminar on Food Security and Sustainability in India, GAD institute of Development Studies, Amritsar.

Educational System for Sustainable Development

—Rupali Rathod and
—Safiya Begum

ABSTRACT

Education is an essential tool for achieving sustainability. People around the world recognize that current economic development trends are not sustainable and that public awareness, education, and training are key to moving society toward sustainability. This would be antithetical to the nature of ESD, which, in fact, calls for giving people knowledge and skills for lifelong learning to help them find new solutions to their environmental, economic, and social issues. Sustainable development is a difficult concept to define; one of the original descriptions of sustainable development is credited to the Brundtland Commission: "Sustainable development is development that meets the needs of the present without compromising the ability of future generations to meet their own needs" (World Commission on Environment and Development, 1987, p 43). Sustainable development is generally thought to have three components: ***environment, society, and economy.*** *The well-being of these three areas is intertwined, not separate. For example, a healthy, prosperous society relies on a healthy environment to provide food and resources, safe drinking water, and clean air for its citizens. Thus considering sustainability to be a paradigm for thinking about a future in which environmental, societal, and economic considerations are balanced in the pursuit of development and improved quality of life.*

Objectives of the Study

1. *To know the concept and three pillars of sustainable development of Educations for sustainable development Programmes.*
2. *To know the major issues related to the sustainable development.*
3. *To discuss various strategies of education for sustainable development*

Introduction

While many nations around the world have embraced the need for education to achieve sustainability, only limited progress has been made on any level. This lack of progress stems from many sources. In some cases, a lack of vision or awareness has impeded progress. In others, it is a lack of policy or funding. According to Charles Hopkins, who has spoken with people at many levels of involvement in education (i.e., ministers of education, university professors, K-12 teachers, and students), twelve major issues stymied the advance of ESD during the 1990s and new millennium. By addressing these critical impediments in the planning stage, governments can prevent or reduce delays or derailment of ESD efforts and, ultimately, the attainment of sustainability. In addition to these generic issues, governments at all levels will need to address issues that are specific to local conditions (e.g., the quality of the relationship between the school governors and the teacher union).

Role of Education for Sustainable Development

Issue 1—Increasing Awareness: ESD is Essential

The initial step in launching an ESD program is to develop awareness within the educational community and the public that reorienting education to achieve sustainability is essential. If government officials or school district administrators are unaware of the critical linkages between educations and sustainable development, reorienting education to address sustainable development will not occur. When people realize that education can improve the likelihood of implementing national policies, regional land and resource management programs, and local programs, then education is in a position to be reoriented to help achieve sustainability. This awareness forms the essential first step in the reorienting process.

Fortunately, at the international level, ESD is recognized as important and central to the success of sustainable development around the world. At the sixth meeting of the UN.

Commission on Sustainable Development, delegations from countries worldwide repeatedly mentioned the importance of ESD in achieving goals of sustainability. It was apparent that they were ready to move forward with the next steps; however, the importance of ESD must reach beyond the delegations and permeate the educational community and the general public.

Inherent in building awareness are efforts to outline important linkages between education and more sustainable societies (e.g., increases in female literacy reduces birthrates and improves family quality of life).

In large part, perceiving a need brings about a corresponding change in educational systems. Unfortunately, the need to achieve sustainable development is not perceived today as sufficiently important to spark a large response in the educational community. If leaders at all levels of governance are to make progress, the recognition and active involvement of the education sector is imperative.

Response to an Educational Crisis

Issue 2 - Structuring and Placing ESD in the Curriculum

Each country faces a fundamental decision in addressing an ESD strategy. Each country must decide on a method of implementation whether to create another "add on" subject, (e.g., Sustainable Development, Environmental Education, or Population Education) or to reorient entire education programs and practices to address sustainable development.

Nations also need to clarify whether their educators are being asked to teach about sustainable development or to change the goals and methods of education to achieve sustainable development. The answer to this question will profoundly affect each nation's course of action.

In reality, education related to sustainable development will be implemented in a wide range, in both depth and breadth. In some communities, ESD will be ignored; in others it will be barely addressed. In some, a new class dedicated to ESD will be created, and in others the entire curriculum will be reoriented to address sustainability. Communities must be aware of the limitations of educating about sustainable development. Teaching about sustainable development is like teaching the theory behind an abstract concept or teaching the principles of sustainability by rote memorization. ESD in its real and effective forms gives students the skills, perspectives, values, and knowledge to live sustainably in their communities. At the same time, true education is not indoctrination or inculcation.

Issue 3 - Linking to Existing Issues: Educational Reform and Economic Viability

The effectiveness of the world's educational systems is already critically debated in light of the changing needs of society. The current widespread acknowledgment of the need for educational reform may help advance ESD. If it can be linked to one or more priorities of educational reform, ESD could have a good chance for success. However, if promoters try to add another issue to an already over-burdened system, the chances of success are slim.

One current global concern that has the potential to drive educational reform in many countries is economic security. Around the world, ministries of education and commerce are asking: What changes will prepare a workforce that will make my country economically viable in the changing economy of the new millennium?

One educational effort that can boost the economic potential of entire nations is educating females. During the past decade, some national leaders have recognized that educating the entire workforce, both males and females, is important for economic viability. In addition, Lawrence Summer of the World Bank says, "Once all the benefits are recognized, investments in the education of girls may well be the highest-return investment available in the developing world" (King and Hill, 1993, p vii). Accordingly, some nations are removing barriers to girls attending school and have campaigns to actively enroll girls in school.

Further, aligning education with future economic conditions is difficult, because economic and technological forecasting is an art based on imprecise science. Answers are elusive.

To be successful, ESD will need to catch the wave of educational reform. ESD proponents need to identify and illustrate the linkages between the principles of sustainability and the long-term economic well-being of each nation. If ESD can be linked to the current global educational reform movement, educating for sustainability will be swept along with the energy of the reform effort. If, however, the wave is missed, proponents of ESD will be looking for a foothold in the curriculum and trying to convince teachers to wedge sustainability principles, knowledge, issues, skills, values, and perspectives wherever possible. Linking to the reform movement can guarantee ESD to every child in school, while inserting ESD into the curriculum will be left to the whim of individual teachers. In the case of the latter, ESD will be characterized by huge gaps or possible redundancies.

Issue 4 - Facing the Complexity of Sustainable Development Concept

Sustainable development is a complex and evolving concept. Many scholars and practitioners have invested years in trying to define sustainable development and envisioning how to achieve it on national and local levels. Because sustainable development is hard to define and implement, it is also difficult to teach. Even more challenging is the task of totally reorienting an entire education system to achieve sustainability.

When we examine successful national education campaigns, we find they often have simple messages. For example, messages that encourage us to vaccinate our children and boil our water, or discourage us from driving drunkand taking drugs, are simple concepts compared to the complex range of environmental, economic, and social issues that sustainable development encompasses. Success in ESD will take much longer and be more costly than single-message public-education campaigns.

National Education Campaigns

When we examine successful national education campaigns, we find they often have simple messages. For example, AIDS education focuses on prevention. The message is, "people can prevent the spread of the HIV virus by taking certain precautions." To convey this message, national governments, nonprofit organizations, and schools spend millions of dollars. The AIDS prevention message is extremely simple. Nevertheless, AIDS is on the rise in many countries, not because the education programs are ineffective, but because the problem is complex.

Rather than being clear, simple, and unambiguous, the concepts involved in ESD are complex. Their complexity stems from the intricate and complicated interactions of natural and human systems. The challenge to educators is to derive messages that illustrate such complexity, without overwhelming or confusing the learner.

Issue 5 - Developing an ESD Program with Community Participation

Perhaps the greatest obstacle to reorienting the world's educational systems is the lack of clarity regarding goals. In simple terms, those who will be called upon to educate differently (e.g., the world's 59,000,000 teachers or agricultural instructors or water-treatment trainers) eventually will ask, "What am I to do differently?" "What should I do or say now that I didn't say before?" These simple questions leave most "experts" in a quandary and the questioner without an adequate response.

Education for sustainable development remains an enigma to many governments and schools. Governments, ministries of education, school districts, and educators have expressed a willingness to adopt ESD programs; however, no successful working models currently exist. Without models to adapt and adopt, governments and schools must create a process to define what education for sustainability is with respect to the local context. Such a process is challenging. It calls for a public participation process in which all of the stakeholders in a community carefully examine what they want their children to know, do, and value when they leave the formal education system. This means that the community must try to predict the environmental, economic, and social conditions of the near and distant future.

Public participation processes whereby stakeholders examine the needs and desires of a community and identify essential elements of basic and secondary education can be adapted and implemented in many types of communities. Seeking the opinions of parents and workers to shape the education of their children will be a totally new idea in some cultures. Although community consultation and other forms of public participation can be effective tools, they should be introduced slowly and in accordance with local traditions and cultures where they have not been used previously. However valuable, the community consultation process is not without pitfalls. For example, an organized, educated, and articulate few might dominate the process; people who have received little formal education may not feel they have the expertise to take part in or contribute to the process; and the worldviews and life experiences of some people might prevent them from perceiving or accommodating the changes that will come to all regions of the planet in the coming decades. In these cases, how the outcome of the process is used becomes important. A continuum of implementation exists, ranging from ruthlessly implementing the results of a skewed process to totally ignoring the outcomes of the process. The interpretative, political, and interpersonal skills of the implementation team are key in this effort.

Issue 6—Engaging Traditional Disciplines in a Trandisciplinary Framework

ESD by nature is holistic and interdisciplinary and depends on concepts and analytical tools from a variety of disciplines. As a result, ESD is difficult to teach in traditional school settings where studies are divided and taught in a disciplinary framework. In countries where national curriculums describe in detail the content and sequence of study

in each discipline, ESD will be challenging to implement. In other countries where content is described generally, ESD will be more easily implemented, although doing so will require creative teachers who are comfortable and skilled at teaching across disciplines.

Issue 7—Sharing the Responsibility

Popular thinking promotes the myth that an informed society is solely the responsibility of the ministry of education. In reality, however, the ministries of environment, commerce, State, and health also have a stake in ESD, just as they have a stake in sustainable development. By combining expertise, resources, and funding from many ministries, the possibility of building a high-quality, successful education program increases.

Every sector of the government that is touched by sustainable development (i.e., every ministry and department) can play a role in ESD and the reorienting process. At the UN meeting of the Commission on Sustainable Development, ministries of the environment have taken the lead in stating that education, awareness, and training are essential tools in bringing about sustainable development. Ministries of the environment need to work with both formal and non formal sectors of the education community to implement ESD. In addition, it is absolutely essential for teachers to be involved in the process of building consensus concerning ESD.

Issue 8 - Building Human Capacity

The successful implementation of a new educational trend will require responsible, accountable leadership and expertise in both systemic educational change and sustainable development. We must develop realistic strategies to quickly create knowledgeable and capable leadership. It is unrealistic to expect nations to retrain 59,000,000 teachers and thousands of administrators in either - or both - ESD and educational change. We must find ways, such as employing the strengths model, to use existing skills.

Issue 9 - Developing Financial and Material Resources

The good news is that many countries are spending a larger percentage of their gross national product (GNP) on education. Two-thirds of the 123 countries listed in the UNESCO World Education Report 2000 that reported public expenditures on education as a percentage of GNP in both 1990 and 1996, reported spending more in 1996 than in 1990. Although governments are prioritizing education in terms of funding, how much of this funding is going to reorient education to address sustainability? As we pointed out in the "Education: Promise and Paradox" section, simply providing more education does not reduce the threat high resource consumption poses to sustainability.

One of the reasons why many experts perceive that little progress has been made regarding ESD since the Earth Summit in 1992 is that few financial resources have been dedicated to reorienting education to address sustainability. In fact, national and local governments have spent little on ESD beyond improving basic education.

In addition, many countries are evaluating new educational technologies (e.g., distance learning, computers, Internet, TV) and strategies to implement them. ESD is already woven into many of these technologies. For example, many free sources of environmental data are available on the World Wide Web as are other teaching resources such as lesson plans. Governments and school districts investing in these technologies will offset expenditures with access to free ESD information and materials.

Funding for New Educational Programs

ESD is a cross-curricular effort. Historically, other cross-curricular efforts (e.g., educational technology) have been expensive. Bringing computers and the Internet into classrooms has required substantial investments by national, state, and local governments. For example, in the 1980s, Tennessee Governor Lamar Alexander decided that every classroom in the state should have a computer. He knew that in many rural areas communities would resist spending large amounts of money on educational technology; in some areas of poverty, the schools could afford neither the hardware nor the software. Rather than waiting for individual districts to prioritize and fund technology, the state government paid for a computer for each classroom. In the 1990s, Tennessee also paid for an Internet connection for each school, because the state realized the importance of all students learning to access, manage, and use information from the World Wide Web.

Issue 10—Developing Policy

To succeed, ESD must have an authoritative impetus from national or regional governments that will drive policy development. The omission of such an impetus proved to be the downfall of the 1970s global effort to infuse environmental education into the elementary and secondary curriculums. This same fate could befall the ESD effort. The reality of any educational reform is that success depends on both "top down" and "bottom up" efforts.

Issue 11—Developing a Creative, Innovative, and Risk-Taking Climate

In order to bring about the major changes required by ESD, we need to nurture a climate of safety. Policymakers, administrators, and teachers will need to make changes, experiment, and take risks to accomplish new educational and sustainability goals. They need to have the authority and support of the educational community to change the status quo. Teachers must feel that the administration will support their efforts if parents or vested interest groups in the community question or criticize their initiatives.

We need to develop and implement policy to ensure administrators and educators at all levels have the right to introduce new or controversial topics and pedagogical methods. Of course, an over-zealous few could abuse these rights; therefore, a system of checks and balances within professional guidelines and cultural context should also be in place.

Issue 12—Promoting Sustainability in Popular Culture

Perhaps the most difficult obstacle to address in implementing ESD is that of popularity. While many countries agreed that ESD is important, the themes of sustainability are not prevalent in popular cultures or governmental policies. For example, one principle of sustainable development is that the rates of use of renewable resources should not exceed their rates of regeneration. Yet, many societies have developed or are developing a "disposable culture." Disposable beverage containers, food wrappers, plates, and eating utensils pass through our lives daily. We use them once and then discard them to be buried, burned, or dumped in the water. This disposable culture is using such resources as trees and fossil fuels more rapidly than they can be replaced.

Strategies for Future Education

The strategies envisaged here are anticipated to improve competence in the education sector, enhance its impact in the target area, and explore the scope for its extension and consolidation through seven policy measures.

1. Sensitization

Active advocacy at the mass level to increase public awareness on education-related issues and mobilization of resources through talks, seminars, and use of media and publication.

2. Enablement

Efforts at capacity building of professionals and to increase human capital through courses, trainings, and workshops.

3. Entitlement

Effective use of legislation, enforcement, and adjudication measures to implement laws, rules, policies, programs, and decisions made.

4. Empowerment

Focusing on concrete and empirically measurable improvement in the professional competence of individuals, agencies, and organizations through the increased level of collaboration and solidarity building.

5. *Mainstreaming*

Targeting and channelizing the new generations (children and youth) in an inclusive manner, and also women, disadvantaged groups, and minorities as well as communities at the local level.

6. *Reenforcement*

Strengthening the capacity building of the key educational agencies, organizations, and institutions by consolidating their policy, decisionmaking, and implementation mechanism focused on the promotion of a healthy self-through civic, security, and scientific education.

7. *Networking and Synergizing*

Linkaging the stakeholders at the local, national, regional, and global levels in a coordinated framework of proactive communication, creative interaction, and productive collaboration for sustained flow of the resources and assistance needed in the education sector and integrating the educational policies. Also, development of programs and activities with other existing and upcoming initiatives in the field at home and abroad.

Conclusion

This paper has highlighted the latest educational concepts and pillars of sustainable development and major issues related for sustainable development. However as this is an emerging field much R&D needs to be done.

REFERENCES

Allenby, Braden R. "Industrial Ecology: The Materials Scientist in an Environmentally Constrained World," *MRS Bulletin* 17, No. 3, March, 1992: 46–51.

Ehrenfeld, J.R. 1995. Industrial ecology: A strategic framework for product policy and other sustainable practices. In *Green Goods*, edited by E. Rydén and J Strahl. Kretsloppsdelegationens rapport 1995:5. Stockholm

Graedel, T. and Allenby,B. 1995. *Industrial Ecology*, Prentice-Hall, Englewood Cliffs, NJ, USA

Harry Freeman, Teresa Harten, Johnny Springer, Paul Randall, Mary Ann Curran, and Kenneth Stone, "Industrial Pollution Prevention: A Critical Review," Air and Waste (*Journal of the Air and Waste Management Association*) 42, no. 5 (May 1992): 619.

Managing the Human Resources for Poverty and Socio-economic Development of Mayurbhanj District in Orissa, India

—Sandeep Kumar Patnaik
—Dr. Upendra Nath Sahu
—Dr. Priti Ranjan Hathy

ABSTRACT

One of the major concerns of Indian planning has been the removal of disparities among different sections of population especially the weaker sections like the scheduled tribes and scheduled castes. The basic features common to these tribes as listed in the constitution were that they were having tribal origins, primitive ways of life, habitation in remote and less easily accessible areas and generally backward - socially and economically. The main objective is to analyse the present socio-economic conditions of the tribals in the district and to find out the innovative schemes for Human Resources Development by way of education, training and other social facilities to the tribals of Orissa in India.

***Keywords** : Karl Pearson's Coefficient of Correlation, Analysis of Variance (ANOVA), Human Development Index (HDI), Socio Economic Development.*

Introduction

Mayurbhanj is located at Northern region of Orissa in India. This study covers the district of Mayurbhanj where the concentration of tribal population is the highest (56.6%) among all the 30 district of Orissa. The district is called Mayurbhanj after the name of the ex-state which on its merger with Orissa in 1st January, 1949 constituted the entire district. According to 2001 census, the district covers an area of 10418 sq. km which constitutes 6.69 percent of the state territory. The total population was 22.34 lakhs that constitutes 6.08 percent of the state's total population. Density of population in the district is 213 per sq. km of area as against 236 at the state level. It is rural based district where the rural population constitutes 93 percent as against state average of 85 percent. Mayurbhanj is said to be a land of tribals. Out of 62 tribal communities of Orissa, 45 communities are found in Mayurbhanj alone. Among the major tribes Santal, Ho, Bhumija, Bhuiyan, Bathudi, Kolho, Munda, Gond, Kharia and Lodha are important. The mountainous and forest in land regions of the district have been considered ideal by the tribal inhabitants for centuries.

Table 20.1 : Details of surveyed villages

Block	GP	Name of village	Total population	ST population	No. of BPL holders	Sl.No. of households surveyed
Shyamakhunta	Godipokhari	Kuchilaghaty	3786	2080	518	1-30
Kuliana	Dumurdiha	Andhari	1462	1268	305	31-50
		Tulasibani	1620	1415	418	51-65
		Jampada	1000	642	230	66-80
	Marangtandi	Bhuyangoda	1082	732	229	81-90
		Marangtandi	960	888	133	91-100
		Jhenei	1216	895	229	101-110
	Baiganabadia	Jaganathpur	214	202	32	111-120
		Balipal	432	147	68	121-130
		Bankasole	335	185	64	131-140
Bangiriposi	Bhuasuni	Purunapani	344	322	90	141-160
		Chakdar	492	480	94	161-180
		Bhuasuni	908	327	188	181-200

***Source:** Panchayat office of all villages.

As per 2001 census Mayurbhanj district has a total population of 22,23,456 number of which rural population has 20,67,756 and Urban population has 1,55,700. Out of total population 12,58,459 belong to ST and 1,70,835 belong to SC and rests belong to other communities. The percentage of ST and SC to total population of the district is 56.6 percent and 7.68 percent respectively. The sex ratio shows a total of 980 female per

1000 males. The Tribal education in Mayurbhanj at present is obstacle by a number of factors like poverty, tribal eco-system, language and distance, etc. (Agarwal, 2001).

Review of Literature

According to "Orissa Human Development Report – 2004", jointly prepared by the Planning Commission, UNDP, State Government and Nabakrishna Choudhury Centre for Development Studies, the Human Development Index (HDI) of the State stands at 0.404 while Kerala tops the chart with 0.638 followed by Punjab 0.537 and Tamil Nadu 0.531. Orissa occupies the fifth place from bottom among 15 major states. The analysis of the states' development is based on three basic parameters – livelihood, health and education. (*The New Indian Express*, 25th March, 2005).

Mayurbhanj is vulnerable to repeated natural calamities like droughts, floods and cyclones. A large number of ST people of Mayurbhanj lack access to growth centers and service centers as they live in remote and hilly areas. Tribal communities residing in hilly terrains of Mayurbhanj are physically excluded, as they demand for connectivity and other infrastructural support. As a result, the poor in general and ST and SC people in particular lack access to growth centers and service centers. Though extensive forest resources are an important source of sustenance to a majority of rural poor especially tribals are highly degraded and lack desired financial and managerial inputs. Optimal exploitation of its vast natural resources demands heavy investment in infrastructural development. However, the State Government's capacity to develop infrastructure is very weak and limited. (Bairathi, 1991).

Objectives of the Study

The main objectives of the chapter is to examine the following:

(*i*) To analyse the present socio-economic conditions of the tribals in the Mayurbhanj district of Orissa in India ;

(*ii*) To assess the various problems faced by the tribals and to suggest suitable measures for solving them;

(*iii*) To examine the Strategic planning such as developing an overall plans and programmes of government machineries and their implementation;

(*iv*) To study the involvement of existing agencies and their support for upliftment of tribals;

(*v*) To identify innovative strategies with regard to the Human Resources Development by way of education, training and other social facilities to the tribals.

Sources of Data

Consistent with the objective of the study different techniques are used for the analysis of the primary data collected by authors from 200 selected respondents of thirteen villages by direct observation and interview of the tribal people according to a well set questionnaire under three blocks of Mayurbhanj District in the year 2008. The secondary data (1998 to 2008) are collected from several published sources such as books, journals, bulletins, reports and publications of Government and Research Institution.

Statistical Methodology

The data analysis is undertaken mostly with the help of several managerial and statistical devices, comparative and experimental methods of analysis are adopted. Various statistical tools like Coefficient Variation, t-test, Correlation coefficient, Regression analysis and Analysis of Variance (ANOVA) are adopted for analysis. Economics-Statistics like Human Development Index (HDI), which is an innovative method, have been used to calculate to know the development rank. Here, for analysis the statistical tools SPSS (Statistical Package for Social Science) software package is used for calculation in order to plot different graphs and charts.(Bajpai).

Empirical Results

The data after collection has been processed and analysed in accordance with the outlined laid down for the purpose. The computerized processing implies editing, coding, classification and tabulation.

Family Size

Family Size of Respondents in the Study Area

Member Size	Percentage(%)
Up to 2	5.0
3 to 4	23.0
5 to 6	40.0
7 to 8	30.0
Above 8	2.0

Land Holding

Land Holding of Respondents in the Study Area

Member Size	Percentage(%)
0 to <1	47.5
1 to <2	16.5
2 to <3	19.5
3 to 4	10.0
> 4	6.5

It reveals that the majority of the respondents have more family members who helps in earning from different sources.

Own Land Cultivated

Own Land cultivated by the Respondents in the Study Area

Size in Acres	Percentage(%)
0 to <1	40.0
1 to <2	24.5
2 to <3	20.0
3 to 4	10.0
> 4	5.5

Main Occupation

Main occupation of Respondents in the Study Area	Percentage (%)
Agriculture	44.5
Collection of MFP	12.5
Daily Labour	25
Business	11.5
Others	6.5

The majority of respondents have cultivated their own land having less than one acre, Hence it is observed that most of the respondents depend on agriculture. Daily labour is the second main occupation and the collection of minor forest produce is the third occupation.

Subsidiary Occupation

Subsidiary occupation of Respondents in the Study Area	Percentage (%)
Agriculture	22
Collection of MFP	28.5
Daily Labour	23.5
Business	19.5
No subsidiary occupation	6.5

Annual Earnings During the Year 1998 & 2008

Annual Earnings during the Year		
Earnings in Rs.	1998 (% of Respondent)	2008 (% of Respondent)
Upto Rs. 5,000	21.5	1.0
Rs. 5,000 to Rs. 10,000	51.0	5.5
Rs. 10,000 to Rs. 15,000	20.0	39.0
Rs. 15,000 to Rs. 20,000	3.0	33.0
Above Rs. 20,000	4.5	21.5

The majority of respondent's subsidiary occupation is from the collection of minor forest products (MFP). The earnings of the respondents has increased due to implementation of several poverty alleviation programmes adopted by the Government during 9th and 10th Plans in the year 2006.

Earning from Agriculture During the Year 1998 to 2008

Earning from Agriculture during the Year in Rs.	% of Respondents	
	1998	2008
Upto Rs. 2,500	53	34
Rs. 2,500 to Rs. 5,000	24.5	16.5
Rs. 5,000 to Rs. 7,500	15	26.5
Rs.7,500 to Rs. 10,000	4	11
Above Rs. 10,000	3.5	12

Earning from MFP (collection of minor forest products)	% of Respondents	
	1998	2008
Upto Rs. 2,500	87	76
Rs. 2,500 to Rs. 5,000	6.5	9
Rs. 5,000 to Rs. 7,500	6	6
Rs. 7,500 to Rs. 10,000	0.5	4
Above Rs. 10,000	0	5

It indicates that the agricultural income of the respondents has increased significantly.

The comparative figure from secondary source of data indicates there is no such difference in earnings from collection of minor forest produce between 1998 and 2008. Only few respondents were able to earn above Rs.10000. It is observed from this the dependency on forest still exists in the study area.

Earning from Wages during the Year 1998 and 2008

Earning from Wages during the Year	% of Respondents	
	1998	2008
Upto Rs. 2,500	66.5	50
Rs. 2,500 to Rs. 5,000	17	8
Rs. 5,000 to Rs. 7,500	13	14.5
Rs. 7,500 to Rs. 10,000	3	9
Above Rs. 10,000	0.5	18.5

Earning from Business during the Year 1998 and 2008

Earning from Wages during the Year	% of Respondents	
	1998	2008
Upto Rs. 2,500	67.0	58.0
Rs. 2,500 to Rs. 5,000	14.0	5.5
Rs. 5,000 to Rs. 7,500	14.0	8.5
Rs. 7,500 to Rs. 10,000	4.0	4.5
Above Rs.10,000	1.0	23.5

The comparative figure shows that there is a increasing trend in earnings from wages due to implementation of NREGS programme by the Government in recent years.

It is also observed that the paying capacity of the respondents has increased due to their increase in income.

Education Status of Children of Respondents

Qualification	% of Respondents
Undermatric	57
Matriculate	25
Graduate	4
Dropout	14

Education Status of Children of Respondents

Qualification	% of Respondents
Dugwell	46.5
Tubewell	53.5

The education status of children of respondents shows that there is a trend up dropout from UP & ME classes.It also observed that the respondents have not to move for distance places to acquire water for drinking, which they had faced earlier. As the supply of safe drinking water is prioritized by

Major Diseases

(Sufferings from a disease by the respondents and their family members)

Major Diseases	
Sufferings from a disease	**% of Respondents**
Malaria	41
Other Diseases	20.5
No-Disease	38.5

Health Centers

(Sufferings from a disease by the respondents and their family members)

Health Centers	
Health Centre Facilities Available	**% of Respondents**
PHC	18.5
CHC	6
Anganwadi Centre	75.5

the government the safe drinking water is available is all the villages under study.

The major diseases table shows that in spite of several precautions are taken by the district malaria office the percentage of sufferings from malaria is not reduced to that extent.More persons are dependant on anganwadi as compared to PHCs and CHCs. So anganwadi workers should be more service oriented and dutiful to provide their reliable service in desired time.

Only few respondents are residing in good sanitary condition. They are aware of insanitation and its causes. But majority of the respondents are residing in poor sanitary condition. They are ignorant about the consequences of poor sanitation and unhygienic condition. The unhealthy practices of personal and environmental hygiene resulting the suffering of the respondents in different diseases which sometimes causes death.

Sanitation	
Awareness of sanitation	**% of Respondents**
Yes	24
No	76

The child mortality table shows that only 6.5 percentage of respondents have faced child mortality and 93.5 percentage of respondents have no child mortality during pregnancy. Hence, the tribal people even if they reside in remote and forest area, they are now aware of different health measures through the anganwadi workers of their locality. (Bakshi and Bala, 1999).

Child Mortality	
Child mortality during pregnancy	**% of Respondents**
Yes	6.5
No	93.5

Use of Medicines

From the preference of medicines at the time of disease by the family members of the respondents, it reveals that 54.5% respondents prefer allopathic medicines, 34% respondents prefer ayurvedic medicines, 7% respondents prefer homeopathic medicines and only 4.5% respondents prefer prayer being upon superstitious during their sufferings from any disease. It also is observed that the tribal people are also stepping towards scientific development as majority preferred to allopathic medicines which is prepared scientifically.

The NREGS table reveals that 30% of the respondents are listed and getting jobs under NREGS. Whereas 70 respondents are not availing the facility of NREGS. This indicates that the respondents are unaware of this new scheme which can give 100 days guaranteed wage to each listed labourer. As the scheme is newly introduced at the time of survey, mass advertise has not been done, so ignorance regarding the scheme has increased the percentage of non-listed wage earners. (Chaku, 2005).

NREGS

(Respondents listed under NREGS)

Respondents listed under NREGS	
Facility of NREGS	**% of Respondents**
Yes	24
No	70
Yes	30

Sources of Borrowings

(Loans availed by the respondents from different sources)

Sources of Borrowing Money	
Borrowing Money	**% of Respondents**
Moneylender	75
Bank	9
Co-operatives	4
LAMP	3
No borrowing	9

The above table shows the sources from which the respondents are borrowing money for their livelihood. It reveals that 75% of respondents are borrowing money from the local money lenders. It also found at the time of survey they expressed due to excessive law imposed by the banks, they preferred to take loan from the money lenders even at high rate of interest. Due to lack of land deeds bank also refused them for sanction of loan. 4% of respondents are availing loan from Co-operatives some are specifically from TRCS for tasar rearing and only 3% of respondents taken loan from LAMPs for agriculture purpose. (Datt 2001).

Benefited from Government Development Programmes

It is found that 85% of the respondents are benefited by different development programmes undertaken by the government through its schemes like IAY, JRY, SGSY, SGRY, PMRY, NREGS and ITDA and DRDA programmes. Only 15% are not availing these facilities due to lack of their awareness and ignorance. As they are very simple and ignorant they are not able to understand the objectives of the programmes which are specifically implemented for them.

Electrification of Houses

Even though all the villages under study are electrified the respondents are not able to get the electric connection due to lack of land records in their own name and lack of funds as well.

Postal Services Availed

Most of the respondents are not availing postal services in their villages due to poor communication .

Facilities availed by the respondents from the LAMPS (Large Area Multi Purpose Cooperative Societies)

It is found that 70% of the respondents have their scope to get the facilities from LAMPs established in their areas. But 30% of the total are not able to get assistance from LAMPs, as no activities of LAMPs are functioning in their area.

Old Age Pension Facility

It is observed that 11.5% family have availed old age pension benefit from the government through their Panchayat. But due to improper selection of beneficiaries at the panchayat level some respondents are debarred to get such benefit.

Benefits availed from Antyodaya Anna Yojana

Under Antyodaya Anna Yojana (AAY) the poorest of the poor families in the State are supplied with 35 kg of rice per family per month at Rs. 3 per kg since September, 2001. It reveals 91 percentage respondents are getting benefits from Antyodaya Anna Yojana and the rest are not availing this benefit as they belong to APL group. Thus this study observed that all BPL families under study are getting subsidized rice as per government norms.

Expenditure incurred in Food and Beverages

It reveals from the study that 12.5% of total respondents spend the major earnings on drink. Generally there people are very poor and totally ignorant about the different development programmes undertaken for their upliftment. They spend the total amount on drinks. The percentage of respondent who spend money on food is 87.5%.

Major Findings

Mayurbhanj is a tribal concentrated district, which is covered with dense forest and hilly areas. It is not possible to contact with the tribals of the remote areas of the district. Co-efficient of variation is used to know the data variation collected from thirteen selected village of the district. The data are primarily collected by direct oral investigation from the respondents through interview with the help of a well set questionnaire.

Mean, Standard Deviation and Coefficient of Variation (C.V.) and t-test of the indicators

Mean

$$\left(\text{or } X = \frac{\sum X_i}{n}\right),$$

Where $\bar{X}$ = The symbol we use for mean

Σ = Symbol for summation,

X_i = Value of the ith item X, $i = 1, 2, \ldots, n$

n = total number of items

Standard deviation

$$*(\sigma) = \sqrt{\frac{\sum f_i (X_1 - \bar{X})^2}{\sum f_i}}$$

where f_i means the frequency of the ith item

Indicators	Mean	S.D.	C.V	t-test
Health (X_1)	1.83	± 0.08	4.53	5.89
Income (X_2)	2.31	± 0.29	12.71	6.43
Education (X_3)	0.59	± 0.20	33.44	7.15
Family Size (X_4)	3.03	± 0.59	19.45	6.29
Socio-Economic Status (X_5)	1.76	± 0.18	10.39	4.67

The collected data are clubbed into five indicators such as Health, Income, Education, Family Size and Socio-economic Status and its consistency and variation are tested by the help of t-test with a tabulated value given in the table at 5% and at 1% level of significance.

Coefficient of variance

$$C.V. = \frac{\sigma}{X} \times 100 .$$

From the above table it is observed that there is a less variation in the data collected in case of indicators like Health (X_1) and Socio-economic Status (X_5) which are 4.53 and 10.39 respectively. It is also found that there is a slight variation in case of Income (X_2) and Family Size (X_4) that is 12.71 and 19.45 respectively. Finally, the indicator Education (X_3) shows more variation that is 33.44 which results a less consistency of the data in the study area.

All the indicators values are tested with t-test at 5% level of significance = 1.782 and for 1% level of significance = 2.681. Since, the t-test values of all the indicators are more than that of 5% and 1% level of significance. So we accept the variation and the level of consistency.

Karl Pearson's Coefficient of Correlation

Correlation in statistics refers to relationship between any two, or more variables. Two variables are said to be correlated if with a change in the value of one variable there arises a change in the value of another variable.

Economic development means sustained and sustainable growth in per capita income, accompanied by diversion of production, reduction of absolute poverty and expanding economic opportunity for all the tribals of the district.

Karl Pearson's Coefficient of Correlation

$$(r) = \frac{N\Sigma XY - \Sigma X.\Sigma Y}{\sqrt{N\Sigma X^2 - (\Sigma X)^2}.\sqrt{N\Sigma Y^2 - (\Sigma Y)^2}}$$

X = given, or reduced values of the first variable

Y = given, or reduced value of the second variable, and

N = number of pairs of observations of X and Y.

The value of 'r' lies between ±1.

Correlation Coefficient ('r' value) between indicators in the study area

Categories	Health (X_1)	Income (X_2)	Education (X_3)	Family Size (X_4)	SES (X_5)
Health (X_1)	1.00				
Income (X_2)	0.41	1.00			
Education (X3)	0.10	0.79	1.00		
Family Size (X4)	0.50	0.87	0.75	1.00	
Socio-Economic Status (X_5)	0.23	0.79	0.80	0.93	1.00

Positive value of 'r' indicates positive correlation between two variables, changes in both the variables take place in same direction, where as negative values of 'r' indicates a negative correlation, i.e. changes in the two variables taking place in opposite direction.

Inferences

There is a strong correlation between family size and socio-economic status as co-efficient of correlation where $r = 0.93$. Also the table reveals that there is a strong and positive correlation between the family size and income which is 0.87. As because the family size is on an average is 6 and the members are able to earn more from different source of income like from agriculture, collection of MFP, wages and business etc. collectively and managed themselves with their combined incomes keeping all the expenditure in a balanced way.

Development of education system means introduction of mass education that is education for all, DPEP, mid-day meal system, Ekalabya Model School with an aim to increase class room enrolments and attendance. In Mayurbhanj Government as well as NGOs are constantly utilizing their resources to uplift the tribals through education and awareness and organizing various cultural programmes. It show a strong between education and socio-economic status in the study area.

For a society, a transition from high incidence of morbidity and mortality to a state where people generally enjoy long-term and disease free lives is desirable. But in the study area the major disease like malaria (41%) child mortality (7%) are marked due to very poor health care facilities. Even though the Government and NGOs try their level best to educate the tribals, their health to education relation is only 0.10, which is a very poor correlation. As they are unable to avail the health facilities in time due to bad communication and transportation, they are affected indirectly, which caused their relation family size to health 0.50 and health to income 0.41. So due to the poor health and income, the social status sometimes dropped abruptly, which shows a weak correlation ($r = 0.23$) between health and social status. (Dubey, 1967).

Multiple Regression

The simple correlation between two variable is sometimes misleading and may be erroneous if there is little or no correlation between the variables other than that brought about by their common dependence upon a third or several variables. Since a combination of variables usually results in a more accurate prediction than two variables, prediction studies often result in a prediction equation referred to as a multiple regression equation.

The hypothesis is tested with available evidence and a decision is made whether to accept this hypothesis or reject it. In the context of hypothesis there are basically two types of errors occur.

We may reject H_0, when H_0 is true (Type-I, error)

We may accept H_0, when H_0 is not true (Type-II, error)

Type-I error means accepting the hypothesis which should have been rejected and denoted by alpha (a)

Type –II error means accepting the hypothesis which should have been rejected and denoted by beta (b).

Below table describes the main regression results. It shows the effect of the indicators adopted for the study.

The specification and justification of variables included in the analysis are used as

$$Y = f\,(X_1\ X_2\ X_3\ X_4\ X_5)$$

Where Y = Dependent variables, X_i = Independent variables,

C_i = Constant, X_1 = Health

X_2 = Income, X_3 = Education

X_4 = Family Size, X_5 = Socio-economic status

The form of equation fitted for production is given below linear model

$$Y = C_0 + C_1X_1 + C_2X_2 + C_3X_3 + C_4X_4 + C_5X_5$$

Regression results - Effect of indicators in case of development in the study area

(*i*) Dependent Variable – All Development

Coefficients

Indicators	Standardized Coefficients	t-statistic
	Beta	
X_1	.238	9444.624
X_2	.235	5184.304
X_3	.247	6158.273
X_4	.236	5356.842
X_5	.259	7361.506

Inferences

In the present observation more than two independent variables (Health, Income, Education, Family Size and Socio-economic Status) are studied against each other with respect to dependent variable (All Development). (Jhingan 2006).

For that multiple regression with T-Statistics is implemented.

Null Hypothesis H_0 :- Standard health services is worst even though there is a proper education environment and awareness created by Government and NGOs, with an average family size which results with a satisfactory income in group or family as a whole results a developed socio-economic status.

H_1 :- There is a good health facility availed by all the family members, as all the family members are educated with the help of Government and NGOs, their income increases significantly.

Even though they have good income, due to lack of communication, transportation and other socio-economic factors, their socio-economic status does not contribute much to the all development in the study area.

The calculated value of the co-efficient b of variables in the multiple regression is either perverse or insignificantly different from Zero. The value is tested with respect to the t-statistics and is found that the socio-economic status ($\beta = 0.259$) have more impact on the overall development is the study area.

So finally it is observed that the indicator socio-economic status has significant contribution towards the development in the study area, which accepts the hypothesis H_0.

Analysis of Variance (Anova)

In the present study two way ANOVA Technique is used i.e. data are divided into both columns and rows to study the effect. The dependent variable 'All Development' is assumed and classified on the basis of the independent variable indicators Health, Income, Education, Family-Size and Socio-economic Status, in order to determine which one of the above indicator is more effective on 'All Development' of the tribals of the Mayurbhanj district.

Analysis of Variance (ANOVA) for the indicators in the study area

Source of variation	Sum of Square	Degree of Freedom	Mean Square	F-statistic (Calculated)	Table value of F	
					5% level	1% level
Between Row	4.0200	12	0.3350	8.3750	3.2592	5.4119
Between Column	0.2704	4	0.0676	1.6913		
Residual (error)	1.9182	48	0.0400			
Total	6.2086	64	0.0970			

It is important to understand the principles and techniques of analysis of variance (ANOVA) to test the hypothesis by calculating F-statistics. It involves the computation of F-ratio.

F-statistic is computed as

$$F = \frac{\text{Mean sum of square of explained sum square}}{\text{Mean sum of square of residual sum square}}$$

Inferences

From the ANOVA table it is found that in between row and column, the row indicator is significant. The calculated value of between the row is 8.3750.

The calculated 'F' Ratio value is higher than the table value of 'F' values, both at 1% and 5% level of significance. So it is concluded that from the row indicators the socio-economic status has more significant contribution towards the 'All Development' of the tribals of study area (Khare 1991).

Human Development Index

Human Development Report (HDR) broadly focuses on the overall human well being. According to UNDP's HDR 2001, India placed 115th rank among the 162 countries. The report also examined the progress made by developing countries towards targets set in the UN Millennium Declaration goals for poverty eradication. The report notes that around one-third of people in developing countries continue to live in 'income poverty'

Since human development includes several factors contributing towards human welfare, measuring human welfare poses a great problem. The most recent endeavour in this line of approach is the Human Development Index (HDI) as formulated by UNDP to measure relative deprivation in overall perspectives (UNDP, 1990). Among many indicators to measure relative deprivation, five indicators like health, income, education, family size and socio-economic status of the respondents of thirteen villages of Mayurbhanj District under survey are brought into focus.

$$\text{HDI} = \frac{(X_1 - X_{min})}{X_{max} - X_{min}}$$

Where X_i refers to each variable for the ith village X_{min} to the lowest value of the variable and X_{max} the highest value.

We have worked out a physical quality of life index using indicators like Health (X_1), Income (X_2), Education (X_3), Family Size (X_4) and Socio-

Economic Status (X_5). It shows the distance of the concerned village from the most developed village with a view to measuring its backwardness in regard to each one of the variables, besides working out a simple composite index.

The deprivation with regard to the five indicators for each village are next indexed in a scale. By construction the scale ranges from the minimum value of 'zero', in case of minimum deprivation to the maximum value of 'one' in case of maximum deprivation for these indicators and the human development index is calculated as per the formula given in the methodology. The thirteen villages of Mayurbhanj District are ranked in a descending manner as per their indicator on the basis of the overall measure of backwardness. The calculated index is given in the following table.

Human Development Index of the villages in the study area

Vill_ code	Health (X_1)	Income (X_2)	Education (X_3)	Family Size (X_4)	SES (X_5)	All Develop-ment	HDI Rank
3	0.8295	1.0000	0.9465	1.0000	0.4991	0.8550	1
8	0.7209	0.7803	0.8036	0.8276	1.0000	0.8265	2
4	0.2403	0.9306	1.0000	0.6897	0.9480	0.7617	3
5	0.4419	0.8324	0.9375	0.7759	0.8073	0.7590	4
6	1.0000	0.5896	0.8840	0.5690	0.5076	0.7100	5
2	0.5581	0.5636	0.8974	0.8017	0.5775	0.6797	6
12	0.8140	0.5289	0.3080	0.7241	0.2294	0.5209	7
7	0.5817	0.5029	0.4822	0.4655	0.3853	0.4835	8
9	0.3023	0.6069	0.6935	0.3103	0.3431	0.4512	9
1	0.1783	0.4046	0.4822	0.3966	0.0000	0.2923	10
13	0.0000	0.1040	0.5739	0.2586	0.2584	0.2390	11
11	0.7209	0.2254	0.0000	0.1034	0.0734	0.2246	12
10	0.1628	0.0000	0.2143	0.0000	0.0000	0.0754	13

Inferences

The human development index of thirteen villages of three blocks against five indicators i.e. Health, Income, Education, Family Size and Social Development of Mayurbhanj District are studied and found with the following observations. The index is ranked in descending order with respect to the column 'All Development' index and the villages are ranked from 1 to 13 accordingly. As far as HDI is concerned Tulasibani village is ranked one where as Bankasole village is ranked thirteen, both the villages are under Kuliana block. This indicates the physical quality of life of tribals of Tulasibani village is best among the 13 villages surveyed and the physical quality of life of tribals of Bankasole is worst. Similarly in case of health index, Marangtandi village ranked one, which indicates the tribals of that village are more cautious regarding health and hazards. But tribals of Bhuasuni village are more prone to disease like Malaria and ranked last as it comes under forest area of Bangiriposi block.

Tulasibani village is also indexed top as regards income and family size of the respondents. It is because out of 20 respondents, surveyed in that village, four are well placed as government servant and coming under APL group. Statistical table shows that most of them are literate and aware of birth control. Hence, their family size is also small. But the income and family size of respondents of Bankasole village is very precarious, the respondents are mostly landless and are marginal labourers. Their income is also very poor due to their ill health. The respondent and their family members are illiterate, even though the scope of education facility is nearer to them, they are unable to avail such facility due to their acute poverty. As they are illiterate and unaware of the birth control, their family size is big which again drug them to poverty.

The HDI rank of education status of the children of the household of Jampada village is highest. It is possible due to the said village is sorrunded with UP, ME, High School and one college. But as Purunapani village is situated in forest area of Bangiriposi Block, the education status of the children of that village is very poor. There is more dropout and children are generally prepared to collect minor forest produce instead of going to school.The socio-economic index of the respondents of Jagannathpur is highest as compared to Bankasole village, which is lowest so far as HDI is concerned (Mohapatra, 1987).

Summary and conclusions

The scheduled tribe population continues to have nearly double the incidence of poverty compared to the non-tribals of Mayurbhanj district of Orissa in India. The incidence of poverty is more in northern and southern regions of Orissa compared to the coastal region.The growth rate of tribal population in Mayurbhanj district during the year 1998 was 10.30 percent, which increased to 17.98 percent during 2008. The per capita income of Orissa is very low. Agriculture under Primary sector continues to be the mainstay of the rural economy (Padhi, 2000).

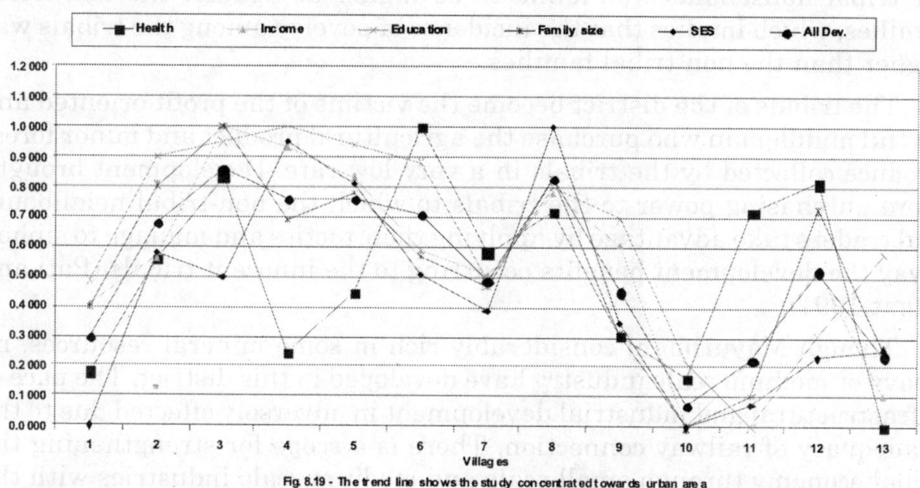

Fig. 20.1 : The trend line shows the study concentrated towards urban area

The literacy rate of the district has been a steady improvement. So, there is an improvement in literacy rate, which can help in reducing the poverty among masses.

The health picture of the district is far from the satisfactory. Further, while naturally female life expectancy should be more than male life expectancy it is the opposite case in Orissa. Pointing towards discriminatory practices against both the girl's child and women, leading to higher mortality then nature would otherwise determine.

The tribals in the district depend mostly on collection of forest produce for their livelihood. Pisciculture has not been developed to a considerable extent for want of suitable fishery resources as most of the areas of the district are having lateriate soil and full of hill locks.

The child labour is a major obstacle in the path of educational development in the district. Cattle and goat rearing and agricultural work are the main activities of child labourers, whereas household work is done mainly by the girls and partly by term as maidservant. Most of the primary school of the district do not have the basic facilities like drinking water and sanitation, play ground, science equipments etc. The economically worse off tribal parents need the assistance of their children who contribute their share towards the family income.

The estimates of average expenditure on various commodities spend by non-tribal families are higher proportion of income on consumption in comparison to tribal families. The largest item of expenditure was on food for both tribal and non-tribal BPL families. The Income/poverty gap ratio for tribal households was found to be higher as against the non-tribal families, which implies that the incidence of poverty among the tribals was higher than the non-tribal families.

The tribals of the district become the victims of the profit oriented and tactful middleman who purchase the agricultural product and minor forest produce collected by the tribals in a very low rate. Development brought more purchasing power to the tribals to which the non-tribal neighbours and traders take advantage by applying their tactics and manage to siphon away the development benefits occurring to the innocent tribals (Pati and Jagat,1991).

Though Mayurbhanj considerably rich in some mineral resources, no heavy or medium scale industry have developed in this district. The pace of infrastructural and industrial development in adversely effected due to the inadequacy of railway connection. There is a scope for strengthening the tribal economy through small scale and medium scale industries with the optimal utilization of sabai grass, sal leaves, silk cocoons and various other forest products, which are plentily, available in this area.

The development personal cannot have a through idea about the socio-economic status of the tribal because of lack of knowledge. They have the conception that the tribal societies are ideal community practicing some sort of primitive communism. As a result there is a growing development in the well to do families who win the confidence of development agents and the needy poor remains in dark making a wide gap between the two. In some cases the poor fellow tribals of the district are exploited. The negligence and failure for the upliftment of the tribals have given rise to the Maoist activities in the in the Similipal area who have become a constant threat to the civilization.

The foregoing analysis reveals that the tribals of Mayurbhanj district of Orissa in India confront some major problems like poverty, illiteracy, unemployment, alienation, displacement, malnutrition, disease etc. The Central Government and State Government are putting sincere efforts to uplift the economic condition of the tribals through different ITDAs of the district under TSP approach and through DRDA of the district by implementing different anti-poverty schemes. Despite the fact, the tribal people in the district remain backward socially and economically.

Suggestions

1. As the tribals of the district have land problems minimum 2 acres of land should be distributed to landless or marginal tribals on priority basis to increase the agriculture income of the district as well as to reduce the dependency on forest by the tribals.

2. The district has possessed plenty of mineral resources and a good number of tribal labour forces. So steps may be taken by the government to include the district under SEZ.
3. More incentives should be given to SHGs especially to tribal women SHGs to undertake more income generating occupations.
4. To fulfill the object of 'Vision 2020', steps should be taken to educate all the children of the district above 7 years whole-heartedly by the local educationist, politicians, NGOs and government through awareness.

REFERENCES

Agarwal, A.N., *Indian Economy - Problems of Development and Planning*, Wishwa Prakashan, New Delhi, 2001.

Bairathi, Shashi, *Tribal Culture, Economy and Health*, Rawat Publications, Jaipur & New Delhi, 1991.

Bajpai, S.R., *Methods of Social Survey and Research.*

Bakshi, S.R. & Bala Kiran, *Development of Women, Children and Weaker Sections*, Deep & Deep Publications Pvt. Ltd., New Delhi, 1999.

Chaku Pariaram M., *Tribal Communities & Social Change*, Sage Publications, New Delhi, 2005.

Datt, Tara (Dr.), *Tribal Development in India (With special reference to Orissa),* Gyan Publishing House, New Delhi, 2001.

Dubey, S.C., *India's Changing Villages: Deals with Human Factors in Community Development*, Allied Publisher, Bombay, 1967.

Gedam, Ratnakar, *Poverty in India (Myth and Reality, Definition and Identification, Critical Evaluation*), Deep & Deep Publications Pvt. Ltd., New Delhi, 1998.

Gupta, V.S., *Communication Development and Civil Society*, Concept Publishing Company, New Delhi, 2004.

Jain, P.C., *Planned Development among Tribals*, Rawat Publications, Jaipur & New Delhi, 1999.

Jhingan, M.L., *The Economic of Development and Planning*, Vrinda Publications P Ltd., 2006.

Joshi, Vidyut, Tribals Situation in India- Issues in Development, Rawat Publication, Jaipur & New Delhi, 1998.

Khare, P.K., *Social Change of Indian Tribes (Impact of Planning and Economic Development*), Deep & Deep Publications Pvt. Ltd., New Delhi, 1991.

Lakra, Paulamuni, *Tribal India-Communities, Castes and Culture*, Dominant Publishers, New Delhi, 2000.

Mahalingam, S., *Tribal Cooperative System*, Rawat Publications, Jaipur & New Delhi, 1992.

Mohapatra, Prafulla Chandra, *Economic Development of Tribal India*, Ashish Publishing House, New Delhi, 1987.

Mohapatra, Sitakant, *Modernization and Ritual Identity and Change in Santhal Society*, Oxford University Press, Calcutta, 1986.

Padhi, Kishore.C., *The Challenges of Tribal Development*, Swarup & Sons, New Delhi, 2000.

Panigrahi, P.K., *Political Elite in Tribal Society*, Commonwealth Publications, 1998.

Pati R.N. & Jagat Dev Lalitendu, *Tribal Demography in India*, Ashish Publishing House, New Delhi, 1991.

Role of Job Re Design in Enhancing Job Satisfaction and Productivity

— Prof. C. K. Roy

When the job of a person in an organization is of repetition nature, the person who is engaged works will for the beginning of the time period. Due to monotonous nature of his job he starts getting frustrated. This happens because these is no change factor in his job which he has to perform daily. One of the great poet 'Kiets' says "variety is the spice of life" and this means change. In other words the job satisfaction is available when these is variety in his job or we may say that lack of variety results in to job monotony or job dissatisfaction. Frustration with the job is not .... to the Indian corporates only rather it is more common elsewhere and is a global phenomenon. To exactly understand the frustration from the job, a few illustrations shall be of good value which shall help in explaining and understanding this problem which is expending widely.

One old strong to illustrate the meaning of monotony leading to frustration is being narrated as a suitable case study:

In a kingdom (estate), one hawker used to visit the palace-estate of the king where several family used to live inside the fort like a township. The hawker was selling fish. On the gate the guard was not allowing him to enter in the palace township easily and he used to allow him after getting one coin only. This act was followed by the guard service past several months. One day the king was standing on his palace corridor and observed this act of guard and notice the event. The king called the mantri (minister) and asks him about the decision to be taken to curb this act. The king's minister takes a decision that the guard should be posted near the river ganges and asked to count waves of ganges only. The king agrees to this decision. This punishment had a big meaning about the characteristics the job change used for punishing the guard and the major factors under this were that the job was highly monotonous in nature which creates quick frustration in the person. Counting the river wave through out the while day and recording it daily expresses the monotony evolved in this job. Reverse to this punishment is the conversion of monotony in to non monotonous work and this means variety of job and room to add values in a person in terms of knowledge base and an increase in the future status and which he is expected to earn, means creating a money power. Also the changes and varieties allows you to progress and more importantly growth with social approval. It generates self esteem and self actualization in a person. To show such problems proper job design and job redesigns are necessary tools which shall helps in enhancing job satisfaction.

The second case is of a bank clerk who is working on a cash counter. If you observe what a cashier does in a bank for the entire day. He sit in a steel netted (cell) termed as cubical which is locked from inside. His job is to receive checks and issue the currency after counting them and posting in the ledger. The daily routine follows. Can you imagine the monotony evolved in a banks' cashier working on a cash counter. It becomes a most monotonous job sitting alone in a steel netted cubical having no variety in work and that too alone like a cell in a jail. There is no room to learn or grow in terms of knowledge. This is the reason that these cashiers are compensated for this monotony by extra wages/salary in the term of cash handling allowance. Also, the bank employees treat the cash handling job of the bank of a lowest category and due to this monotonous nature, the cashier jobs are rotated.

The third case is an example of general post office (GPO) of a big town where there are many counters to sell postal stamps. Earlier days, from one counter all types of postal stamps such as post cards, inland letters, envelops and stamps were dispensed but today due to increase in volume of work and population several counters have been opened where only one type of material will be available at on counter and it is either only postcard or inlands or stamps etc. All the counter clerks are also supplied with a ready recorder for computations. The result is that the employee has no variety in his job, even no different materials to handle or no different calculation to perform, for calculation it is ready reorder and even there is no occasion or opportunity to create an argument with the customer over the calculation for payment. It is so simple, there, can you imagine the level of monotony and expected level of frustration.

The simpler and monotonous jobs do not provide an opportunity to add knowledge to the activities being performed. The simplified approach provides fast and easy to understand the took to be performed but at a long term it becomes non productive. The workers who have monotonous work due to its monotony get retarded in their performance. Also due to non addition of knowledge base, the growth aspects is negligible and the future carriers graph is blocked. The person does not grow with the organization. The ultimately loses his interest in the work and growth is curbed. The suitable examples are gate keepers or guards of a company who sits on the gate and carries out his routine work for the entire day and earns of fixed monthly income – his growth in the sense of knowledge, role play and earnings is limited. In the same company, if a person enters as a helper to a skilled worker, he gradually learns how to operate the machine, how to lubricate and maintain it and ultimately he becomes an skilled operator. During the process he broadens his knowledge base, he is a fully satisfied person due to variety in his job, changes in knowledge base and a better carrier path in his future.

The Human Resource Experts of the opinion that:

One of the reasons for strikes and rough industrial relation in the job frustration which is caused due to job dissatisfaction in a worker. This is because there is no challenge in the job and such person can not get job else where due to its monotony and poor skill level. The only alternatives left is demand for higher wages and is the only symptom in the cause of dissatisfaction. In other words we may say that the demand in enhancement of pay is a compensation for the lack of challenge in the job or in a simpler way it is an allowance for monotony.

Bipolarization of job and job redesign:

To tackle the problem of job satisfaction the job knowledge enrichment because important. There, under advance technological achievements, a shadow affect is an automatic creation of "bi-polarization" which is nothing but de-skilling some of the lower level jobs and increasing the skill requirements at higher levels of job. To provide a satisfaction at all level of jobs the periodic job redesign based on ability of the work force, their knowledge base and their training needs is the solution to the problems. A suitable example shall be the steps taken by banks in the process or time mechanization using information technology (computes and net working) where the skill of bottom level uses diluted due to mechanization but at the same time due to automation and machine based calculation the clerks were trained using bank-master software where the skill was up graded at higher levels. The time used in physical writing and checking of ledgers was utilized for other analytical and decision-making process. Initially, these was resistance from the trade union and by providing a mechanization allowance the matter was sorted out. Today the bank staffs are fully satisfied and their growth is also faster. The time saved is used for marketing and other services.

Usually job redesigns are of three types. Which are:

1. Enrichment of job.
2. Enlargement of job.
3. Rotation of job.

Enrichment of Job

The job enrichment in creases the proportion of job "satisfiers" related to a particular job a person is performing. Here is will be important to understand the job 'satisfiers' which are relevant factors contributing towards job satisfaction in a human being. The major job satisfiers based on Herzberg's motivators:

(*i*) Achievement.
(*ii*) Recognition.
(*iii*) Work itself.
(*iv*) Responsibility.
(*v*) Advancement.
(*vi*) Growth.

Achievement

A person who is performing a job must feel that by performing the task he handled these is an achievement for him and for the society. The achievements are in the terms of values and social achievements. Example – if a worker is contributing in producing a "Jaipur" foot which is an artificial foot for disabled of new design his achievement level shall be high for self because he has contributed for creating something new and here the social achievement mattes more than money. The satisfaction level is high.

Recognition

The performer needs credit when due and this credit giving is nothing but his recognition. In a rural artisan work if the artist who is performing some artistic work is awarded by the Government of India or some recognized Society or Organization he feels esteemed and here, his recognition plays a more added role than even job. Apart from money he earns his recognition boosts his eggo of performance and he turns to be a better performer for the future to came. For a job satisfaction the recognition helps in building a better performance in to the performer. Similarly in the military organization 'medals' on the recognition of bravery and this alone adds to the motivational values more than the cash benefits, no doubt at a longer term the up gradation or promotion brings same monetary benefit too.

Work itself

Work itself is the mental positioning of a worker where he performs happily and takes his own decision in performing better jobs. The job is not imposed on him rather he happily accepts the challenges of the day. This type of approach is only available in a fully motivated person. Such persons are dedicated persons towards their job.

Responsibility

The workers perform the work in two ways. Firstly, they accept the job for a job shake means earning their wages without taking any responsibility towards the job, which means performing in a casual manner with little responsibility. Secondly, the loyal worker performs his job from the core of his heart and sole and do so he takes the full responsibility. In other words he proves to be a responsible person for the job he is performing. A responsible person performs better and his quality of work improves daily and is always better than yesterday. In his work rejections are also less. The responsible person are more co operative, dedicated and suggest for better way of doing the same job. Usually he accepts the responsibility, even without delegating it.

Advancement

It relates to growth of a person or employee and this means his future placement related to responsibility, authority and monitory gains. A human being is a social animal and he always desires to look different than others which is only possible by way of his advancement. There are persons who joined a n organization in a clerical cadre and retired as chief, one of the burring example is the case of Mr. Ram Rakha who joined the SBI, Calcutta circle as a clerk cum godown keeper and retired as Secretary and Treasurer of the SBI Bengal circle and this post is redesigned today as Chief General Manager, who is head of a circle. This advancement was a result of his dedication, added educational achievement, hard work and sincerity. For advancement are has to adopt following characteristics:

(*a*) Increase your knowledge base on continuing basis

(*b*) Learn the task of proper management

(*c*) Improve your productivity by providing quality work and timely performances

(*d*) Hard work

(*e*) An excellent relationship with juniors, colleagues and seniors – move smoothly with others

(*f*) Adopt ethical practices

(*g*) Core for institutions mission and vision

For advancement learning variety of tasks given is another important factor which helps in speedier growth of carrier. Here in other words it is the job redesign or changing job to adopt job redesign or broader job span which creates an environment which pushes you up and up with a higher speed of growth or advancement leading to job satisfaction and eagerness to take up new challenges.

Growth

Growth of a person is co related to advancement. For total satisfaction the growth should be in multiple directions. For all dimensional growth following characteristic prevails in a person.

(a) Spreading the knowledge base.

(b) Keep up with time.

(c) Organizational inter relation and be fitting in to the organizational structure.

(d) An excellent human factor.

(e) An unique way of performing a job – different then others.

(f) Maintaining quality of the work.

(g) An extra ordinary dedication to the work and the organization as a whole.

Thus the responsibility level which is self controlled and steered result in to utilize the continued learning opportunities which helps in achieving a good growth level. The job challenge level could be increased thus enriching it of course employees should be capable of handling these higher level demands of the enriched job for which they have to enhance their experience, knowledge base and dedication to the organization which is only possible if the job-redesigns are happily provided and accepted by them.

A suitable example shall be, if a technician in a large industry is performing a simple maintenance job involving welding, soldering, drilling and assembling etc under the supervision of a junior engineer who is his supervisor, the technicians job can be enriched by de designing his job by the way of giving him an independent charge of maintenance, may be partially in the initial stage as these technicians are diploma holders in engineering and if their carrier path is not elevated they may leave the organization. Such qualified technicians and supervisor s deserve such privileges but is only possible if by job-redesigning their skill and responsibilities are enhanced. Such a decision making may need some short term management orientation or management appreciation training.

One job enrichment leads to another at a higher level and it is a continuous process. The entire chain of management gets activated and galvanized. In the above example, if the technicians job is enriched the junior engineer shall also be elevated. Some times, where there is a gap in the middle rank caused due to labour fluctuation, it is filled by junior level without replacement and only successful through job redesign, training and enrichment process.

Jot Enlargement

Sometimes, it is not possible to enrich the jobs. Instead the management may think of enlarging the job by increasing the variety of tasks in a job. These jobs do not differ widely in their level of responsibility. This phenomenon is termed as job enlargement.

A suitable example shall be – if a wireman and lineman are doing indoor and outdoor jobs related to electricity requiring similar knowledge base of an electrician, there is an opportunity to club there jobs and enlarge the base. This will also help in putting the responsibility on a single person.

Job enlargement is gaining much support, mainly the pull type of production management adopted by Japan using CANBAN system is nothing but job enlargement. At a particular production level keep all facilities and the workers are trained to operate all facilities. When the job comes a single man performs all operation and his job is widely enlarged. In other words organizations are carrying for variety of jobs to be performed by a single man. This is nothing but job redesign with job enlargement. This provides maximum satisfaction to the worker and completely illuminates the monotony. Most of the automobile industries in Japan are adopting this process of job enlargement. The enlargement process tries to make the job as "Complete" as possible. In this situation, the worker here gets variety as well as he becomes responsible for the complete job. Though the skills, knowledge and decision making level have not gone through major changes, the identification of the worker with his product is more complete raising his level of achievement which is the Herzberg's satisfier rules. This also provides a feeling of having more control over his job. He becomes a responsible person and feels his stronger presence in the organization than before.

Today, in most of large organizations the master desires that one man should perform variety of job may be at a higher cost and since he replaces two to three persons this becomes more advantages for the organizations. After mechanization of offices due to use of IT one clerk can post accounts, write letters and keep other records (data base) for the management. One stores man can perform the supervision of stores, materials and finished goods using computerized inventory system. He also maintains the records and data base including re ordering from vendors.

Today, job enlargement is gaining much relevance in the manufacture of automobiles mainly in assembling line. The enlargement process leads to make the job as "complete" and provides a greater level of satisfaction as the worker working is in a position to say that this complete work is mine and he becomes a part of being and not only doing. Also due to one man's complete job the quality is improved and accountability and responsibilities are enhanced to a greater level. Though the basic knowledge, skill and decision making level has not changed, the identification of the worker with his product is more complete raising his level of (Herzbeng's) motivation and satisfaction in the form of higher achievement and satisfaction.

The help in building a higher "satisfier" and provides the worker a feeling of having more control over his job. The job re design method produces a higher motivated person (worker) resulting in to better quality of product (less rejections) and higher productivity as well. The job re design also leads to lesser supervision and lesser movement of men and materials. How ever, there shall be added cost on training for skill enhancement which is quite small compared to the long range benefits or gains.

Job Rotation

Performing similar nature of job every day creates a monitory and the job rotation helps in minimizing such monotony. Under job rotation system at a periodic interval the workmen are assigned at a job of variable nature at the similar levels. For example a person in bank handling savings bank account may be rotated for current account job where the customer base and accounting system changes and result in to a changed job or product. Similarly a machine operator may be rotated to perform the maintenance job. These are situations where job enlargement may not be possible due to physical hurdles the variety in nature of job is brought through a well thought periodic rotation of job. Since there are changes in nature and magnitude of job, the monotony is reduced and the job rotation results in to job re design. Where one activity is replaced by another activity the workers understand the difficulties and problems of each job which is only possible by job rotation.

A Typical Case Study

From a village two young children Ram and Shyam who were of the same age group and friends traveled together to get a job. They met a *Jamindar* who employed both of them. Ram was assigned the job of cow boy to carry a cow for grazing in a forest and Shyam was assigned the job of irrigating a small piece of land using a well water located inside the land. Both started their work. Ram's cow was undisciplined and used to run like a horse in the treed and it was not easier to control it. The entire day Rama used to get completely tired. The Shyam tasks was irrigation of small land but the entire day he used to lift water from well, still the land remained dry. The Jamindar had made a hole in the land connecting his larger farm house. After s[pending a few days both Ram and Shyam started describing their activities to each other with an intention to enter change the job (job rotation). How they narrated their job profile was as under:

Rams says that his cow which he accompanies for grazing is very gentle and when she grazes he sleeps all the day beneath a tree shadow. He describes the extreme comfort level of job which was with an intention to change it with irrigational activity which Shyam was performing. Now Shyam narrates his role. He says that land size is so small that he is able to irrigate within two hours and all the time he remains sleeping and enjoys the life. Again here the intention was a job change. Both of them exchanged the job and after a few days they could realize the difficulties of each and jointly they left the job of *jamindar* who was unethically using them.

Job Re design leads to human resource development:

A re-design in job means changes for a workman. Usually in India the employees resist to any changes which can be won over by continued training input and preparing the employees and staff to meet the challenges of change gladly. For this an affective communication and transparency between the employees and the management of the corporate helps in achieving the objective of acceptance of job redesign. One of the most positive approach is the participation of employees or workers in the redesigning schemes. Human resource needs an intelligent approach to take care of the employees in which the role of management as whole and related manager in particular plays an important role. The manger develops it and the past human 'potential' is easily turned in to a real strength today. Job re design is not just a jugglery of different tasks or jobs. It has to be a commitment on the part of management towards continuous development of the human potential to meet the never challenges created by research and development of process, designs and human skill etc.

An effective job redesign is possible through enhancement in the quality of employee and his motivational factors. Following approach may lead to a better result:

1. Training of workers/employee.
2. Enhancing his wages in relation to new job challenges.
3. Promotion at higher level – a position of higher responsibility.
4. Motivational training for being with the organization than doing.
5. Adoption of newer technology which leads to better comfort to the employee and a higher productivity.
6. Always follow "positive approach".

The detailed discussion follows:

Training

When the job redesign is decided, the present worker with little orientation picks up the new process easily and fills honoured. Suppose a new machine is introduced which needs some training. The worker is told that you are the right person to take this responsibility and it is an opportunity for you for which the company shall send you for training in the suppliers original plant. Training in the suppliers original plant. This change shall motivate the operator. The training helps in easy acceptability of job redesign. Talk the example of "SUKOI" fighters introduced in Indian Air Force for which training was provided to Indian Air Force Pilots and maintenance engineers at Rusia. This was an exact case of job re design and the pilots who were selected felt proved of it by way of piloting the latest defense fighter plane. Similar impressions are to be given where ever there is a job re-design whether small or large.

Better Wages Promotion

Once the job re design is offered to a worker on employee, the productivity increased due to newer job. Some of the employees agree to accept newer job along with their existing job profile. Since the job re design is going to improve the productivity and profitability of the corporate same proportionate enhancement in wages brings happiness in the workmen.

Also if the job redesign is a big changes and an extensive training is imported, under job evaluation the status of the employee if elevated, results into an excellent satisfaction.

Motivation

Usually, under present circumstances, there are very few emplcyees who are fully satisfied and they just 'do' their job. In IT segment the job hopping was quite frequent and common. The engineers or software developers . . . package in terms of money (package) and they used to 'do' the job and by the time they become a 'being' person to the organization, he hopes to another organization. Here being means belonging to the organization and he is always a motivated person and he can not think of snap[ping the ties easily if he is a 'being' person. A being person always carriers out his day's job for eight hours with total dedication and happiness where as a 'doing' person carries out his work for shake of work and wages. When a 'doing' person leaves the job he hardly repents but when a 'being' person leaves his job or even he superannuates he has affection for the organization and there are tears in his eyes. It has been observed that 'job re design' a 'doing' person can easily be changed to a 'being' person for the organization.

Adoption of Newer Process - Technology

A newer technology enhances the productivity of a company but at the same time it provides a better comfort and working condition for the workmen. This 'comfort factor' enhances the quick and easy acceptance of job redesign. A suitable example shall be introduction of computes in mechanization of banking and insurance sector. The mechanization provided comfort and quality in banking sector along with the efficiency. The type writers turned to be a history and show pieces.

Positive Approach

To adopt job re design the management must have a positive approach which is nothing but to achieve something better. The job redesign must give same positive results in terms of productivity, quality, job efficiency, operator comforts and over all operational satisfaction to employer and the management, otherwise it is an useless exercise.

Case Study

One of employee Mr. Jaidev Shato joined the SBI as Hindi Typist in the category of clerk cum typist. He used to type matters in Hindi and English both languages. After six months of his joining he got conformed in his job and become a permanent employee of SBI. After his confirmation he refused the typing of English based letters and drafts telling that he has been appointed as Hindi typist. The Boss was Assistant General Manager, Mr ARLAL and he had meeting with the author and proposes me that since Mr. Saha has refused to type English typing or record – data entry etc. Also the number of Hindi letters were very few, and his manners and productivity was poor, he should be transferred. I was in the capacity of chief Manager and after going through the talks of Mr. Lal, I told him that Mr Saha shall turn productive within ten days and he may prove to be an excellent and outstanding, personnel of the Bank. He provided me this opportunity to mend him with authority to act freely.

Next day, I called Mr Saha in my chamber and had detailed talk about his family and self, From the talk it appeared that Mr Saha was an artist, t he was suffering from stomach disorder and sleeplessness. All his family embers were at Calcutta and one of his sister was in Mumbai. He was feeling loneliness and shielded him self from the society. He appeared to be in depression. After well defining and understanding his social, personnel and skill requirement. I took the challenge of correcting him.

I suggested him to print some artistic figures on tassor cloth locally available which I arranged from cut piece stocks. Also from same cloth merchants I arranged fabric painting work on sarees. He got a job to partially satisfy his hidden artistes ego. Second step I took was his health problem for which I suggested ayurvedic medicines which he took and started improving. After meeting his social needs, I took up the office work which was typing and data / file maintenance. I narrated him the carrier path of Mr Ram Rakha of Calcutta who joined the SBI as on godown keeper and retired as Secretary and Treasurer of one of the local head offices (Calcutta). Also I designed his carrier path. The next step was his job- redesigning and provide a different look to him about his job. Actually what happened that one new computer was being installed in the AC Chamber of Asstt. General Manager, Mr. Lal and could educate Saha to accept this job which was actually a job re design. I put before him the advantages of this approach (Computer Operation) which were:

(a) One of a few persons who shall work on computer aided typing and data entry
(b) Shall live in an AC atmosphere
(c) Shall be close to Boss Mr. Lal
(d) Based on an excellent performance – a chance to be posted at Mumbai Central Office where he will line with his sister may get a chance to show his artist carrier a better path.

The resultant effect was that within a week Mr Saha started working and through out the whole day he was now a very busy person and fall all files and typing work he was personal secretary to the Boss. His health and habits improved to a level that he transferred himself from a 'doing' person to a 'being person' for the organization. Mr. Lal was surprised to see this achievement which was a result of motivation and job redesign.

Later on just after about nine months Mr. Lal was elevated and posted at Mumbai Central Office of SBI where he also got Mr. Saha posted there. Mr. Saha started working at Central Office and he became a key person in the personnel department of SBI. Today I don't know his exact posting but he must be at a reasonably good position. At Mumbai he acted in a few TV serials. His eggo was fully satisfied and it was the result of "Job redesign" and motivation which brought such a tremendous changes. On well painting painted by Mr Jaider is changing in my drawing room well – which always reminds me about this success story of a "Job redesigning" and job re defining.

Conclusion

The 'job redesing' is an approach which reduces monotony in the worker's mind and creates a change in his work situation. It may be adopted by job rotation, job enrichment and job enlargement. Today under fast industrialization and growth in the service sector, the job satisfaction is only possible through one of the best process which is job redesign which reduces job monotony and leads to a higher productivity. By performing the similar job each day the monotony has to happen and it is job re design only which provides a better job satisfaction to an employee.

Time Management (with Reference to Project Management)

—Prof. C.K. Roy

Introduction

The time available with an executive or any person is limited and need to be utilized very intelligently. It is said that time is the essence of life and once not utilized it can not be retrieved back. For Project work or day to day management of your work you have to plan well to utilize the time available with you. Several authors have talked or written about the time management and all of them reach to a conclusion to utilize the time in meaningful way. Here in this article the totality about the time management based on behavioral pattern of Indian society and different activities performed has been covered. A person with proper time management can only perform well and reach the highest ladder of his success.

In a project management timely completion of project is very important. Any delay in the project or even crashing the project increases the cost of the project and may result in to financial problem to the firm as they have limited resources. Also in most of the projects based on social objectives for the country the delays compels to revise the project cost upward and the losses to the society turns abnormal in the form of direct losses due to delay of the purpose for which it was being created. Also the cost of the project, here mainly government projects jumps high and the additional cost incurred is recovered by way of taxes. This also creates inflation in the market. Most of the projects of importance under our five years plan have faced such threats leading to cost over run. Several projects were started and lying half done due to political shifts or shortage of funds under planned expenditure head.

Crashing or Expanding the Time

It increases the cost of the project and time over run is obvious. There are two divisions of costs one being variable cost and the other fixed cost. The variable costs are related to direct cost or expenses such as raw material, man power cost, power and fuel etc., and these costs are proportionate to the volume of output. In case of delay of the project, which means loss of time, due to improper and unplaned approach the cost of such input increases. Other costs are indirect costs which is also termed as fixed cost and should not vary if project is completed as per schedule as planned. In case the project is delayed the fixed cost or indirect cost expands in proportion to the time extended for the project.

While crashing or expanding the time limit of a project the time cost relation ship widely changes. The main characteristics of these costs are:-

(a) Direct cost reduces with reduction in the time of the project and expands when the time expands beyond planned time.

(b) The indirect cost increases with the time of the project.

The co-relation between the cost and time are:

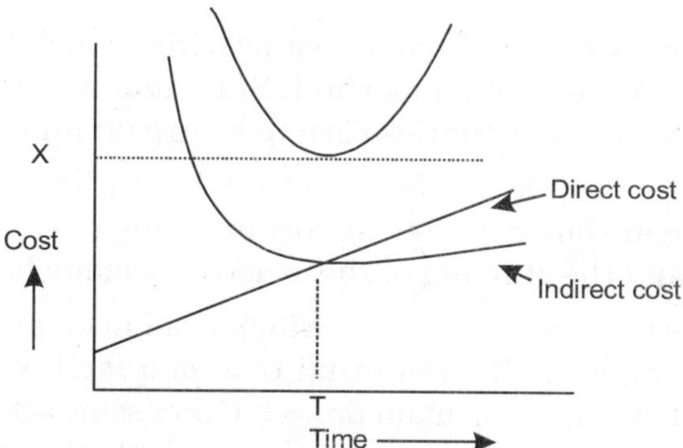

X is the lowest total cost

Y is the point of most accepted project time and is the point of optimum benefits.

This proposition is an indicator as to low the time not in terms of time only rather in terms of cost of a project is important.

Value-based Approach

Principle of value based approach is that you can have a good project management only if every one linked with the project, means all departments and people involved practices good time management.

For proper value approach and time management break all the activities in to four different categories and mark their priorities:

(a) urgent and important.

(b) urgent but not important.

(c) important but not urgent.

(d) neither urgent nor important.

It is easier to categories but difficult to understand. In the organization for different level the scale of importance of work and its urgency changes and it shall be wise if the team as a whole takes a decision in such categorization. The team of project management should take a decision in tabulating the activities in the four categories. After tabulation of each activities or the project in accordance with its urgency and importance the action if taken in order to it saves time and helps in proper time management of the individuals, each department and the organization as a whole. To under stand these four categories following illustrations may help in decision making.

Urgent and Important

According to PERT/CPM, mark all those activities which fall on the critical path of a PERT as urgent and important. Since in a critical path there is no slack available, all these activities turn to be urgent and important.

All activities which do not fall on critical path have some slacks and they become urgent but not that important. This is so; because there is slack available and the starting of these activities may be delayed.

There are certain more activities which are important but not urgent. The suitable example shall be internal road of a factory premises as this shall not have much impact on main project. Other some activities are neither urgent nor important such as gardening and plantation of the project premises. This activity is a part of the project cost out can be differed for some time as it is not going to effect the commissioning of the project.

Some times due to whimsical misunderstanding of the cause and effect the category of urgency and its importance is changed. The suitable case story can be:

A ECO of a firm goes to a Management Institute to deliver a talk and she was gifted with a beautiful wall painting. She returns to her project office and order the skilled operator who was engaged in a heavy earth moving machine maintenance work, to hang the beautiful painting on the wall of her office. The skilled operator was performing a most urgent and important work which was repair and maintenance of a heavy earth moving machine taken on hire and to perform foundation digging work for a major machine. The worker leaves this job and start hanging the painting in the chamber of the ECO. This action by a Boss converts the urgent and most important work in to a important but not urgent activity of the project. The decision at senior level some times changes the importance of activity and helps in creating delays in project time and cost as well. In the case discussed, the heavy earth mover was on hire at a cost of Rs.5000/- per hour and if the wall hanging has taken four hours, the monitory loss to the project shall be Rs. 20,000 and time loss shall be about one day.

Value-Time and Life Management

After all we are human being and the time available with us needs to be managed in a way that it provides maximum value to it. For life there are different factors and areas where value matters. The time available needs to be valued and distributed to all these factors honestly.

Value factors are:

Children and Family.

Education and learning.

Religion and spirituality.

Freedom and independence.

Health and fitness.

Spouse.

Financial security.

Quality of life and standard of living.

Achievement.

Equality.

Forgiveness and Beauty.

A person must devote justified time to add values to all these factors such that his total value remains maximized. There again priority of devotion of time varies from person to person depending on his personality and social environments. A person must devote adequate time for his family and children to justify the family bond and understanding. For a person if there is peace in the family, only then, he can be productive at the project work or his other place of working. Divide your time for the family in an intelligent way and plan it in such a beautiful way that maximum happiness is poured in to the family's happiness. A person with a unhappy family can never be productive.

Another area of success is education and leaning. The project manager and for this purpose any person who is at job needs to up date his knowledge beyond what he is performing presently. For this there are professional course and self study materials which helps in enriching his knowledge base. It has been found in the corporate history that a person entering at a clerical level reaches the highest place in his organization. Example Late Ram Rakha joined SBI as a clerk at Kolkata and he became secretary and treasurer highest post as a controller of four states. This he could achieve due to his educational and learning attitude. There are several such examples. This indicates that a portion of time available with you should be utilized for the purpose of your on going educational and learning development. This part of time management is equally important for a person whether he is in project work, self employed or employed in any organization.

Region and spirituality plays an important role in maintaining over all harmony in your attitude, behavior and character etc. No religion guides you to make a sin out of your time available rather all most all religions invariably stresses on sin-free act of life. Apart from religion if you read any religious book which may be Geeta, Ramayana, Bible or Quran the message is similar and always positive. The religion helps in character building and keeps your soul and mind free of sadness and with an attitudinal change to achieve some thing different than others. Once you follow religious and spiritual system of living on this earth your time management touches the highest productivity and performance level. With this route following achievements are realized.

1. We perform our job in an ethical manner.
2. We don't get involved in an unethical practice which ultimately saves our time and keeps our thinking free and positives.
3. The fear of failure is translated in to hope of success and once the success is achieved it saves time.
4. Out attitude towards juniors and management is always positive which helps in enhancing the group productivity resulting in to better time management.
5. We turn loyal to over work and this loyalty brings longevity.

6. We live in a stress free environment which helps in utilizing our time properly.
7. Spiritualism, moral value and culture are supreme and the corporate management should adopt this while performing their responsibilities.
8. Using spirituality and spiritual values the relationship between corporate, stake holders and shore holders shall turn stronger leading to higher productivity to the organization.
9. Today the physical and mental stress has attained a level that most of the corporate have adopted path of yoga which is an answer to spiritual system being adopted.
10. If we go through our spiritual literatures shastras, it gives a wonderful out look on the basis of our ancient culture and wisdom. We start our morning with prayer and end our day with prayer and for any achievement we thank God the almighty. By adopting spirituality we achieve purity in soul and an elevated work performance leading to higher productivity within the limited time available.

What so ever has been learnt from our culture, that stands good even today and helps in an excellent time management. A few quid lines summarized from our religion are:

1. Wealth should be used for 'Dharma'
2. Non violence is the tool which Gandhi and Budha adopted.
3. Sacrifice for self, society and nation (land today for the globe)
4. Simplicity – there is no end to luxury but the simplicity has an end.
5. Adopt truth – truth is the path which enhances your ethical values – transparency is possible only through truth ness.
6. Honesty – Where there will be truth, honesty, will follow.
7. Satisfaction – be satisfied with what God has given to you but don't stop "Karma" In other words interms of 'Karma' achievement remains dissatisfied.
8. Forgiveness - once you for give, it gives ethical values to them whom you forgive.
9. Love – provides strength and reduces stress.
10. Trust – If you want to manage a larger span of control, trust is the only way to perform. If you leave trust you loose time.
11. Operation and Harmony – Cooperation and harmony help in utilizing your and your team time.

These thoughts co-relate today's scientific and modern management theories. If these thoughts are followed by an individual, it will prove to be durable for the group and organization as a whole and ultimately help in best utilization of time. Time is scarcer than even money. We can not elongate the time span available with us. It is running and can not be stopped. Even a second spent without work shall not be repeated again. To utilize it in best manner we must plan our time management in an intelligent way.

Freedom and independence also needs some time slot. One has to keep himself free and independent for some time. This helps in his stress relieving system. The man lives in a society, he is not a slave and needs freedom and independence which provides him a sense of belongingness to this nature.

Health and fitness is important for time management. If you are not having good health and you are not fit the entire day's time is painful and cannot be utilized in perfect order, out of the time available you must provide time for your good health and fitness. This means Yoga and Exercises etc.

Spouses has a vital place in your life. Apart from family she has an important place as she is said to be "Ardhangini" and for her happiness some time plan is needed. In Indian condition majority of spouses are house wives and they run the family in an organized way and deserve happiness for which the husband or wife has to use a time slot such as entertainment, and understanding the problems and needs of the family. Unless she or he is fully involved in decision making process the family management remains in complete.

Finance is the most scarce commodity and a person can not live stress free if he is financially in secured. Take the cases of farmers committing suicide due to loan load. This indicates that financial security helps in time management as financially secured person is stress free and is more productive.

Quality of life and standard of living also brings in to you the sense of time management. The way your quality of life improves your health and happiness is also enhanced and your time utilization is oriented in right direction which means optimum results from minimum use of time. On the similar lines achievements, equality and beauty (here internal beauty) enhances your performance which means a better time utilization or management.

Equality means equal opportunity to each sex which means both the sex whether male or female to be given equal importance in decision making, responsibility sharing and even accountability. This helps in creating total bond and belongingness to the family and society.

Distribution of Time for Value and Life Management

Out of the total time available per day which is twenty four hours the intelligent decision shall be its distribution and from person to person it varies. Out of twenty four hours each value factors need certain allotments. The working on time management should be:-

Total time available (non flexible and fixed)	=	24 h
Time for attending office or work (as per factory act 1948)	=	8 h
Time for travel (average) home to office and back	=	1 – 2 h
Time for morning and evening Routine changes and work	=	2 h
Time to sleep	=	8 h
Total time consumed	=	19 – 20 h
Balance time available for attending to value factors	=	4 – 5 h

For each factor based on weightage the distribution should be as per under noted break ups.

Factor	Range %	Time utilized range in h
Children & Family	25 – 30	1 to 1.50
Education and learning	20 – 30	1 to 1.50
Religion/Spirituality	10 -15	0.50 to 1.00
Health and fitness	10 – 20	0.50 to 1.00
Spouse	10 – 15	0.50 to 1.00
Quality or Life-forgiveness and beauty	5 – 10	0.30 to 0.50
Achievement	5 – 10	0.30 to 0.50
Freedom and Independence	10 - 20	0.50 to 1.00
		4.60 hrs to 8.00 hrs
Time range available	4 to 5	
Gap (deficiencies)	.60 to 3.00	

This time may be compensated using the Sunday and holidays available but the range required must be utilized intelligently and in a planned way. For ranking the factors which varies from person to person you have to give them priorities which shall help in maximization of the utilization of the time available with you. You must rank the factors and then use it.

The 80/20 Principle

It was Pareto's principle which says "Eighty per cent of results will result from twenty per cent of our action" stands good, even today. Another way to express this statement is that about eighty percent of what we do yields negligible results which is only twenty percent of the total results and is an indicator that most of us waste a tremendous amount of time. Pareto principle can be applied to almost every activity of our lives. For example, we tend to get the greatest enjoyment from just a small number of our leisure activities. Similarly we gain eighty percent of our revenues from twenty percent of our customers. In a project there shall be eighty percent of return from only twenty percent good ideas we apply. Again an eighty percent of progress in planning a project will come from the twenty percent of the work that goes in to it.

With this reason and analysis Richard Koch (1998) argued that we must deliberately select these activities which gives the "biggest band for the buck" and concentrate on doing them. There we have to follow the rule "I can do any thing, but not everything" and this is because time is non elastic and the most scarce. By concentrating on these activities which provides the greatest leverage and ignoring or minimizing these that give small returns. Following these rules one can greatly improve his outcome (result) in every facet of his life.

In a project work do not start with the most difficult or problematic task first, because for a new team it may lead to a starting failure resulting in to de-motivation. Here for a new team or other wise select a smoother task first and succeed and gradually tackle the more complex problem. With initial a few successes the handling and solving the difficult problems also becomes easier. In such a situation the pareto principle should be ignored momentarily. Here after the team has achieved some 'wins' follow the 80/20 principle.

To apply the pareto principle following steps may be followed:

- To improve the use of time prepare a list of all activities.
- Identify those that give the greatest return on your investment of time.
- Concentrate on performing those activities which have better return and drop the others.
- It will provide the greatest result you had ever dreamed – impossible turns possible.

Maintaining a Time Log

For follow up and control of time and to understand where your time is going it is important to maintain a time log. It is more important to understand that each day how much time was really productive or how much time was wasted or turned non productive. The activities which proved to be time waster, eliminate it.

Time planning

One must plan his time. It has been usually observed that people do not use their time in planning. If you ask a question to a manager – How much time are you spending on planning your time? And if the answer is non, you have a problem. Most of the managers have a habit to say "I do not have time to plan. I am doing all I can do to keep from drawing". Here, the general rules of project management is that one hour spent an planning will save three to four hours in execution. The reason of such savings is simple. You work more efficiently and effectively when you have a plan, and you reduce rework and false starts. Here it is important to quote, "If you think you do not have time to plan, you are wrong, you do not have time not to plan".

Feed back and Time Estimate

The data we get from the time log maintained, the feed back is necessary to compare the time and work done (progress). Where you practice without feed back on results or progress of work completed. You are in darkness and can not plan well. The feed back helps in sharpening your skill. Estimating can not improve unless the tracking of actual time spent is followed. No learning takes place without feed back on performance.

A suitable example as to how the feed back helps in improving the time management is:

> Suppose you are trying to improve the speed of your running 400 meter race. You daily go in the field run and come back. You do not know whether you are getting better or worse. You could be getting worse and do not know it. It may be that you may be learning an ineffective way of running. Here, you might be getting better at doing it wrong. The feed back helps in best utilization of time and also improves your skill in doing it better.

Tackling the Big Jobs

Larger projects are quite complex in nature and it is difficult in senses to its time management. There is a tendency to avoid big jobs, as these appear to be unpleasant. This phenomenon is usually called procrastination and there are two ways to get out of this dilemma. One way is to out source the job if you have that luxury and the other way is to approach a job the way you would eat an elephant – one bite at a time. The question arises – can you eat an elephant in one bite? Answer invariably shall be "NO". Trying to eat the whole elephant in one bite is simply over whelming and we tend to avoid over whelming tasks. To perform such project work Break Down system is the only process and it means breaking down the work in to manageable bits. Then tackle a couple of easy pieces to give yourself a sense of accomplishment and go on from these to the bigger ones.

Achieving Balance or Balancing

Under 80/20 principle of time management the major problem is "what am I willing to give up so that I can do those things that really matter to me and that gives the greatest return? A common approach shall be to use the ABC classification of activities or jobs after breaking it down and give priority to 'A' class activities. These A class becomes urgent and important and B class also urgent but not important. C class items are neither urgent nor important.

Covey

Covey (1989) suggested that you never fully schedule your week, leave some slack. It is known that nothing is ever going to go exactly as planned and if you don't have same slack, you will wind up with a constantly rolling priority list and feel that nothing ever gets done.

Another area to think is the situation of a rat race. Here the matter to realize is that "even if you win the rate race, you remain as a rat". If you have desire to come out of rat race, come out of the race and think different than common rats.

The ultimate of time management is the proper utilization of time in relation to return. By proper time management only a battle of project can be won successfully. Remember, those who wasted time during their different age carrier, they are the biggest repenters, because they are lagging for behind others, who are his colleagues. Proper use of time permits you to rise above the present level before time.

Common Property Rights in the Communal Deed for Economic Development

Special Reference to Employment Guarantee Scheme

—T. Rajasekar
—Dr. Malabika Deo

ABSTRACT

The role of the common property concept and its policy implications as a tool in the economic analysis and solution of natural resources policy problems is examined. The formulation and implementation of the Employment Guarantee Scheme constitutes a significant step to poverty alleviation by providing an institutional framework for guaranteeing supplementary livelihood opportunity to the rural households. The study focusing through common property how the rual households get the economic benefit. For that the study mainly concentrates on the Employment Guarantee Programme. The data required for the study were collected from both the primary and secondary sources. The total numbers of samples were 50 from the members of Employment Guarantee Program and the information is collected by adopting snowball sampling. The statistical tool like percentage analysis used to analyse and interpret the data.

Key words: *MGNREGP, Socio-economic condition, Common Property, Rural households*

Introduction

The role of the common property concept and its policy implications as a tool in the economic analysis and solution of natural resources policy problems is examined. Common property is defined as resources subject to the rights of common use, but not to a specific use right held by several owners. The concept is considered as a second level decision system, aimed at maintaining and increasing welfare by continuously influencing decision making on the first level, the operating level, under constantly changing conditions. Whether welfare decreased under common property institutions or whether earlier societies over-used their resources because of common ownership is examined by looking back into economic history. It is the concept has been capable of satisfactory performance in the management of such natural resources as grazing and forest land. Elements of the common property concept are also being employed currently to solve groundwater and fisheries resource problems. This approach would have the advantage of forcing bureaucracies to take the interests of all common owners into account, and allow quality criteria to be incorporated into resource problem solutions. (Luedtke-Wisconsin, 1975)

India accounts for an over whelming number of the poor in the world. The causes of poverty have been traced lack of adequate employment opportunities and limited access to markets by the poor. With the expansion of economy, poverty in India has declined from 54.9 percentages in 1973-74 to 27.5 percentages in 2004-2005. But the absolute number of the poor continues to remain high. The formulation and implementation of the National Rural Employment Guarantee Act (NREGA) constitutes a significant step to poverty alleviation by providing an institutional framework for guaranteeing supplementary livelihood opportunity to the rural households. The NREGA was notified on 7th September 2005. The Act provides a legal guarantee of 100 days of wage employment in a financial year to every rural house hold whose adult members volunteer to do unskilled manual work at the minimum wage rate notified for agricultural labour prescribed in the State or else an unemployment allowance. The objective of the Act is to supplement wage employment opportunities in rural areas and in the process also build up durable assets.

The Act will extend to the entire country within five-years of its notification. In the first phase, the Act was notified on February 2nd 2006 in 200 districts. In the second phase, the Act is to be notified in 130 additional districts. The list of 113 districts has been tabled in the Parliament. For the Act to become effective in these additional districts a separate notification will be issued by the Government of India and the Legal processes delineated in the Act will come into force from the date of that notification. The notification.

Employment Guarantee Act

The Government on the advice of the National Advisory Council has passed the National Rural Employment Guarantee Act. The Main Features of the proposed Act are:

1. Every household in rural India will have a right to at least 100 days of guaranteed employment every year for at least one adult member. The employment will be in the form of causal manual labour at the statutory minimum wage, and the wages shall be paid within 7 days of the week during which work was done.
2. Work should be provided within 15 days of demanding and the work should be located within 5 Kilometer distance.
3. If work is not provided to anybody within the given time, he/she will be paid daily unemployment allowance, which will be at least one-third of the minimum wages.

Performance of NREGA (National Overview)

Employment Provided to households	**(FY 2006-07) 200 Districts**	**(FY 2007-08) 330 Districts**	**(FY 2008-09) 615 Districts**
	2.10 Crore	**3.39 Crore**	**2.93 Crore**
Person days (In Crore):			
Total:	90.5	143.59	109.30
SCs:	22.95(25%)	39.36(27%)	33.40(31%)
STs:	32.98(36%)	42.07(29%)	26.24(24%)
Women:	36.79(41%)	61.15(43%)	53.52(49%)
Others:	34.56(38%)	62.16(43%)	46.65(45%)
Budget Outlay: (In Rs.Crore)	11300	12000	16000
Cental Release: (In Rs.Crore)	8640.85	12610.39	16060.85
Works break up			
Water conservation:	4.51(54%)	8.73(49%)	8.42(44%)
Provision of Irrigation facility to land owned by SC/ST/BPL and IAY beneficiaries:	0.81(10%)	2.63(15%)	3.35(18%)
Rural Connectivity:	1.80(21%)	3.08(17%)	2.83(15%)
Land Development:	0.89(11%)	2.88(16%)	4.42(23%)

Source: *Kurukshetra*, December 2008

4. Workers employed on public works will be entitled to medical treatment and hospitalization in case of injury at work ,along with a daily allowance of not less than half of the statutory minimum wage. In case of death or disability of a worker an exgratia payment shall be made to his legal heirs as per provisions of the workmen compensation Act.
5. Five percent of wages may be deducted as contribution to welfare schemes like health insurance, accident insurance, survivor benefits, maternity benefits and social security schemes.
6. For non-compliance with rules, strict penalties have been laid down.
7. For transparency and accountability all accounts and records of the programme will be made available for public scrutiny.
8. The District Collector/Chief Executive Office will be responsible for the programme at the district level and
9. The gram sabha will monitor the work of the gram panchayat by way of social audit.

Role of State Government

For the implementation of the Scheme, each state Government shall prepare an Employment Guarantee Programme within six months of enactment. The main Features to the included in the programme are:

(*i*) Only productive works that are based on economic, social and environmental benefits, contributing to social equity, and have the ability to create permanent assets will be taken up under the Programme.

(*ii*) The works shall be located in rural areas and.

(*iii*) When wages are directly linked with the quantity of work, they shall be paid according to the schedule of rate fixed by the state government. For unskilled labourers, this schedule shall be so fixed that seven hours of work shall fetch wages equal to the statutory minimum wage fixed by the state.

A Scene from the South

NREG Scheme in Tamil Nadu

Tamil Nadu has a well rehearsed routine of wage payment on a fixed day every week. Tamil Nadu has put in place a good monitoring system. For instance, every worker is required to put his signature or thumb impression on the muster roll every day (by way of marking attendance), making it difficult to fudge muster rolls. The employment guarantee assistant ("Makkal Nalla Panniyalar") in each gram panchayat is expected to phone the block office every day before 10a.m to report worksite attendance figures. This information is immediately collected at the district level and officials from different department to random checks the same day to verify these reports.

Most importantly, in Tamil Nadu a strong message has been sent from the top that NREGA works are unlike other schemes and that corruption will not be tolerates. This has been done by taking strict action against panchayat presidents, employment guarantee assistants and block development office's who have been found guilty of major fraud. Another special feature of the NREGP in Tamil Nadu is that an over whelming majority (about 80 percent) of NREGP workers are women. Most of them have no comparable work opportunities in the private sector. Indeed Tamil Nadu's strong tradition of active involvement in the social sector is finding a new expression through the NREGP. There is much to learn from this experience, just as Tamil Nadu itself has much to learn from pioneering experiences elsewhere. "In Tamil Nadu, Three Districts (Dinducal, Sivagnagai, Kadalur) received for best performance a word in the NREGP (2007-08) by the central Government".

Wage Rates Number of Person days in Southern States

State	Average Daily Wage Rates in Agricultural Occupations in Rural India, 2004-05 (RS).		NREGP wage Rate (RS)	Employment provides – number of persons-days per Household	
Andhra Pradesh	36.61	27.83	80.00	31.4	39.6
Karnataka	49.00	27.85	74.00	41.1	44.4
Kerala	55.89	27.99	125.00	22.8	28.6
Tamil Nadu	60.79	31.23	80.00	26.9	57.2
All India	61.23	44.59	-	43.1	41.8

Source: Wage Rates in Rural India (WRRI), Labour Bureau, Ministry of Labour and Employment for daily wage rates in rural India, 2004-05; NREGA, 2005, Ministry of Rural Development (MORD) for NREGA wage and employment provided – Person days.

There is a long history (of at least four decades in post-Independence India) of wage employment programmes and reviews of these programmes had shown the following perennial weaknesses:

(*i*) Low Programme coverage.

(*ii*) More than 50 per cent beneficiaries not form most needy group.

(iii) Bureaucracy dominated planning, little participation of community in planning.
(iv) Work to women lower than stipulated norm of 30 percent and
(v) Only 16-29 days employment provided to household.
(vi) Assets created not durable.
(vii) Corruption; reports of false muster rolls; contractors persisted; payment offer less than prescribed wages.

Review of Relevant Literature

A literature is account of what has been published on a topic accredited scholars and researches. The purpose of writing the literature review is to convey to the readers matters what knowledge and ideas have been established on a topic and what their strengths and weakness areas. As a piece of writing, the literature review must be defined by a guiding concept.

Rajanna and Gundeti (2009) had found that "NREGP – Fact Of Inclusive Grouth A Study Of Karimanagar District In Andhra Pradesh" by selecting 500 beneficiaries of the programme random only to assess the impact of the NREGP. Out of 500 NREGP worker's 68.6% were women and the rest of the workers were men. This programme helped a but in reducing the seasonal and disguised unemployment in the agricultural sector and also contributed to empower the women folk in the rural areas. Further this also reduced the wage dissimilarity between men and women workers by increasing the minimum wages. The study revealed that 51.6 percentage of the workers were from backward class communities and 46.6 percentage of workers were scheduled class (S.C.) category and the rest were from scheduled Tribe (S.T.) and other communities.

Pant (2009) with joint support from Allah bad University and the National Commission for Enterprises in the Un-Organized sector (NCEUS) entitled NREGA server 2008 was conducted in May-June 2008. It covered 10 districts spread over Six North Indian States (Bihar, Chhattisgarh, Jharkhand, Madhya, Pradesh, Rajasthan and Uttar Pradesh) concluded that 81 per cent of the sample workers live in a *kaccha* house, 61 per cent are illiterate and 72 per cent have to electricity at home. Scheduled Caste (S.C) and Scheduled Tribe families are also joining the NREGA in large numbers. Clearly, the NREGA is a powerful tool to economic redistribution and Social equity.

Anish Vanaik (2008) analysed NREGA and the death of Tapas Soren, a tribal of Birakhap in Jharkhand, committed self-immolation recently, impoverished by the constant demand for bribes by local officials for work done uncover the National Rural Employment Guarantee Act. His death soon after the murder of Lalit Mehta who had exposed corruption in NREGA schemes in Palama is damming comment on how the scheme is being implemented in Jharkhand.

Santhosh Mehrotra (2008) entitled NREG two years on where do we go from here? Concluded that it is perfectly possible to put in place a system to minimize corruption in the NREG (and in fact other Schemes). Gopal (2009) entitled “NREGA Social Audit: Myths and Reality”, concluded that much had been said and written about the social audits conducted in Andhra Pradesh under the National Rural Employment Guarantee Act. But on the ground these audits had achieved much less than advertised and they had ignored many important aspects of implementation of NREGA. The Social audit process had a long way to go before it can claim to have contributed to transparency, empowerment and good governance.

Sudha Narayanan (2008) analysed “Employment Guarantee, women’s work and childcare” she examined that the provision of effective childcare facilities at NREGA worksites was an important issue that calls for creative thinking and action. Tamil Nadu was well placed to take the lead in this field; given it were earlier achievements in the domain of childcare. This would not only be a step forward for Tamil Nadu but also an example for the country as a whole. Mihirshan (2007) entitled “Employment Guarantee, Civil Society and Indian Democracy”, concluded that Even as we had celebrated 60Years of Indian democracy, with millions of our people hungry, cynical and insecure, and living the barrel of the gun (of the state or the extremists), we needed to worry about the reach and quality of our political process. The National Rural Employment Guarantee Act had the potential to provide “big bush” in India’s regions of distress. For NREGA to be able to realized its potential, the role of civil society organizations is critical. But this calls for a new self-Critical politics of fortitude, balance and restraint.

Chaya Datar (2007) analysed “Failure of National Rural Employment Guarantee Scheme in Maharashtra”, he examined that the Maharashtra Rural Employment Guarantee Scheme (MREGS) had not yet picked up momentum because government machinery is paralysed. In the past circumstances, the MREGS would acquire life only if there was a grounds well of the poor willing to pressurize the sarpanch and gram sevaks and make life impossible for the Chief Executive Officer (CEO) and Block Development Officer (BDO). It was expected that the sarpanch and gyam sevaks would be happy to receive such a large sum to develop village assets. But it is sad to know that they are resisting because of the increased burden and the lack of kickback through the contractor. It is high time that something is done to wear out present amnesia and push the state to implement the scheme in a vibrant manner and reclaim the old glory of the innovative idea.

Das and Pradhan (2007) entitled "Illusions of change" concluded that the National Rural Employment Guarantee Act as implemented by the Orissa Government has resulted in grandiose claims of expenditure but very little to show in reality. The government has taken, as pointed out earlier, several progressive steps. But, it should not sit back and count its laurels. The government of Orissa must rise to the occasion, and take immediate steps to this most hypothetical and cruel joke on its poorest and most vulnerable communities.

Methodology

Objectives of the Study

The main objectives of this paper as follows:

(*a*) To study the important features of (National Rural Employment Guarantee Programme) NREGP

(*b*) To analyze the socio-economic conditions of workers under the NREGP

(*c*) To study the knowledge about NREGP and major achievements.

Data and Data Source

The data required for the study were collected from both the primary and secondary sources. The primary data has been collected from the respondents through interview schedule. The Secondary data used for the study were collected from various websites and the published journals, books related to the Topic. The total numbers of samples were 50 from the members of National Rural Employment Guarantee Programme and information is collected by adopting snowball sampling. A pilot study was made before carrying out the actual study. The interview schedule was used in the pilot study among 10% of the total respondents. From the pilot study, the necessary changes were made in the interview schedule before making the data collection for this study by knowing the obstacles.

Tools for Analysis

The statistical tool like percentage analysis used to analyse and interpret the data. The researcher feels that only percentage analysis shows the total percentage in each and every individual question. So this study fully based on the percentage analysis and makes it needful findings of the study.

Data Analysis and Interpretation

This chapter is for analyzing the data collected. The investigator has made every effort to bring out the objectives of the study through all possible means of analysis and subsequent interpretation.

Table 23.1 : Socio-Demographic profile of the sample respondents

Sl.No.	Particulars	Number of respondents	Percentage of respondents
A.	Age distribution		
	(i) Below 20 years	0	0.0
	(ii) 21 – 40 years	14	28.0
	(iii) 41 – 60 years	28	56.0
	(iv) 61 and above	8	16.0
	Total	**50**	**100**
B.	Marital Status		
	(i) Married	42	84.0
	(ii) Unmarried	8	16.0
	Total	**50**	**100**
C.	Occupational Details		
	(i) Agricultural Workers	28	56.0
	(ii) Beedi RollersDaily	8	16.0
	(iii) Wage Labours	14	28.0
	Total	**50**	**100**
D.	Educational Qualification		
	(i) Illiterate	18	36.0
	(ii) Primary Education	27	54.0
	(iii) Secondary Education	5	10.0
	(iv) Higher Secondary Education	0	0.0
	Total	**50**	**100**
E.	Sex Wise Classification		
	(i) Male	8	16.0
	(ii) Female	42	84.0
	Total	**50**	**100**

Source: Primary data.

Table 23.1 shows among 50 NREGP respondents, 56% of the respondents are at the age of 41-60 years, 28% of the respondents are at the age of 21-40, 16% of the respondents are at the age of above 60 and no one of the respondents are at the age of below 20 years of age. This shows aged rural households mostly depend on the National Rural Employment Guarantee Program. Marital status of the NREGP workers 84% of them are married and 16 % of them are unmarried. Thus, most of the sample respondents of NREGP workers are married. Out of the total sample respondents, 56% of them are depending the agricultural and its related works when they are not getting NREGP works, 28% of them are having the daily wages works and 16% of them are working in the rolling of *beedi* works most of south tamilnadu people having the beedi and its related works. Mostly south side of tamilnadu people they are doing this beedi rolling works at the part time basis. This shows NREGP created a significant portion of workers in rural areas. Since the villages are the backbone of the Indian economy, the contribution of NREGP for the rural development is appreciable. Among the 50 respondents 36% of are not formally educated and 64% of them are educated. It is appreciable that involvement of educated women workers in the NREGP. This table also reveals that all the respondents have not crossed the school level education. This shows the hard works is not necessary for the educational qualification, therefore those who are not completed people they only depend on the NREGP.

Table 23.2 : Monthly Income Details of the Sample Respondents

Sl.No.	Income (Rs.)	Before NREGP		After NREGP	
		No. of Respondents	Percentage	No. of Respondents	Percentage
(i)	Below 1000	26	52.0	0	0.0
(ii)	1000 – 1500	20	40.0	38	76.0
(iii)	1500 - 2000	4	8.0	12	24.0
(iv)	Above 2000	0	0.0	0	0.0
	Total	**50**	**100**	**50**	**100**

Source: Primary data

Table 23.2 reveals the income wise classification of sample respondents before and after joining under the NREGP works. The table shows that 52% of the NREGP workers are having the income of below 1000 before joining the NREGP works. Forty per cent of the sample respondents reported that they are having the income range Rs. 1000-1500 when they are not enrolled in the NREGP. Only 8% of the respondents have Rs. 1500-2000 monthly income range. In the comparison of after joining NREGP out of the sample respondents majority 76% of workers getting the monthly income Rs. 1000-1500. Remaining 24% of the sample respondents having the income range of Rs. 1500-2000. From this table compare to before and after NREGP reveals that after joining NREGP works the sample respondents really gets empower on the economic related. The NREGP sample respondents get economic empowerment from this national employment guarantee program.

Table 23.3 : Savings and Debt details of the sample respondents

Sl. No.	Particulars	Number of respondents	Percentage of respondents
A.	Mode of Savings		
	(i) Self-help Groups	37	74.0
	(ii) Banks	5	10.0
	(iii) No Savings	8	16.0
	Total	**50**	**100**
B.	Debt details		
	(i) Bank debt	5	10.0
	(ii) Money Lenders	33	66.0
	(iii) Self-help Groups	12	24.0
	Total	**50**	**100**

Source: Primary data

Table 23.3 reveals the savings and debt details of the sample respondents those who are working under NREGP. From the table it can be seen that 74 per cent of the NREGP workers are savings their income to the self help groups because majority of the workers availing SHG facilities in their own place. Ten per cent of the sample respondents saving their income to the public and private sector banks because only these workers knowing the banking operations. Remaining 16% of the sample respondents not savings their income, because the workers earning income its necessary to spend their daily expenses. They have to spend their NREGP income to their daily routine activity. Out of the sample respondent's debt details 66% of the sample respondents reported that, they are borrowing from the money lenders for their necessary needs. Twenty four per cent of the sample respondents borrowing the money from self-help groups because (SHGs) SHG giving loan facility to their members at the low interest rates. Only 10% of the respondents getting money through bank in respect of gold, land etc. from Table 23.3 its concluded that majority of the respondents still borrowing the money through money lenders because majority of the respondents not having adequate knowledge so the money lenders also use these people and getting more interest.

Table 23.4 portrays details of the NREGP among 84% of the workers reported that the work were doing one only member of their family, 12% of the workers doing this work two of the family members and remaining 4%

Table 23.4 : NREGP Details of the Sample Respondents

Sl. No.	Particulars	Number of respondents	Percentage of respondents
A.	No of Family members working under NREGP		
	(i) One member	42	84.0
	(ii) Two members	6	12.0
	(iii) Three members	2	4.0
	Total	**50**	**100**
B.	Category under NREGP		
	(i) OBC	10	20.0
	(ii) SC	13	26.0
	(iii) ST	5	10.0
	(iv) MBC	22	44.0
	Total	**50**	**100**
C.	Motivation to join NREGP		
	(i) Through Panchayat	16	32.00
	(ii) Self Help Groups	11	22.0
	(iii) Family members	8	16.0
	(iv) Others	5	10.0
	Total	**50**	**100**
D.	NREGP improve standard of living of member?		
	(i) Yes	41	82.0
	(ii) No	9	18.0
	Total	**50**	**100**

Source: Primary data.

of the employees working the NREGP in three members of their family. Out of 50 respondents 44% National Rural Employment Guarantee Program belongs to most backward community, 26% of the workers belongs to Schedule Caste families 20% of the workers belongs to Other Backward Caste only 10% of the workers belongs to Schedule Tribe community. This shows the government primary aim to give the jobs those who are backward position in respect of economic. So from this table we can conclude all the community people working together without any problems this is another ways of getting peaceful from the workers. Out of 50 respondents majority 32% of the workers motivated by the panchayat authorities because once the government announce any new scheme the local government have full responsible. Twenty two per cent of the NREGP workers gets motivate from the self-help groups, the SHG also responsible to take care of the people those who are not knowing such a thing, 16% of them getting motivation from their family because the family people always giving torture to get any work another think is they are not having regular work. Only 10% of the workers motivated from the other groups like friends, organization and its related. So this is reveal that the panchayat government always willing to reach the government schemes. From the table majority 82% of the respondents reported that their standard of living has been improved after joining this NREGP 18% of the respondents did not get any improvement from their present work. This shows majority of the employees feels better, because they are getting the job 100 days in the year. This work will be helpful to take necessary expenses in their family.

Conclusion

From this study the researcher found the important findings like as follows:

(*i*) increased living and economic conditions by reducing the income imbalances in the rural area.

(*ii*) Reduction of wage differences in various works by creation equal wages to male and female works.

(*iii*) Helped to overcome the uncertainty in the employment.

(*iv*) Work culture norms in bringing cohesiveness among the workers in the rural areas irrespective of caste and freedom gender and age.

(*v*) As a subsidiary activity it helped a lot in improving the main occupation of the workers in enhancing their income levels.

(*vi*) Helped to some extent in reducing the disguised and seasonal unemployment.

The study also giving some suggestion to the government as well as those who are organizing this NREGP program in the formal way:

1. At present the Government provides employment opportunity for 100 days per year. The days should be increased from 100 to 150 days. As a result of this income and standard of the people can be increased.
2. As the rural people are getting work for 100 days only, they are not in a position to get loans from any scheduled bank. So the government must provide loan at low interest level to those people.
3. Under this scheme, different wages are paid in different states. There is a vast difference between the states regarding the wages

paid under NREGP. For example, in Kerala the wage is Rs.125 per day At the same time people in Tamil Nadu are getting Rs.80 as wage per day. Even in North sates also the wages are very lower than in Tamil Nadu.

(4) Awareness about the minimum wage should be created and spread among the rural people in their "Gram Shaba Meeting"

Clearly the NREGA is a powerful tool of economic redistribution and social equity. All the policy makers should engage in truly improving the living conditions at the masses through improved per capita income.

REFERENCES

Das, Vidhya Pradhan Pramod. (2007) "Illusions of Change", *Economic and Political Weekly*, Vol. XLII, No. 32, p. 3283.

Datar, Chhaya, (2007) "Failure of National Rural Employment Guarantee Scheme in Maharashtra", *Economic and Political Weekly*, Vol. XLII, No. 34, p. 3454.

Gopal, K.S. (2009) "NREGA Social Audit: Myths and Reality", *Economic and Political Weekly*, Vol. XLIV, No. 3, p. 70.

Mehrotra, Santosh (2008) "NREG Two Years on: Where Do we Go from Here?" *Economic* and Political Weekly, No. 31, p. 27-35.

Mihirshah (2007) "Employment Guarantee, Civil Society and Indian Democracy" *Economic and Political Weekly*, Vol XLII No. 45, p. 43.

Narayanan, Sudha, (2008) "Employment Guarantee, women's work and childcare", *Economic and Political Weekly*, Vol. XLIII, No. 9, p. 10.

Pant, G.B. (2009) "NREGA Survey 2008". *Frontline*, p. 4-17.

Rajanna and Gundeti Ramesh (2009) "NREGP – Fact of Inclusive Growth A study of Karimanagar District in Andhra Pradesh". *Kurukshetra*, Vol. 57, No. 4, p. 33-35.

Vanaik, Anish (2008) "NREGA and the Death of Tapas Soren", *Economic and Political Weekly*, No. 30, p. 8-10.

Wisconsin, Luedtke (1975) "Common Property as a Concept in Natural Resources Policy" *Natural Resources Journal,* Vol. 15, p. 713-727

Sustainability of Common Property Resources with Special Reference to Forest in Arunachal Pradesh

— Dr. Ram Krishna Mandal

Introduction

Ever since man appeared on the earth, he has been harnessing the natural resources to meet his basic requirements. Reference to soil, water and air as basic resources, their management and means to keep them pure are mentioned in the *Vedas* and *Upanishads*, the ancient Hindu literature. The phenomenal increase in population of both human beings and animals in the last century and fast growing industrialization and urbanization in the last few centuries have overstrained the natural which are getting degraded much faster than before. With the advent of high yielding varieties, augmentation of irrigation facilities, increased use of fertilizers, adoption of improved agronomic practices, concerted efforts of researchers, planners, government and above all the farming community, green revolution was brought about in the mid 1960s. This led to a quantum jump in food grain production from 51 Mt in 1950-51 to a record figure of 203 Mt in 1998-99. With the adoption of intensive agriculture to meet the varied growing demands for food, fuel, fibre and cattle fodder, natural resource have been put under intense pressure resulting in fast degradation and lowering of production efficiency.

On the other side, the demographic pressure is rapidly mounting on the natural resources. The present population of over 1000 million, accounting for about 18 percent of the world's population, is estimated to become 1.4 billion by 2025 and 1.7 billion by AD 2050, needing annually about 380 Mt and 480 Mt food grains respectively (Yadhav *et al.,* 2000). This scenario along with the increasing industrialization and urbanization will place tremendous pressure on the shrinking natural resources. Unless corrective measures are taken, this will make the damage to the environment and the very resource base irreversible. However, we still have the capacity to produce enough food to meet the basic requirement of the burgeoning population, but the moot question is whether, we can do so while maintaining our natural resources and preserving the bio diversity at the same time.

Common property resources (CPRs) imply local commons line village pond and tanks, pastures and threshing grounds, watershed, river beds, sources of fuel woods, medicinal herbs, bamboo, resin, gum, etc. Local commons are open only to those having historical rights, kinship ties, community membership, etc.

A series of policy intervention along with market focus are likely to be unleashed in the wake of opening up and globalization. This will alter the land use and tenurial system (directed to institutionalization of modern private property) with serious environmental and social consequences to both private and communal property resources. By passing the transitional task of creating an environment for the evolution of co-operation based new 'Common Property Resources Management (CPRM)' institutions may further aggravate the already prevailing unquiet environment of India's North-East.

The Seven North-Eastern States has a geographical area of 2.55 lakhs sq.kms and a population of 384.95 lakhs while 325.23 lakhs of population live in rural areas of this region. Thus, 84.5% of population lives in rural areas. This region is rich in forest and bio-diversity. 64.3% of its geographical area is covered under forest. The region is also recognized as hydro-power house to feed at least one-third of requirement of power in India. The area is rich in mineral resources and maximum of these are yet to be tapped. Under the given condition, the area is rich in natural resources. But over 40% of rural population lives under poverty in the region. The development in the region can be achieved after eradication of poverty from North Eastern Region. Arunachal Pradesh, one of the seven states of North East Region, has vast area of 83,743sq.km. As per the state forest report 1999, published by the Forest Survey of India; forest cover of Arunachal Pradesh is 68,951 sq.km, accounting 82.21 per cent of its total geographical area. The recorded forest area of the state is 51540 sq km, which is about 61.5 % of its total geographical area. Thus, the sate is fortunate to have such high percentage of its area under valuable forests cover against the national percentage of 23.28. Again, out of its area, 70% constitutes broad and narrow valleys, 10 percent foothills and flat areas and 20% snow clad peak areas. The agricultural operations are confined to only five per cent of its total geographical area, out of which 62 % to 65 % are under shifting cultivation (*jhum*).

The dependence of human activities on natural resources is not only recognized but well acknowledged also. Surprisingly, mainstream economists especially a group of engineer cum neoclassical economists rarely pays attention to the importance of natural resources or environmental resources.

Arunachal Pradesh is very rich in terms of natural resources and sustainable use of these resources may make sure sustainable development. These natural resources may be classified as open access or common property resources depending upon property right and the rights and responsibilities for harvesting and conservation.

As per 2001 census, the population of Arunachal Pradesh is 1097968 out of which 40% of its population is living under BPL (Below Poverty Line). Poverty and Sustainable Development (SD) are two socio-economic phenomena drawing global attention of academician, researchers, policy makers as well as human activists. Traditionally, the issues of poverty and SD have been treated separately and singularly but during last one decade there have been conceptual developments and paradigm shifts in these areas. They are now viewed as concepts that are multidimensional and more comprehensive. Also, there is some degree of convergence within and between the two in that the issue of poverty and food security is now considered on integral part of the bigger challenge known as SD. Further, most of the remedial aspects of poverty and SD required direct action and a pro-active involvement on the part of the government, the private sector, the civil society and the NGOs at all levels – local, national and global. This paper seeks an attempt to examine an in-depth study about the degradation of common property resources, poverty and sustainable development in Arunachal Pradesh.

The paper is divided into three sections. The first section concentrates on Common Property Resources (CPRs) especially forest. The second section devotes to examine the meanings and some dimensions of Sustainable Development. The third section deals with the negative correlation between deforestation and sustainable development and finally conclusion follows.

SECTION I

Common Property Resources are those common resources in which a precise group of individuals have the rights as well as responsibility to use and conserve but not for individual possession. The resources are not under any management system and everybody has the equal right to use but no responsibility to conserve it, these are open access resources and termed as only commons. A variety of common resources such as forest lands, revenue lands, lands lying along side railway tracks, roads, water reservoirs, tanks, canals, irrigation ponds, rivers, lakes, streams, etc. are found to happen at varied degrees in rural areas. Majority of the rural poor depend on these commons for at least four purposes such as fishing, livestock rearing (grazing and fodder), fuel wood and irrigation of crops. Conventionally, the rural people of Arunachal Pradesh significantly depend on common resources (CRs) for their livelihoods and the duty of harvesting from the CRs lies on women and children of this impoverished class. It has been estimated that 84 to 100% of poor households are dependent on CRs for fuel, fodder and food items and they obtain 14 to 23% of their income from harvested CR products (Jodha, 1990). Most of these natural resources are 'open excess' and hence the destiny of these resources is supposed to be what has been described by Hardin (1968) as 'Tragedy of Commons'. However, in many parts of the world Hardin's hypothesis proved incorrect as communities, under certain conditions, are found to manage resources like water and forests successfully over a long period of time (Wade, 1988; Ostrom, 1990; Baland & Platteau, 1996) despite the fact that the resources and the management and use system are nearly everywhere facing increasing pressure from growing population and the effects of economic and political changes (Arnold, 1998; Nadkarni, 2000; Lu, 2001).

Forest has been playing an important role in socio-economic development of this region-specially hill tribal inhabited region, as a source of subsistence, employment, and raw-materials for industry. The indigenous people's role in ecological balance, environmental stability and sustainable development has been recognized in National Forest Policy, 1988. The forest resource of the region is under tremendous pressure due to increasing demand for human and livestock. Too much of extraction has led to forest degradation and disaster in ecological balance in recent time in this region. The position of forest cover as per statement of Forest Report (SFR) 1997 is in Table 24.1.

The forest cover has decreased in all the states in this region in 1997 compared to 1991 except Arunachal Pradesh. The trend is observed in all India too.

Forests may be regarded as capital stocks of such a nature that they yield two distinct flows of goods fundamentally different in nature-flow of private good such as timber, fuel wood, other minor forest produce and a flow of public goods like maintenance of environment, causation of rainfall, prevention of soil erosion, etc. There are some unique features of forest situated in Arunachal Pradesh. Around 61.5% of the total geographical area is covered under forest which is the highest among the seven states of North East India. The state contains nearly 16% of the total timber growing

Table 24.1 : Forest Cover in North-Eastern Region in India

State	Geographical	1991	1993	1995	1997
Arunachal Pradesh	83743	68757	68661	68621	68602
Assam	78438	24751	24508	24061	23824
Manipur	22327	17685	17621	17558	17418
Meghalaya	22429	15875	15769	15714	15657
Mizoram	21081	18853	18697	18576	18775
Nagaland	16579	14321	14348	14291	14221
Tripura	10486	5535	5538	5538	5546
Total in NE Region	255083	165777	164842	164359	164043
All India	3287263	639364	639386	638879	633397

Source : *The State Forest Report, 1997.*

stock of the country (the highest among the individual states) and more than 20% fauna of India (Government of Arunachal Pradesh, 1995). In Arunachal Pradesh, the ownership of land as well as the forest land and the individual right to use it are governed by local traditions and custom of the tribes. Under the prevailing land tenure system, there are three types of land ownership namely (*a*) community land (*b*) clan land and (*c*) individual land. Regarding the forest land, almost all the tribes have the community forest land, almost all the tribes have the community forest which is controlled by the village council. In some areas, clan ownership is recognized in the forest areas failing within the village jurisdiction. That is why, if we look at the data on the basis of legal status of forest in the state, it is found that around 62.17% of total forest is under community ownership which is reported as Unclassified State Forest (USF). However, at present there is a growing tendency of individual ownership of forest which is a recent phenomenon in the state. For example, in the Apatani plateau of Lower Subansiri district, the forest has become increasingly privatized.

The reserve forest constitutes 19,236.55 sq.km, i.e. nearly 37.32% of the total forest area of the state. On the other hand Anchal Reserve Forest covered only 256.08 square kilometers (only 0.5% of the total forest area). Such forests are managed by the forest department with the provision for sharing the net revenue in the ratio of 50:50 (share of village: share of government). The classifications of Forests in Arunachal Pradesh are shown in Table 24.2:

Table 24.2 : Classification of Forests in Arunachal Pradesh in 1990-91

Sl.No.	Legal Status of Forest	Area (in sq.km)	% of total of area	% of total geo. area
1	Reserved Forest	19,236.55	37.32	22.97
2	Anchal Forests	256.08	0.50	0.30
3	Protected Forests	7.79	0.01	0.0091
4	Unclassified State Forest (U.S.F.)	32,039.00	62.17	38.27
	Grand Total	**51,539.42**	**100.00**	**61.54**

Source : Arunachal Pradesh Environment Forest Department, Govt. of Arunachal Pradesh, 1993

SECTION II

What is Sustainable Development?

It appears that the term Sustainable Development (SD) was first used in the context of environmental degradation across generations (Raskin, 1996). However, it scope has since widened to incorporate the new realities of changing times in almost all areas of human concern. Before elaborating on the various dimensions of SD we first explore its meanings.

The notion of SD is derived from two words – sustainable and development. SUSTAIN means 'to maintain' or 'to uphold' something (e.g., a life, a system, etc.) by providing a minimum necessary support and /or a conducive environment. Sustainable implies 'capable of maintaining' or 'capable of upholding' and has the objective and subjective dimensions of *viability* and *desirability* respectively. Finally, Sustainability refers to the capacity or capability of systems for achieving the viable and desirable results from an activity under consideration.

Sustainable Development means 'development that needs the needs of the present without compromising the ability and future generations to meet their own needs. World Bank Report speaks the sustainable development "a process of managing portfolio of assets to preserve and enhance the opportunities people face". Sustainable Development includes economic, environmental, social sustainability which can be achieved by rationally managing physical, natural and human capital. This term being used by economists and politicians all over the world and the term is constantly being refined. 'Intergenerational' equity would be impossible to achieve unless the groups stops exploitation of other groups or community living in other parts of the world.

For example, Greenhouse gases generated by highly developed/ highly industrialized countries of the world leading to global warning and flooding of some islands resulting in displacement and impoverishment of entire islands. The situation of profiteering by the Pharmaceutical companies at the cost of millions of poor people being unable to offer medicines required to life threatening diseases. The live examples we can also quote in this regard are Bhopal gas tragedy of 1994, Chernobyl in Russia, Nuclear bomb attack on Nagasaki and Hiroshima during World War II in various forms.

The meaning of development is better understood when contrasted with the notion of growth. Growth (or economic progress) means a vertical change in the economy requiring an efficient use of resources (based on the criterion or cost minimization). It is limited to an increase in the material production of goods and services produced in a year and can be measured quantitatively in terms of per capita income of a country. On the other hand, development is much more than just economic progress. It is a 'holistic' and 'multi-faceted' phenomenon of horizontal change demanding a judicious use of resources (based on the notion of welfare maximization for the society as a whole). Of late, development levels achieved by different countries are approximated with human development index (HDI) that is currently based on three variables – literacy, life expectancy and gender disparity in addition to per capita income. Many other aspects of social concern such as poverty levels and gaps in income-distribution, etc. are also the desired variables of HDI but not included in its calculations so far. However, it is clear that the notion of development requires balance and harmony amongst various components of economy as well as society. Finally, it should be noted that growth is a necessary condition for development and not the sufficient one, i.e. growth is necessary for development but growth need not always lead to development.

Historical example reveals that greater economic development was achieved at the cost of inequality, unemployment, weak democracy, loss of cultural identity, over exploitation of natural resources leading to ecological and economical imbalances resulting in a dire threat for both flora and fauna. To be sustainable, we must rely on certain amount of natural resources available in nature to absorb pollution and regeneration of resources.

Mainstream economists have been primarily concerned with growth and development and neglected the consequences of more production and output on the physical environment. While poverty has to be removed for accomplishment of development and economic development wants production of more goods and services which not only is the cause of environmental pollution but also leads to more extraction of renewable natural resources than their replenishment and directs to exhaustion of non-renewable natural resources that may deprive future generations from experiencing the benefits of those valuable resources. In economics little attention is paid on the problems of excessive natural resources exploitation in long run since to an economist sustainable economic development means extraction of maximum possible benefits over a fairly long period from the exploitation of the available resources in alternative uses. But given the fact that poverty, environment and development are closely connected; environmental problems which is largely caused by increased economic activities appeared as a serious threat to whole mankind across the globe in general and the poor in particular; hence, the costs of worsening environmental quality can no longer be ignored even in underdeveloped counties because unrestricted development may cause harm to environment which in turn may impair the scope of future development. In contrast to economic approach, ecologists are in favour of not using natural resources for economic purposes at least at the cost of loss of bio-diversity as biological sustainability implies conservation of environmental resources for maintaining wide bio-diversity which has vast option and existence values. The World Commission on Environment and Development (WCED, 1987) provided a balanced approach by defining sustainable development that "meets the needs of the present without compromising the ability of future generation to meet their own needs", which accepts obligation to pay attention on improving the economic condition of the poor for better environment recognizing the importance of people and their roles both in economic and ecological consideration. The definition of sustainable development given by Viederman (1996) which states "sustainability is a community's control and prudent use of all forms of capital to ensure, to the degree possible, the present and future generations can obtain a high degree of economic security and achieve democracy while maintaining the integrity of the ecological system upon which all lives and production depends" explicitly signifies management and use of capital by the communities in a democratic structure and may be regarded as an appropriate and comprehensive approach in the context of sustainable development. Though sustainable development needs reduction of industrial pollution, sustainable use of renewable resources and making certain the carry-over of non-renewable resources for all future generations, we will focus on the conservation of renewable natural resources in a participatory scaffold under the leadership of local level self-governing administration.

The equitable and balanced development must continue indefinitely by considering the interest of different groups within the same generations and among the generations taking into account the three interrelated areas i.e., economic, social and environmental. Blending or balancing, economic objectives – growth, stability, efficiency, productivity, per capita income, living standard and so on; social objectives – employment, equity, security, education, health, cultural identify, status and so on, and environmental objectives – healthy environment for both flora and fauna including human beings, rational use of renewable natural resources, conservation of non renewable natural resources, pollution control, treatment of effluents (solid, liquid and gaseous waste), etc., is becoming an enormous challenge for any country in the process of sustainable development otherwise there will be irreparable damage on the environment. Many issues which are becoming more challenging and complicating, because the decisions which are taken at the local level have far-reaching consequences at global level – economic, social and environmental. When these consequences are negative, the situation is referred to as 'exporting un-sustainability'.

In Rio de Janeiro in June 1992, United Nations conference on Environment and Development, 1992, Para 2.1, it is declared, "Human beings are at the center of concern for sustainable development. They are entitled to a healthy and productive life in harmony with nature". Sustainable development assumes high substitutability among different, components of national wealth. Depletion of natural resources can be compensated with high investment on education i.e., human development and physical capital development which make ways for replacement of old technology to new technology to have effective usage of non-renewable resources at lesser level.

SECTION III

Deforestation and general degradation of forests encroachment of valuable forest land, illicit felling, inter-State boundary disputes and their effect on deforestation, timber trade in the District Council areas, shifting cultivations and forest fires due to pressure of increase in human population and increase in urbanization are some of the reasons for the continuous loss of forest cover in Arunachal Pradesh. Due to population pressure, more and more forest lands are being brought under cultivation for increased food supply. The demand for fuel wood is increasing steadily. Virgin forests are being exploited for commercial abuse. The growth of population is shown in Table 24.3 and Table 24.4.

During every tenth year, population census is undertaken in India. The growth behaviour of population is shown above in Table 24.3 and Table 24.4 accounted for this period, which is known as decennial growth of population. From the standpoint of economic development, to know decennial growth rate of population is one of the most essential requirements. Because, the decennial growth rate and the economic benefit out of economic development

Table 24.3: Population Growth Since 1961

NEFA/ State	1961	1971	1981	1991	2001
Arunachal Pradesh	336558	467511	628050	864558	1097968

Table 24.4 : Decennial Population Growth Rate Since 1961

State	Percentage decadal			
	1961-71	1971-81	1981-91	1991-2001
Arunachal Pradesh	38.91 (24.80)	35.15 (24.66)	36.83 (23.86)	26.21 (21.34)

Source: Census Report, Arunachal Pradesh, 2001.

Note: (i) Figures within bracket are at national level.

(ii) Decennial growth = $\frac{\text{(Population of previous census – Population of current census) x 100}}{\text{Population of previous census}}$

at constant rate relate inversely considering that other things remain as constant. That is why, the technique of decennial growth rate is used as barometer to reflect the growth phenomena of population. In the absence of decennial population growth rate, the requirements can neither be identified nor quantified properly. Thus, population is the pivot around which all types of economic activities rotate. Census wise population growth and the decennial growth rate of population of Arunachal Pradesh.

Urbanization

Urbanization indicates technological, institutional, educational, communicational, industrial and organizational development from time to time and is being brought about by modernization and migration. It is so closely related with economic development and social transformation of state or a region. Urbanization and economic development stimulates each other. Structural changes are linked with urbanization. Economic development is generally associated with the growth of urbanization.

Growth of Urban Centres

Till 1961 census the State of Arunachal Pradesh was entirely rural census wise trend in urbanization is shown in Table 24.5.

All these towns are administrative centres in most cases before the establishment of administrative centres, these places were full of jungles. According to 1991 census 12.80% people live in ten urban areas while as per 2001 census 20.41 people live in seventeen urban areas. The decennial urban growth rate in the state has been record as 139.63 in 1971-81, 167.04 in 1981-91 and 101.24 in 1991-2001. The effect of urbanization brings deforestation for the establishment of urban centre.

Table 24.5 : Census-wise Urban Centres

Census	No. of census Towns	Name of the census Towns
1961	NIL	—
1971	4	Bomdila, Along, Pasighat and Tezu
1981	6	Bomdila, Along, Pasighat and Tezu, Naharlagun and Itanagar.
1991	10	Bomdila, Along, Pasighat and Tezu, Naharlagun and Itanagar, Ziro, Roing, Namsai and Khonsa.
2001	17	Bomdila, Along, Pasighat and Tezu, Naharlagun and Itanagar, Ziro, Roing, Namsai and Khonsa, Tawang, Seppa, Daporijo, Basar, Changlang, Jairampur and Deomali.

Source : Census Report

Timber extraction in the State was taken up on a large scale till 1995-96. A large number of wood-based industries cropped up in Arunachal Pradesh. A timber trade in the state had also increased through the operation of tree permits. There was halt on this trade after a Supreme Court judgment on 12th December, 1996 on a writ petition (Civil) No. 202 of filed by Shri T.N. Godavarman Thirumulkpad.

Forest in a renewable resource if properly husbanded, but it becomes a depleting non renewable resource once the process of deforestation brings the stock and its variety below a threshold. Deforestation does not take long, while a forest takes a very long time to develop into a self contained viable eco system. Preservation of the wealth of wild life depends on a scientific management of forest resources. Deforestation invites so many problems which are discussed below:

1. Environmental and Socio-Cultural Problems: Environmental concerns generally comprise of three factors:

(*i*) Depletion of natural resources.

(*ii*) Conservation of the natural state of the environment and

(*iii*) Pollution and its control.

These factors constitute the domain of environmental accounting. The issue of natural resource accounting or environmental accounting become more pressing for a country like India where economic growth is significantly based on natural resources.

In natural resource accounting, besides lack of awareness and proper database, one does not find set of rules which have universal application (which can be applied universally), Norway, France etc, have achieved remarkable success in this field but their geographical and political setup is so different that their framework cannot be adopted by most of the developing countries where the need of environmental accounting is much more pressing. This need becomes exigent considering the fact than in these poor countries the linkage between poverty and environmental degradation is very strong. In this context, World Resource Institute (WRI) has conducted some very useful studies, but it could not adopt a more sophisticated approach because the necessary data were not available. However absence of proper methodology to calculate the value of depreciation of environmental resources does not imply that we should wait for new techniques of natural resource accounting.

The concerns and doubts about environmental degradation were raised in Rome in 1972. These concerns have persisted since then and now it is widely recognized that the environmental degradation has essentially germinated from the failures/inconsistencies of the part of the decision makers. Some writers go to the extents of suggesting that the problems of environmental degradation is more serve than that of inflation, excessive foreign debt or stagnant economic growth. For less developed countries it has become much pressing where rapid deforestation, watershed degradation, loss of biological diversity, fuel wood and water shortages, water contamination, excessive soil erosion, land degradation, overgrazing, over fishing, air pollution and urban congestion are prevalent. Here a pertinent question arises that why this unwanted phenomenon occurs while no economic agent is willing to pay for this to happen.

It has been undisputedly accepted that shifting cultivation creates environmental and socio-cultural problems. The growth in the number of members per *jhumia* family and in the number of *jhumia* families cannot be absorbed in settled and *jhum* cultivation, as a result a consumption gap develops in the hills. The greater food requirements cannot be met out of dwindling yields from smaller plots of land devoted to *jhumming* with smaller and smaller fallowing periods. The over exploitation of forests for *jhumming* and commercial purposes also lead to a deterioration of the condition of the forests. The misuse and destruction of plants cover combined with great increase in human and livestock population has aggravated the problem of eco-system. Ecological damage in the hills, widespread poverty among hill-dwelling tribal, social discontent and the growth of extension has been the fall-out of the development of the hill economy.

There is an urgent need to study in-depth the present environmental crisis related with the misuse of natural resources. A thorough understanding, awareness and perception about environmental issues and natural resources management practices will help in designing suitable extension strategies to make to make the farmers aware and perceive better the issues concerned and adopt remedial practices. Further, studying the present utilization pattern of natural resources by farmers will also give an idea about the status of the existing resources and the exploitation level.

2. Soil Erosion: High rainfall and undulated topography is always associated with problem of severe soil erosion, which affects the environment adversely. The excessive deforestation caused by excessive cutting down of trees for commercial purpose as well as shifting cultivation are resulting in alarming and frightening signals for human survival. Estimates reveal that nearly 181 mt. of soil is lost annually as a result of shifting cultivation from north eastern hill region (Task Force Report, 1983). Developments in the hills and its fall out on the ecology have caused soil erosion, landslides, floods and droughts in the plains. Without forest cover, there would be nothing to resist solid erosion during monsoon months. Forests are necessary to maintain the balance in the agricultural system in North East India and to increase agricultural productivity.

3. Soil Fertility: Burning of vegetation in the process of shifting cultivation chemically alters the plant nutrient supply from organic form to a mineral form in ash, major portion of which is often lost in course of run off. The effect of burning on some soil properties examined at laboratories shows the deficiency of soil fertility.

The shorter the jhum cycle preserves the lower level of soil fertility. Five year jhum *cycle* generates very low level of soil fertility. Thus, jhum cultivation becomes uneconomic progressively. This necessitates switching over to settled cultivation.

4. Loss of Flora and Fauna: Forest is a living resource. A large number of people of the hills and of plain area depend on forest resources. The forest eco-system is to be preserved and managed for wildlife improvement, soil and water resource conservation, maintenance and improvement of bio-diversity, medicinal plant and for what is now termed as eco-tourism to improve the economic potentiality of the people living in and around forest. The extent of deforestation of tropical forest has caused world wide alarm as tropical forests provide more than 50% of modern medicine. Tropical forests are living museums and laboratories that have yielded only a tiny fraction of their treasures to scientific study.

Arunachal Pradesh is, as if, a natural garden of more than 20,000 identified species of medicinal plants and many more still remain unidentified. In course of shifting cultivation remarkable varieties of flora and fauna are disappearing, which need immediate attention for extensive and intensive studies.

The type of vegetations destroyed depends upon the length of *jhum* cycle. A dense forest of long cycle has more tree species than grasses, whereas a forest of short cycle has more number of grasses. About 300 plant species out of native flora in North-Eastern India are used for edible purpose. Of these, over 25 provide tubers/rhizomes etc., which are eaten raw or boiled. Over 50 are consumed as green with their leaves/tender shoots cooked as vegetable; about 170 ripe fruits, which are pulpy and sweet/sub-sweet are eaten raw and many of these are used for pickles/vegetables, when unripe; about 15 have edible seeds are eaten raw or roasted.

Wildlife in the natural system constitutes the most important component of the ecosystem, which participates affectively in the energy flow and bio-geo-chemical cycling. Animal-plant, plant-plant and animal-animal interactions are the basic milestone of the success of an ecosystem and its productivity. As such, the richness of the ecosystem means the capacity of hold high species diversity but deforestation has threatened the very fabric of the survival of wildlife and the ecosystem in the region. This area is the habitat of as many as 55 major mammalian species of which 17 are rare or extremely rare. Twenty one rare species of extremely rare birds are found in this region and there are innumerable species of insects. As such, there are different species of wild lives found in this region. Almost all of them are dared as protected species under the protection Act of 1972. Like flora, other forest resources are also disappearing and become rare.

5. Water Resources: There is ample of water resources in North-Eastern Hill Region. Almost 10% of the total rainfall of the country is received in this region. Soil erosion and deforestation favour in less retention of under ground water and more run off water causing flood in the plains. This causes great loss to human and animal lives as well as crops. Now-a-days, supply of drinking water has become serious problem in every town in the hill region. Due to its geographical location and its hilly terrain, Arunachal Pradesh has an immense hydel potential to use the power of water to produce electricity in comparison to the other states of the country. The state is of turbulent perennial rivers and major streams, which possess enormous hydro-electric generation potential. Therefore, Arunachal Pradesh, having untapped estimated hydro power potential of 49,000 MW, may emerge as Power House of India when this potential is fully harnessed. Deforestation which is seen in different remote areas of Arunachal Pradesh is abolishing the immense source of water not only for drinking but also for generating the hydro power.

Conclusion

Preservation of forest is a heavy task for the state. The interests of people depending on the forest products for their livelihood would have to be protected by providing training and employment opportunities in alternative occupations otherwise corruption would be rampant and the policy of protecting forests would be defeated by way of illegal felling of trees. Those who depend on forest products as a major source of fuel should also be provided with the alternatives. The Supreme Court judgment has to be studied in the context of North-East India's dwindling forest cover and needs of the people in villages. It is equally important to have a honest and strong forest administration prepared to stand up to the crime syndicates operating in the forest. No less important is the need of a sound statistical base on forest for a sound policy formulation to maintain a balanced eco-system and also for meeting the economic needs of the people.

Forest must be protected to conserve soil, environment, wildlife and biodiversity for sustainable development. At the same time, we should remember that the demand for resources yielded by forest is growing along with the growth of population and economic development in order to satisfy direct human wants and requirement of the forest based industries and construction activities. Only sustainable use of forest product can ensure the sustainable development of forest taking into account of the problems created by shifting cultivation, indiscriminate destruction of forest. For sustainability of forest in Arunachal Pradesh, the State having enough potentiality can be developed through setting up of fruit processing industries and nature based tourism industries with least possible disturbing the ecology in hill regions. As Arunachal Pradesh is one of the richest forest resources states in India, a vigorous study is required to make the people aware of how additional income and employment can be generated locally due to the existence of forest resources without disturbing its existence.

We must be satisfied with the intervention of the Supreme Court in preserving ecology and environment in North East India. The forest based industries can be properly planned now. But for achieving the objective of forest resource development, we feel that Forest Protection Force is very much required to check illegal felling of trees. The indigenous people may be trained for generation of entrepreneurial skill in forest based industry and maintaining the environment. The approach should be local need based, eco-friendly and accountability in environment management. There is now an urgent need of create awareness among the people that the forest resources including wildlife belong to the people and are essential for the survival and welfare of the societies of North-east India located in a unique environment zone.

In view of such a fast depletion of natural resources, policy-makers must recognize the impact of their macro policy on the environmental resources. For appropriate solutions, policy planners will have to see the whole problem in an entirely different framework. In a normative determination, policy planners will have to go for new set of economic framework starting from the concept of Environmental Accounting to the Benefit-Cost Analysis of each and every macro policy. In a nutshell all policy packages, yielding net economic benefit, should be preferred subject to the condition that depletion or deterioration in the quantity and quality of natural/environmental resources should be in non-positive.

Till now efforts for conservation of forest resources by strengthening the laws and law enforcement machineries have proved by and large futile. Our experience show that forest management, conservation and development could be successfully handled by concerned authority and decision making processes to the local communities. People-oriented planning and management is necessary tools for the purpose. Sharing the responsibility with local forest communities and strengthening of local bodies can go a long way for sustainable management, preservation and development of forest resources in North East India in general and in Arunachal Pradesh in particular. Ownership pattern of natural resources, community participation in the management of natural resources etc, are such issues which should get its due importance.

REFERENCES

Ali, N. (2005), "An Institutional Approach for Sustainable Rural Development", *Journal of Rural Development*, Vol. 24, No. 2, April – June, pp. 178-179.

Arunachalam. R & Radhakrishnan, T (2006), "Status and Concern for Natural Resource Management", *Kurukshetra*, April, Vol. 54, No. 6, pp. 42.

Azad, N.A. (2004), "Poverty and Sustainable Development", S.Bhatt (ed.), *Poverty and Food Security in India*, Aakar Books, Delhi, pp. 106-110.

Bhattacharjee, R.P. (2002), "Forest Resources in North Eastern Region of India – A case study of Arunachal Pradesh" in B. Datta Ray and K. Alam (eds.), *Forest Resources in North East India*, Omson Publications, New Delhi, pp. 269.

Bhattacharya, R.N. (1999), "Economies of India's North-East Natural Resource Base and Globalization" in Banerjee, A. and Kar, B. (eds.): *Economic Planning and Develop-ment for North-Eastern States,* Kanishka Publishers, New Delhi, pp. 113-14.

Government of Arunachal Pradesh (1990) : *Arunachal Pradesh Forest Statistics*, Department of Forest, Itanagar.

Government of Arunachal Pradesh (1990): *Arunachal Pradesh Forest Statistics*, Forest Department, Itanagar.

Government of Arunachal Pradesh (2003 & 2004), *Economy Review of Arunachal Pradesh*, Directorate of Economics and Statistics, Itanagar.

Government of India (1993): *The State of Forest Report*, Forest Survey of India, Dehra Dun.

Jodha, N.S. (1990), Rural Common Property Resources: Contribution and Crisis, *Economic and Political Weekly*, Quarterly Review of Agriculture.

Kumar, P. (2001), "Environmental Economics for Sustainable Development: Some Issues in Modeling, Accounting and Valuation", Manak Publications, New Delhi, p. 2.

Majumdar, D.N. (ed.) (1990), *Shifting cultivation in North East India*, Omsons Publication, New Delhi.

Mandal, R.K. (2008), *Socio-Economic Transformation of Arunachal Economy*, Omsons Publications, New Delhi.

Mitra, A. (2002), "An Evaluation of Forestry Planning in Arunachal Pradesh" in B. Datta Ray and K.Alam (eds.), *Forest Resources in North East India*, Omson Publications, New Delhi, pp. 258-260.

North Eastern Council (1992-1995), *Basic Statistics of North Eastern Region*, Shillong.

Prakash, H, Venugopal, Ramesh Babu, R.K. and Paramashivaiah, P. (2005, "Integration of Environment for Sustainable Development", *Southern Economist*, Vol. 43, No. 21, March, 2005, pp. 17-18.

Report on United Nations Conference on Environment and Development-1992.

Sustainable Development Report–WDR-2003.

Index